The National Parks of
America

The
National Parks *of*
America

TEXT BY MICHAEL BRETT

JH QO IS VRW CCC TH MM

First published in the United States and Canada in 2001 by Barron's Educational Series, Inc.

Originally published in the United Kingdom in 2001 by New Holland Publishers (UK) Ltd.

All inquiries should be addressed to:
Barron's Educational Series, Inc.
250 Wireless Boulevard
Hauppauge, NY 11788
http://www.barronseduc.com

International Standard Book No.: 0-7641-5421-4
Library of Congress Catalog Card No.: 2001086387

Publisher and Commissioning Editor: Mariëlle Renssen
Managing Art Director: Peter Bosman
Editor: Samantha Hillary
Designer: Lyndal du Toit
Cartography: John Loubser and Carl Germishuys

Reproduction by Pica Colour Separation Overseas (Pte) Ltd, Singapore
Bound in Singapore by Star Standard Industries Pte Ltd

Printed in Singapore

9 8 7 6 5 4 3 2 1

Publishers' Note

For ease of reference by the general reader, species are for the most part referred to by their common,
as opposed to scientific, names throughout this book. In some instances, however, scientific names have
had to be used. In a number of others (where they are likely to prove helpful), both the common and scientific names are given. The maps published in the book are intended as locators only; detailed, large-scale
maps should be consulted when planning a trip. Although the publishers have made every effort to ensure
that the information contained in this book was correct at the time of going to press, they accept no
responsibility for any loss, injury, or inconvenience sustained by any person using this book.

PHOTOGRAPHIC CREDITS
Copyright© of all photographs: **Michael Brett**, with the exception of the following:
Art Wolfe: pp 28 bottom; 35; 115; 173; 177; 215; 223; 225; 229 center; 232 bottom; 233.
Biofotos/*Ian Tait*: p 219.
Colour Library Pty Ltd/Tony Stone Images *(Derke/O'Hara)*: pp 236–237.
David Muench Photography: pp 30; 33–34; 36; 60–61; 64 bottom; 65 bottom; 82 top left and right;
Mark Muench: p 130.
FLPA: *Catherine Mullen*: p 163 top; *David Hosking*: pp 162 bottom; 163 bottom; *Larry West*:
pp 54; 56–57; 58 bottom; *T&P Gardner*: p 203.
Heather Angel: p 131.
Gavriel Jean AWC: p 63.
Holger Leue: back cover (main); 2–3; 8; 10 bottom; 11 top;
84 top; 85 top and bottom right; 86; 88–92; 94–97; 99; 100 bottom left; 101 bottom right; 103 top left
and bottom; 106; 108; 110 top right; 112 bottom; 126 top left; 153; 156–157; 164 top right and bottom
center right; 166 bottom; 168; 169 top; 194–195; 196 center right; 198 top; 199 bottom; 200–201;
209; 210 bottom left.
Inpra: *Jeff Foott*: pp 132; 136 bottom left; 149; 150 top left and bottom; 152; 155 bottom left and right.
Peter Horree: half title (p.1); pp 135; 142 center; 146 center top; 155 top; 158; 160 top and center right.
Peter Mertz: back cover (above center right); pp 6–7; 9; 14–16; 18 top and bottom left; 19–24; 26–27;
28 top; 29; 48–50; 76–79; 83; 84 bottom; 87; 164 left, center top and bottom right; 166 top; 169
center and bottom; 188; 208; 210 top left and right and center; 212–213; 226–228; 229 top right;
230–231; 232 top left; 234.
Courtesy of National Park Service: pp 30; 32 top; 52; 58 top; 59; 64 top; 65 top; 80–81; 82 bottom
right; 161; 162 top; 214.
Olivier Michaud: pp 216–218; 220–222; 224; 225 bottom.
Paul Humann: pp 51; 53.
Photo Access: *Margaret Welby*: p 165; *HPH Photography*: p 167.
David E Rowley: pp 181; 191; *D. Robert Franz*: p 185; *Willard Clay*: p 62.
Sandra Braswell: pp 25; 93; 235.

Page 1: The awe inspiring Grand Canyon was declared a World Heritage Site in 1979.

Pages 2–3: Described by a former president as "the most beautiful country in the world," the Grand Tetons rise majestically above the Snake River.

Right: After plunging down two waterfalls, the Yellowstone River surges through the Grand Canyon of the Yellowstone.

CONTENTS

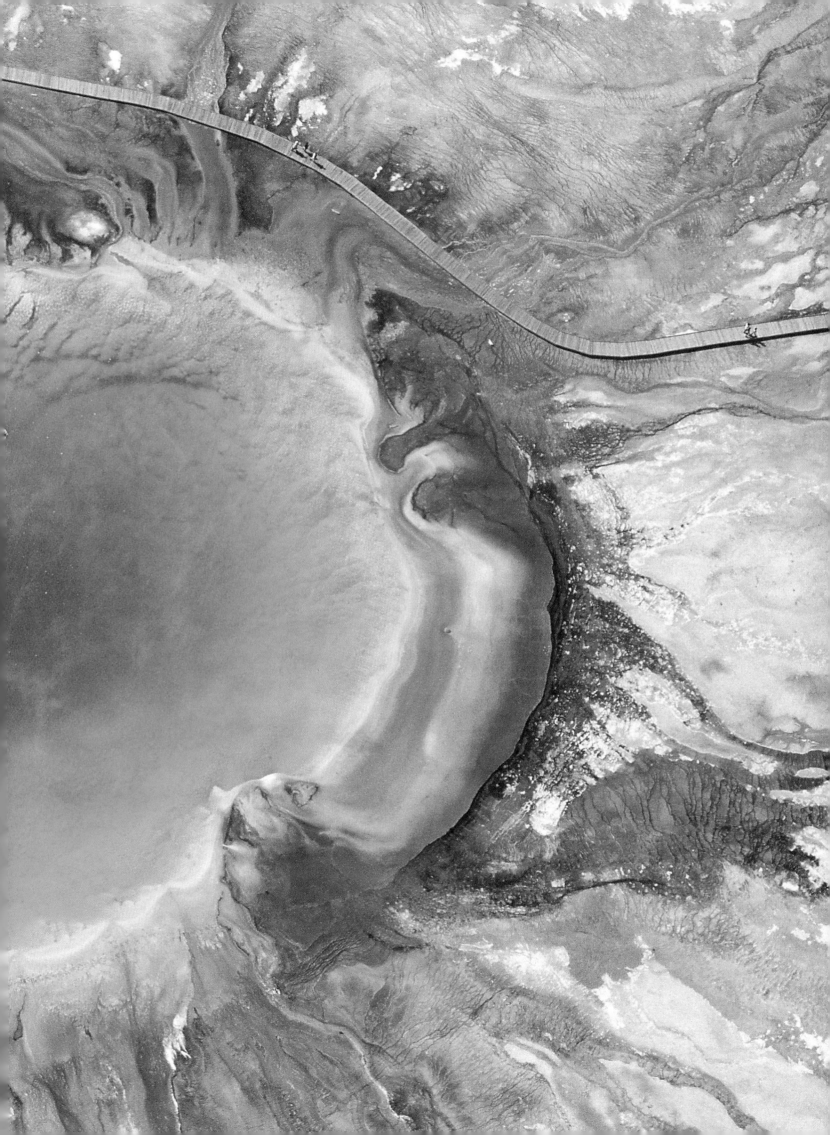

INTRODUCTION

It has been called the best idea that has ever come out of America. Its roots can be traced to the mid-nineteenth century when America's western frontier was still an untamed land where Native Americans on horseback hunted bison, while European settlers laid railway tracks across the prairies and staked out land claims. Extensive regions of the West remained unknown territory, cloaked in vast pine forests and crossed by uncharted rivers. In the 1860s, reports began to surface of a strange otherworld in the northwestern corner of Wyoming, a land where fountains of boiling water burst into the air and steam rose from vents in the ground as if the land were on fire.

To respond to these accounts, Henry D. Washburn, surveyor-general of Montana, led a party in 1870 to investigate the upper catchment of the Yellowstone River. For six weeks, the men explored the natural wonders of the region. One night, they camped along the Firehole River, where steam fumaroles line the banks and streams of hot water cascade into the cobalt blue river. As the men sat around the fire, they discussed ways of exploiting the Yellowstone region's natural resources. One member of the group, Cornelius Hedges, recalled how President Abraham Lincoln had found time during the Civil War to grant the Yosemite Valley to the people of California. Hedges suggested that the federal government should retain Yellowstone in its pristine state for the benefit of the entire nation.

One year later, Dr. Ferdinand Hayden, of the U.S. Geological Survey, led an official survey party of 35 men on horseback to Yellowstone. On March 1, 1872, President Ulysses Grant signed a bill establishing the world's first national park. As no government structure existed that was competent to conserve nature and manage tourists, the United States Army was placed in charge of the park until 1916, when President Woodrow Wilson signed legislation establishing the National Park Service.

From the proclamation of Yellowstone to the formation of the Park Service, 14 additional national parks were established. While national parks were receiving public attention, the government also began proclaiming national monuments. In 1933, all national parks and monuments, and historical and military parks, were placed under the Park Service. By 1960, it administered a total of 187 sites. In 1980, its real estate was doubled when 11 immense parks and preserves were set aside in Alaska by President Jimmy Carter.

A total of 379 units are now maintained by the National Park Service, including 55 national parks. The system preserves a combined land area twice the size of the state of Georgia. National parks have been established in 24 states. Every state except Delaware now has national monuments and recreation areas or national lakeshores and seashores. In a country of immense natural beauty and diversity, these parks safeguard many of the 865 tree species, over 900 bird species, and 350 large mammal species, as well as reptiles, fish, and flowering plants.

Apart from the land set aside as national parks, conservation of wildlife and natural habitats is the responsibility of four other federal institutions. The U.S. Forest Service has jurisdiction over 155 national forests and 20 national grasslands comprising 8 percent of America. Although activities such as logging, grazing, and mining are permitted in some forests, on three-quarters of national forest land no timber is harvested. A total of 624 wilderness areas covering 162,500 square miles (419,250 sq km), three-quarters of which coincide with parks and national forests, have been designated on

Above: The mountain lion is an agile predator that is widely distributed in the mountains and forests of the Rocky Mountains, southwestern desert, and Pacific Coast regions.
Opposite: Grand Geyser is one of 24 geysers within walking distance of Old Faithful in Yellowstone National Park, WY.

land free of any roads or development. These pristine areas comprise 4.4 percent of the United States. The Forest Service plans to prevent road building and logging on an additional 62,500 square miles (161,250 sq km) of forest land. Another agency, the U.S. Fish and Wildlife Service, controls an additional 4 percent of the country apportioned among 500 national wildlife refuges, which are home to large flocks of waterbirds and many endangered mammal and bird species.

Apart from land set aside by state and local governments, the area devoted to conservation by the federal government therefore amounts to 13.5 percent of the United States, an exceptionally high figure for a developed country. There are 43 national parks in the lower 48 states, and California and Utah have the highest number of parks. Ten national parks in Hawaii and Alaska conserve vastly dissimilar environments, from tropical jungles and lava flows to ice-blue glaciers and Arctic tundra.

This rich array of natural attractions brings visitors from all over the world and contributes billions of dollars to the economy. In the mid-1900s, visitors reached the 80 million mark. In 1972, over 172 million visits were recorded and the latest tally exceeds 290 million. About one-third of all visits are to natural areas and the rest to historical monuments and recreation parks. Many national parks have adopted management plans to deal with the ever-increasing numbers of visitors. In 1919, fewer than 45,000 people visited the Grand Canyon. By 1946, visitors surpassed 486,000. In 1969, over two million were recorded. The latest count exceeds 4.5 million. During

Right: Shafer Canyon Trail, in Canyonlands National Park, UT, is an ideal location for four-wheel-drive adventures.

Below: The glacier-studded peaks of the Teton Range dwarf the southern entrance to Grand Teton National Park, WY.

peak summer periods, some parks can be crowded. However, hiking trails and backcountry campsites offer an almost endless list of wilderness alternatives.

Typically, American national parks contain visitor centers, outdoor museums, and a comprehensive array of brochures and books. Free color maps are available for all national parks, even remote wilderness areas in Alaska where there are no facilities. Most parks offer a range of accommodation options and outdoor activities. Even in the busiest parks, though, wilderness areas constitute three-quarters of the area.

This book focuses on the national parks of the United States of America The country has been divided into regional chapters determined chiefly by their natural habitats and geography. In some instances, national monuments, lakeshores, and seashores have been included along with neighboring national parks, where they protect important examples of certain ecosystems. In showcasing the United States' many national parks, this book examines all 13 of the country's natural regions. As country of superlatives, the United States embraces three of the five largest lakes in the world, some of the longest mountain chains and river systems, and vast deserts, frigid ice fields, humid swamplands, and apparently endless windswept prairies. In recognition of the country's unique landscape and commitment to conservation, 13 American national parks have been declared World Heritage Sites by the United Nations.

Above: Death Valley National Park, WY preserves an immense desert wilderness in the hottest and driest region of the United States.

Center: Snow-crowned mountains and extensive ice fields surround picturesque Diablo Lake in North Cascades National Park, WA.

Left: At the end of summer, the Gunsight and Cathedral Rocks flank the thin plume of Yosemite's Bridalveil Fall in California.

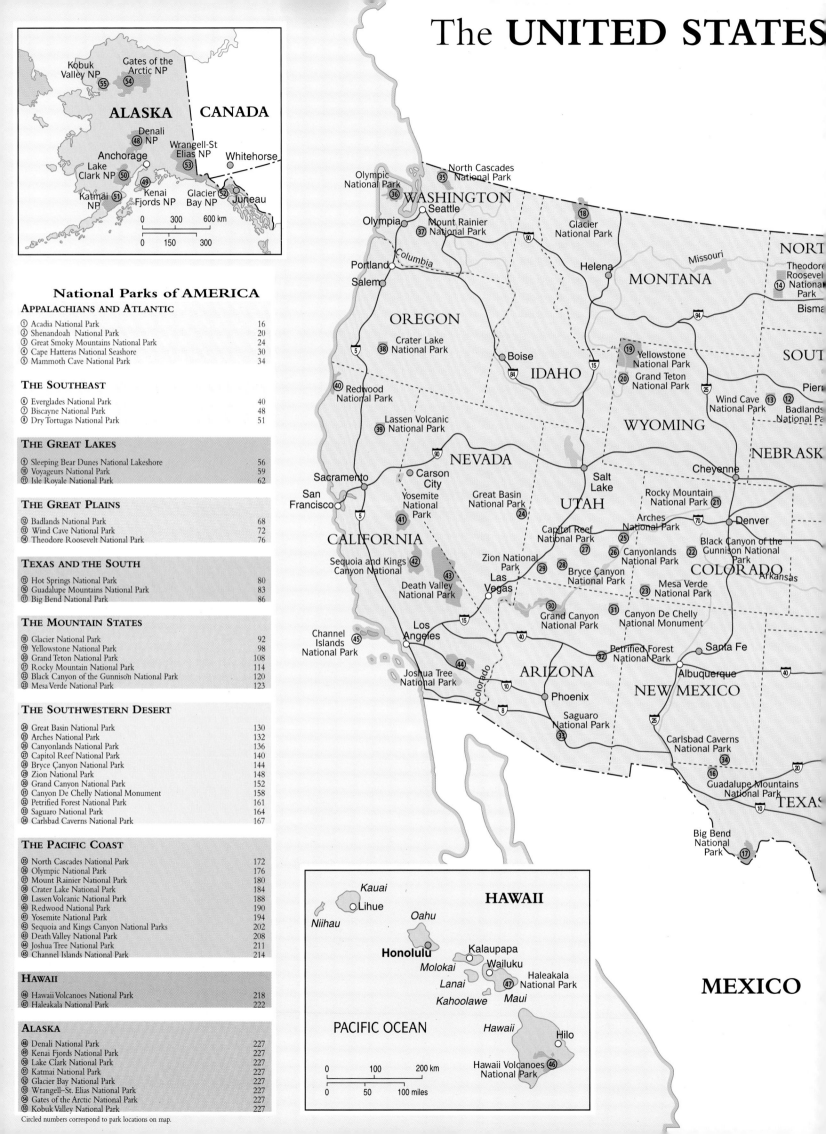

The UNITED STATES

ALASKA   **CANADA**

Kobuk Valley NP (55)   Gates of the Arctic NP (54)

Denali NP (48)

Anchorage
Lake Clark NP (50)   (49)

Wrangell-St Elias NP (53)

Whitehorse

Katmai NP (51)   Kenai Fjords NP   Glacier Bay NP (52)   Juneau

0   300   600 km

0 150 300

National Parks of AMERICA

Circled numbers correspond to park locations on map.

Olympic National Park (36)   North Cascades National Park (35)

WASHINGTON   Seattle
Olympia   Mount Rainier National Park (37)

Glacier National Park (18)

NORTH

Theodore Roosevelt National Park (14)

Bismarck

Portland   Columbia
Salem

OREGON

Crater Lake National Park (38)

Boise

IDAHO

Helena

MONTANA

Missouri

Yellowstone National Park (19)
Grand Teton National Park (20)

SOUTH

Pierre

Redwood National Park (40)

Lassen Volcanic National Park (39)

WYOMING

Wind Cave National Park (13)   Badlands National Park (12)

NEBRASKA

Sacramento   Carson City

NEVADA

Great Basin National Park (24)

Salt Lake

UTAH

Cheyenne

Rocky Mountain National Park (21)

San Francisco

Yosemite National Park (41)

Arches National Park (25)

Capitol Reef National Park (27)   (26) Canyonlands National Park

Black Canyon of the Gunnison National Park (22)

Denver

CALIFORNIA

Sequoia and Kings Canyon National (42)

Zion National Park (29)   Bryce Canyon National Park (28)

COLORADO

Arkansas

Death Valley National Park (43)

Las Vegas

Mesa Verde National Park (23)

Grand Canyon National Park (30)   (31) Canyon De Chelly National Monument

Channel Islands National Park (45)

Los Angeles

ARIZONA

Petrified Forest National Park (32)

Santa Fe

Albuquerque

NEW MEXICO

Joshua Tree National Park (44)

Colorado

Phoenix

Saguaro National Park (33)

Carlsbad Caverns National Park (34)

Guadalupe Mountains National Park (16)

TEXAS

Big Bend National Park (17)

MEXICO

HAWAII

Kauai   Lihue
Niihau   Oahu
Honolulu   Kalaupapa
Molokai   Wailuku
Lanai   Haleakala National Park (47)
Kahoolawe   Maui

PACIFIC OCEAN

Hawaii   Hilo

Hawaii Volcanoes National Park (46)

0 100 200 km

0 50 100 miles

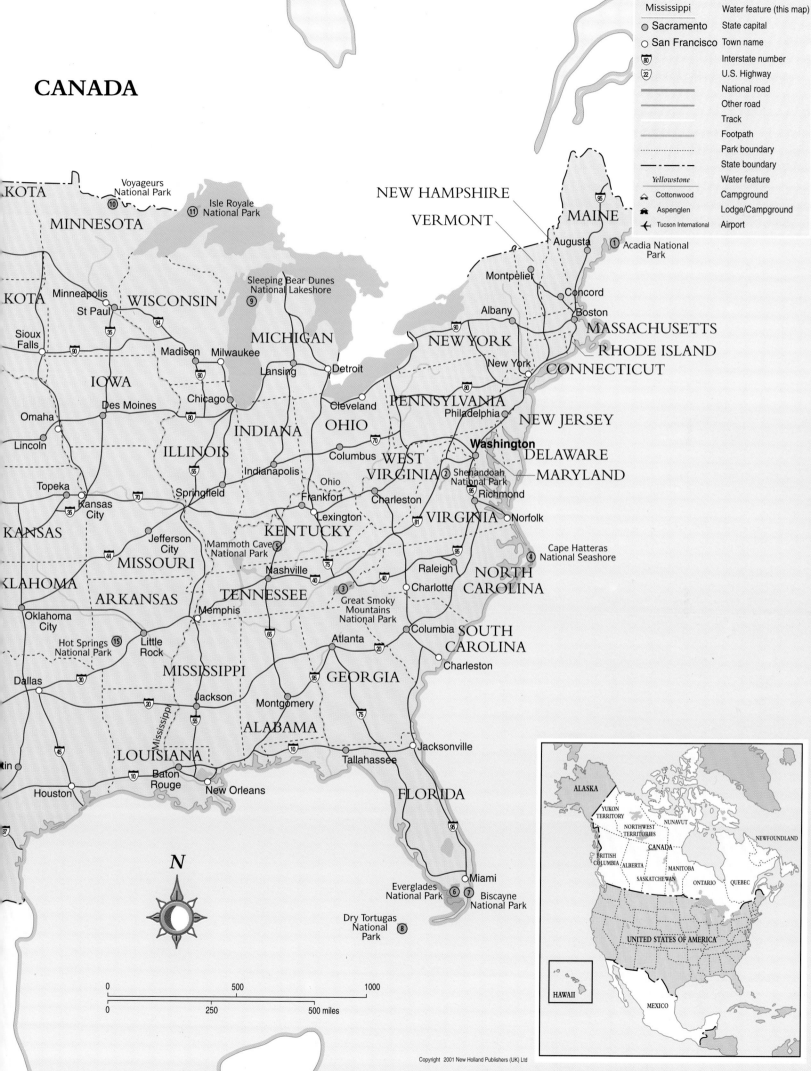

OF AMERICA

APPALACHIANS AND ATLANTIC

Powerful forces of land and ocean have shaped this region. From the Caribbean Sea in the tropics, water heated by the sun's mighty energy is sent northward at a rate of 1,500 billion gallons (6,000 billion L) a second, an immense ocean current that flows as far north as Cape Hatteras before it turns to move in a northeasterly direction across the Atlantic. From the north, the frigid Labrador current flows south before being turned back again. The convergence of these currents sustains a wealth of fish, shellfish, marine organisms, and birds along the Atlantic Seaboard.

On land, before the arrival of Europeans in the seventeenth century, an immense and unbroken temperate forest once stretched westward from the Atlantic Seaboard toward the Mississippi. Where the earth's crust has been folded, tilted, and eroded to form mountain ranges, the forest-clothed Appalachians, the oldest mountains in America, run in a series of high ridges from Vermont to North Carolina.

European settlers began arriving at the beginning of the seventeenth century. The ocean provided a means of trade between Britain and the colonies. Exploitation of the region's bountiful forest and wildlife resources greatly aided the initial economic development of America.

Today, the 16 states that fall within the eastern side of the continent comprise 8.5 percent of America's land area and are home to 27 percent of the population. Despite centuries of settlement and development, in parts of this region, especially northern Maine and even New York State, rivers meander through forested hills rich in deer and bird life. Extensive wetland areas are still found in North Carolina, Maryland, New York, and Maine. Great coastal marshes attract large flocks of wildfowl where five national seashores protect wild beaches and barrier islands of sand.

In an area where few forests escaped the ax over the past 400 years, scattered tracts of virgin forest still occur in northern New York, North Carolina, and Tennessee. The indigenous broad-leaved forests still cover much of the region. Experiments have shown that forests are able to recolonize cultivated land. The two largest national parks in the region protect part of the scenic Appalachian Range, and national forests cover vast tracts of the mountains. In recognition of the natural splendors that have helped shape this part of America, Mammoth Cave and Great Smoky Mountains National Parks were declared World Heritage Sites in 1981 and 1983, respectively.

Left: Acadia National Park preserves the rugged coastline and sheltered coves of Mount Desert Island in Maine. The island's convoluted shoreline incorporates Somes Sound, the only fjord in the lower 48 states.

ACADIA NATIONAL PARK

Maine is one of the coldest states in America. The frigid, nutrient-rich waters of the Labrador current flow down its jagged, rocky coastline, nourishing shellfish such as crab, clam, and lobster and an abundance of fish, including cod, hake, tuna, Atlantic salmon, and mackerel. During the last Ice Age, the immense weight of the continental ice sheet forced the land in this region to subside. As the climate warmed and the ice sheet melted, the oceans flooded many low-lying valleys. The crests of sunken hills now appear as the many islands that dot the coastline. These islands, formed from ice-scoured granite domes, are clothed in forests of red spruce (*Picea rubens*), paper birch (*Betula papyrifere*), and pine. The 48˚F (9˚C) water of the Labrador current causes moisture-laden air to condense, and dense fog often blankets this coastline. The combination of rain and fog produces a luxuriant carpet of green during summer.

It is therefore unusual that a 108-square-mile (278-sq-km) island, the third largest along the Atlantic Seaboard, should be known as Mount Desert Island. The island's somewhat unusual name is derived from a corruption of the French name L'Isle de Monts-déserts, the Isle of Bare Mountains. It was so named by Samuel de Champlain in 1604 after he observed its ice-scoured granite domes. French Jesuits following in his steps set up a mission on the island in 1613 but were later ordered to leave by the captain of an English ship, as the uncharted coastline was considered British territory.

During the 1880s, America's wealthiest industrialists were attracted to the island. Many built palatial summer holiday cottages in the village of Bar Harbor. John D. Rockefeller, Jr., who also helped buy up land for a national park in Wyoming's Grand Teton Mountains, donated about 17 square miles (44 sq km) of his land on the island to the park. The 54-square-mile (141-sq-km) park was established in 1919. It consists of three large blocks of land that cover about half of Mount Desert Island. Offshore, four small islands are also incorporated. Park land protects half of Isle au Haut, 15 miles (24 km) to the southwest, and the Schoodic Peninsula to the east of Bar Harbor.

A dozen large glacier-carved lakes adjoin, or are included within, the park boundary. Somes Sound, the only fjord on America's East Coast, is a 6-mile-long (9-km) finger of the ocean that has drowned low-lying valleys and effectively divides the island, and park, in two. The western section of the island is known for its quiet fishing villages. The eastern section is busier, and activities center on the town of Bar Harbor.

Above, right: Wood ducks nest in hollow trees, often high up. During summer, the ducklings leap from their nest in response to their mother's call.

Opposite: Cadillac Mountain rises 1,530 feet (466 m) above the surrounding ocean, a perfect viewpoint.

Location: On the coast of Maine south of Ellsworth. The park protects three islands and a portion of the Schoodic Peninsula.

Climate: Fog is common in summer, and temperatures are moderate with a range of 50˚ to 80˚F (10˚ to 27˚C). During winter, from November to April, temperatures remain below freezing and an average 60 inches (150 cm) of snow falls.

When to go: Best visited from May to October as many of the roads on Mount Desert Island are closed during winter.

Access: From Interstate 95 to Augusta and Ellsworth on Highway 3 and then south to Mount Desert Island.

Facilities: The visitor center is located near the northern entrance. There are two campgrounds, picnic areas, interpretive trails, and sites for launching boats on five lakes. Accommodations are available in the neighboring town of Bar Harbor.

Outstanding features: Rocky coastline battered by the powerful currents of the Atlantic. Cadillac Mountain, on Mount Desert Island, is the highest point on the East Coast. Along the island shores are tidal pools, seabird colonies, and secluded bays. On land, quaint villages, lakes, lighthouses, and historic stone bridges are added attractions.

Visitor activities: Boat cruises to islands, scenic drives, hiking, swimming, bird-watching, freshwater and saltwater fishing, and seafood dining. Many of the carriage roads are open for hiking, horseback riding, and cycling. Winter activities include ice fishing, cross-country skiing, and snowmobiling.

Appeal of the Ocean

Much of the appeal of Acadia lies in the proximity of the ocean and its natural resources, the island's rugged shoreline and sheltered coves, and the sound and aroma of the pounding waves. Guided boat rides expose visitors to the beauty and power of the Atlantic. Seabirds nest on cliffs, bald eagles and gulls soar overhead, and harbor seals and porpoises swim through the waves. Many bird species are drawn by the interface of sea and shore and the abundant food supplies that this offers. Some of these birds include wood duck, loon, common elder, green heron, herring gull, double-crested cormorant, and spotted sandpiper.

Crab and lobster are abundant in the surrounding ocean. The streets of Bar Harbor are lined with gift shops and seafood restaurants offering clam, lobster, fish, and crab. On summer evenings, the town band plays on the village green while visitors dine, often outdoors, at nearby restaurants.

Around Acadia

Highway 3 crosses a bridge spanning the Mount Desert Narrows, which separates the mainland from Mount Desert Island. The road follows the island's northern coastline to the visitor center where the Park Loop Road begins. A 27-mile (43-km) circular drive that is mostly

laid out for one-way traffic, the road skirts ocean cliffs at Otter Cove that rank among the highest in the country, and passes through spruce forest. On the return leg, the road passes three glacial lakes. A side branch leads to the summit of 1,530-foot-high (466-m) Cadillac Mountain. When the weather is fine, there is a superb view from the summit over the town of Bar Harbor, the surrounding forests, and the blue waters of Frenchman Bay. As the first point in the United States to see the sunrise each morning, this is an ideal spot to enjoy an early breakfast.

A comprehensive network of hiking trails crisscrosses the forests around Cadillac Mountain and the portion of the park west of Somes Sound. Two campgrounds are in the park. Blackwoods is south of Bar Harbor and overlooks Otter Cove. Seawall is at the southern extremity of the island on Highway 102A to Bass Harbor Head Lighthouse. Beach houses, cottages, and motel rooms can be rented in the island's six villages.

West of Cadillac Mountain, visitors will notice many carriage roads meandering through the forests between Eagle Lake and Jordan Pond. The 45-mile (72-km) network of carriage roads is part of the legacy left by John D. Rockefeller, Jr. Rockefeller constructed the roads from 1915 to 1933 and desired that they be kept free of motor vehicle traffic. These roads are open to hikers and cyclists, and certain routes are open to visitors on horseback.

It is possible to fish for both freshwater and saltwater fish on the same morning on the island. No license is needed for ocean fishing, but a state license is required for freshwater fishing. As an average of 60 inches (150 cm) of snow falls in winter, ice fishing, cross-country skiing, snowshoeing, and snowmobiling are popular.

Four lighthouses help to protect ships from this treacherous coast. There is a lighthouse on Baker Island, the island farthest from the mainland, and another on Bear Island near the village of Northeast Harbor. Bass Harbor Head Lighthouse, which can be reached by car, was built in 1858 and stands at the southernmost tip of Mount Desert Island.

Opposite, top: A continental ice sheet once covered much of this area.

Opposite, bottom left: The beautiful eastern shores of the island south of Bar Harbor.

Opposite, bottom right: The common eider, restricted to colder regions of the United States.

Left: Schooner Head, and the Schoodic Peninsula to the east, guard the entrance to Frenchman Bay.

Below: The bright flowers of the mountain laurel.

SHENANDOAH NATIONAL PARK

In the state of Virginia, the Blue Ridge forms the eastern edge of the Appalachian Mountains. A long, narrow, irregularly shaped park protects the mountain crest. Virginia was one of the 13 original colonies founded by European settlers along the Atlantic Seaboard. At first, new arrivals settled on the fertile valley farmlands. As immigration increased and land became less easily obtainable, people began to move onto the steep slopes of the mountains. By the end of the nineteenth century, the Blue Ridge Mountains were inhabited by several thousand people. After considerable areas of the mature deciduous forests were chopped down, it became apparent that the mountainous soils were shallow and difficult to cultivate. The state of Virginia made the decision, unusual in the 1920s, to acquire a considerable area of the mountains and donated the land to the federal government as a national park. Over half the population of the Blue Ridge had already left in search of better prospects elsewhere. However, the state still had to buy 3,870 properties, which comprised 90 percent of the park's total area of 304 square miles (784 sq km).

Shenandoah was proclaimed a national park in 1935 and dedicated by President Franklin Roosevelt as an innovative experiment in land reclamation. As the government was actively pursuing the New Deal at the time, which sought to remedy the economic problems caused by the Great Depression, many land restoration and water conservation projects were carried out in the Appalachian region. Skyline Drive, the northerly exten-

sion of the scenic Blue Ridge Parkway, which ends at the Great Smoky Mountains National Park in North Carolina, was completed in 1939. It runs directly through the center of Shenandoah National Park for 105 miles (170 km).

Over the past seven decades, the land has responded well to protection. Forests now blanket virtually the entire park. Where forests had been razed and open fields had once been cultivated, pioneer shrubs and pines were the first plants to colonize. These plants were then replaced through natural succession by forests of oak and hickory. About 100 species of trees now occur in the park. Rehabilitation of the once decimated broad-leaved forest has been so successful that 40 percent of the park is now a designated wilderness area. Wildlife is once again abundant in the forests of the Blue Ridge, where the dappled shade shelters white-tailed deer, black bear, eastern chipmunk, eastern gray squirrel, raccoon, and gray fox. To the south and west, George Washington National Forest protects 1,648 square miles (4,252 sq km) of the Appalachians, including many historic Civil War sites.

Above, right: A member of the rhododendron family, the pink azalea blooms in summer.

Opposite, top: Shenandoah safeguards the misty peaks of the Blue Ridge Mountains in the state of Virginia.

Opposite, bottom: In spring, wildflowers add a blaze of color to far-reaching views across mountain and valley.

Location: In northern Virginia near the towns of Waynesboro, Front Royal, and Harrisonburg.

Climate: The climate is moderated by altitude. Temperatures in January drop to 20°F (–7°C). In July, temperatures are moderate to comfortable, and highs of around 80°F (27°C) can be expected.

When to go: Summer and fall, especially in October, when the forests are splashed in an array of autumn leaf colors.

Access: The northern entrance is close to Interstate 66 from Washington, D.C.; Interstate 64 from Richmond passes near the southern entrance. Two other highways cross the park, and Skyline Drive runs down its length and connects to all access roads.

Facilities: Visitor centers; lodges at Skyland, Big Meadows, and Loft Mountain; and four campgrounds. Picnic areas, viewing sites, restaurants, and gift shops are evenly spaced along Skyline Drive.

Outstanding features: A range of forested mountains that gives rise to dozens of streams and waterfalls and offers panoramic views over the surrounding countryside.

Visitor activities: Scenic drives, tree and wildflower identification, hiking, overnight backpacking, birdwatching, fishing, and horseback riding. A section of the 2,144-mile-long (3,430-km) Appalachian Trail passes through the park.

Vistas from the Blue Ridge

The mist-shrouded valleys and forested ridges that often appear as a hazy blue are immortalized in John Denver's song "Country Road." Although the park stretches for 70 miles (112 km) along the Blue Ridge, it mainly occupies the narrow crest and varies in width from 1 mile (2 km) to 6 miles (10 km). From the northern entrance around Dickey Ridge, Chesapeake Bay is less than 55 miles (90 km) away, but the rise in topography is quite sudden. Hogback Mountain, at 3,474 feet (1,059 m), is the highest point in this region. Hawksbill Peak, in the center of the park between Skyland and Big Meadows, is the highest park summit at 4,051 feet (1,234 m).

The scenic drive follows the crest down the entire length of the park. It provides superb views of the summits and forested valleys bordered by a patchwork quilt of farmland and towns. A 101-mile (161-km) section of the world-famous Appalachian Hiking Trail, which runs from Maine to Georgia, closely follows the route of the road. As Shenandoah is within easy reach of several major cities, it attracts many visitors, who are tempted merely to drive along the park road or to pause briefly at some of the 88 viewing points that offer sweeping

Right: Spring comes to the low-lying valleys in March and advances slowly up the mountain slopes, reaching the high summits by late May.

Below: A forest creek near Dark Hollow Falls, one of the many that originate on the mountains, begins the journey east to join the Rose River.

views across the landscape. However, the true beauty of the park is discovered away from the road. Four hundred miles (640 km) of hiking trails crisscross many of its hills and valleys or follow small streams and tributaries that lead to the tight meanders of the picturesque Shenandoah River in the valley below the park.

Facilities for Visitors

Four entrance stations are located on strategic access roads leading to the park. The Byrd Visitor Center is near Big Meadows in the northern half of the park. Four campgrounds, picnic areas, and a number of restaurants are located at regular intervals along the park road. At three of the service centers—Skyland, Big Meadows, and Lewis Mountain—lodges or cabins provide overnight accommodations. Large picnic grounds for day visitors, nature trails, and supply stores are also located at Big Meadows, Lewis Mountain, and Loft Mountain. Visitors hiking on the park's comprehensive trail system can overnight anywhere in the park. A free permit is issued for backcountry camping, and hikers must ensure that they leave campsites in a neat condition.

Top: Wildflowers, such as the yellow azalea, are at their stunning peak during spring in April and May.

Above: A typical Virginia mountain cabin. Before the park became a reality, the state government purchased 3,870 properties in the 1920s.

GREAT SMOKY MOUNTAINS NATIONAL PARK

Containing some of the best-preserved examples of deciduous forest in America, this park encompasses the undulating crests and valleys of the Great Smoky Mountains. Straddling the watershed that forms the border between the states of Tennessee and North Carolina, the park protects 814 square miles (2,100 sq km) of forested peaks and secluded valleys. Because altitude ranges from 900 feet (275 m) to 6,645 feet (2,025 m), over 4,000 species of plants and five distinct forest types occur in the park. Changes in forest type are mainly determined by increasing altitude—to experience the equivalent variety of vegetation would require a land journey from southern Georgia to northern Maine.

The Smoky Mountains were once home to the Cherokee, until they were forcibly removed from eastern America in the 1820s. European settlers later moved into the area and began clearing and farming the valleys. By 1850, the population of Cades Cove had risen to 685, and many smaller settlements were established in suitable locations. After the Civil War, many residents of the mountains avoided contact with the outside world. At the beginning of the twentieth century, widespread logging cleared two-thirds of the mountain slopes, resulting in extensive soil erosion.

In the 1920s, several people began to campaign for a national park in the Smoky Mountains. Although the federal government was unable to provide money for land acquisition, a Park Commission raised $2.5 million toward buying the 6,600 portions of land that were incorporated within the proposed boundary. North Carolina and Tennessee allocated an additional $2.5 million. Final consolidation was made possible by a $5-million donation from the Rockefeller family. Some of the mountain residents were opposed to the concept of a national park and were granted lifelong residence rights. The Great Smoky Mountains National Park was finally established by Congress in 1934 and officially dedicated by President Franklin Roosevelt in 1940. This beautiful park was declared a World Heritage Site in 1983.

Each year, nearly 10 million people enter the park, three times the number that visit Yellowstone. However, 95 percent of all visitors keep to the Newfound Gap Road between Cherokee, North Carolina and Gatlinburg, Tennessee. This road provides the easiest and quickest route across the park, with side roads to Cades Cove, Cherokee Orchard, and other isolated corners offering an insight into the park's settlement history. Historic churches, cabins, and mills surrounded by green pastures complement the dappled leaves of the surrounding forests. White-tailed deer and many birds are attracted by an abundance of food that grows at the juncture of meadow and forest.

Above, right: A wide variety of forest types helps sustain a significant population of black bears.
Opposite: The remarkable view at sunset from Clingmans Dome, the highest peak in the park, across the aptly named Smoky Mountains.

Location: Straddles the border between North Carolina and Tennessee. Gatlinburg and Pigeon Forge, in Tennessee, are the closest major towns.

Climate: Temperatures in January may drop to 26°F (–3°C), while in July average highs of 80°F (27°C) can be expected. Rain occurs on most days during summer and mist is common. Thunderstorms can be expected on an average of 50 days per year.

When to go: Summer and fall when the forest foliage is at its best. This park attracts the greatest number of visitors in the United States. During summer weekends, it can be extremely busy. Snowfalls close many roads in winter. Some of the visitor centers and campgrounds are closed until mid-May.

Access: Between Asheville and Knoxville, Interstate 40 skirts the eastern border of the park. Newfound Gap Road, known as U.S. Highway 441 within the park, provides access to most of its attractions; side roads lead to Cades Cove and Cherokee Orchard.

Facilities: Most of the park's 10 campgrounds are located near the southern and northern boundaries. Overnight accommodations in the park are available only to hikers. There are three visitor centers and a number of self-guided interpretive trails.

Outstanding features: As the best example of a broad-leaved deciduous forest in the United States, the park protects a large section of the picturesque Great Smoky Mountains. Secluded valleys give rise to many streams and cascades and provide a haven for many species of plants and animals.

Visitor activities: Scenic drives, hiking, short walks to waterfalls, overnight backpacking, demonstrations of frontier life, tours of historic settlements, cycling, fishing, river tubing, horseback riding, wildlife viewing, and bird-watching. A section of the Appalachian Trail passes through the park.

Forests of the Smokies

Over 130 tree species are included in the five forest types occurring in the park. Increasing altitude results in a drop in temperature and an increase in precipitation. As this means that a gain in altitude of 1,000 feet (300 m) is the equivalent to travelling 250 miles (400 km) north, all the forest types found in eastern America can be seen in the park.

The most diverse forest is found in the low-lying valleys and includes trees such as tulip poplar (*Liriodendron tulipifera*), red maple (*Acer rubrum*), and flowering dogwood (*Cornus florida*). Warm temperatures, sufficient rainfall, and an extended growing season produce a forest that supports an abundance of wild animals. Along stream banks, a forest of eastern hemlocks (*Tsuga canadensis*) can be found. Unfortunately, these trees are threatened by an invasive insect from Asia, the hemlock woolly adelgid. At altitudes ranging from 3,500 feet (1,050 m) to 5,000 feet (1,500 m), a forest of northern hardwoods grows on the mountain slopes. This forest contains fine specimens of sugar maple (*Acer saccharum*), yellow birch (*Betula alleghaniensis*), and American beech (*Fagus grandifolia*) and is very similar to the forests of New England. During the autumn months, the maple trees are renowned for their brilliant displays of orange and red leaves.

On the crest of the Smokies, a forest occurs that is closely related to the forests of northern Maine and parts of Canada. The red spruce and Fraser fir (*Abies fraseri*) are the dominant trees. However, in recent years, the balsam woolly adelgid, a relative of the hemlock woolly adelgid accidentally imported from Europe, has destroyed most of the Fraser firs in the park. As these trees are restricted to the southern Appalachians, rangers have begun planting them in areas where they can be easily treated against the destructive pest.

Opposite: Newfound Gap Road climbs to the summit of the Smoky Mountains and offers panoramic views over much of the park.

Below: More than 130 species of trees have been identified here in the most important broad-leaved forest in the United States.

Top: The Newfound Gap Road closely follows the course of the Oconaluftee River.

Opposite, top: The historic cabins in Cades Cove have been preserved as a part of the park's heritage.

Opposite, bottom: The forest boundary provides an ideal habitat for white-tailed deer and many species of birds.

Below: Attempts have been made to release the red wolf into the Smoky Mountains.

Black Bears and Red Wolves

A total of 61 mammal species have been identified in the park. The black bear is the most popular animal among tourists. The park is home to an estimated 600 of these animals, which is one of the highest densities in America. After their long winter sleep, bears begin to emerge in March. They are active mainly in the early morning and late afternoon The Cades Cove and Cherokee Orchard areas provide some of the best localities for bear sightings.

The red wolf was reintroduced to the area by the U.S. Fish and Wildlife Service. Unlike the gray wolf, the red wolf does not hunt in packs, and its shy habits make it difficult for biologists to study in the wild. From a mere 17 wolves nationally, the population now numbers about 300. The red wolf was successfully reintroduced to a national wildlife refuge in North Carolina. The Smoky Mountains were selected as the second release site. About 20 wolves were released across the park. Apparently, the wolves could not locate sufficient prey and preferred to range outside the park. Over an eight-year period, 28 pups were born but only two survived.

While the red wolf reintroduction was unsuccessful, other reintroduction attempts have succeeded. A total of 137 river otters have been reestablished along the

700 miles (1,100 km) of streams that course through the park. Three species of fish that were locally extinct have also been released.

White-tailed deer are common and favor the diverse habitat that is found along the forest edge. Between 400 and 800 deer live around Cades Cove, where former farmlands create an ideal habitat. Other mammals present in the park include bobcat, opossum, red and gray fox, raccoon, long-tailed weasel, striped skunk, eastern chipmunk, woodchuck, gray squirrel, southern flying squirrel, eastern cottontail, and New England cottontail. Two recent arrivals are the beaver and coyote. Beavers were reintroduced to North Carolina in the 1960s and migrated upstream to the park. In recent years, the coyote has been extending its range into the eastern half of the country and was first recorded in the park in 1985.

Discovering the Smokies

From the Newfound Gap Road, which runs across the middle of the park, a 7-mile (11-km) side road leads to Clingmans Dome. The 6,643-foot-high (2,025-m) summit is the park's highest, and the highest peak in Tennessee. A trail leads to a 54-foot-high (16-m) observation tower that provides a superb view over the

Smokies. The Appalachian Trail, meandering down the center of the park, crosses Clingmans Dome, which marks the highest point attained along this 2,144-mile-long (3,430-km) hiking trail. At the northern entrance to the park, an interesting diversion along Little River Road leads to Cades Cove, where many historic buildings have been preserved. During summer months, there are demonstrations of traditional skills such as the making of lye soap and sorghum molasses. Cades Cove is also known as an ideal spot for wildlife sightings.

Campgrounds are provided in ten locations, including the ever-popular Cades Cove, although some of these sites are open only in summer. Le Conte Lodge is the park's only lodging and is accessible only to hikers. There are 149 official trails in the park, and backcountry camping permits are available free from the visitor centers. Innumerable streams and waterfalls cascade through the Smokies. Ten short trails, ranging in length from 0.5 mile (1 km) to 8 miles (13 km), explore some of the finest cascades. Bicycles may be hired at Cades Cove, and horses can be hired from the five stables located in the park.

Fishing in the many streams is permitted—a Tennessee or North Carolina license is required. However, either license is accepted throughout the park.

CAPE HATTERAS NATIONAL SEASHORE

North Carolina's convoluted coastline is characterized by the Albemarle and Pamlico Sounds, two fingers of the ocean that extend inland for 50 miles (80 km). This section of the coastline was drowned at the end of the last Ice Age. At that time, the oceans rose to flood low-lying coastal valleys. Coastal sand dunes, washed by the ocean currents, were reshaped into narrow sandbars and islands.

About 13 miles (20 km) south of Kitty Hawk in North Carolina, not far from the place where the Wright brothers tested their first aircraft in 1903, a long, narrow sandbar forms a fragile arc that runs parallel to the mainland for 78 miles (125 km). At Cape Hatteras, this spit is 3 miles (5 km) wide. For most of the way it is little more than 0.5 mile (1 km) across. Its distance from the mainland ranges from 8 miles (13 km) to 19 miles (30 km). Between these islands of sand and the mainland, the sheltered waters of Pamlico Sound are a haven for waterbirds and marine life.

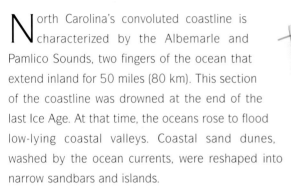

Cape Hatteras National Seashore is divided into two sections. The Pea Island National Wildlife Refuge protects the spit between Bodie Island, in the north, and the major portion of the park south of Rodanthe. Bodie Island boasts the highest sand dune in the United States, Jockey's Ridge, which rises 138 feet (42 m) above the surrounding ocean.

In 1585, Sir Walter Raleigh sent a group of settlers to Roanoke Island, between Bodie and the mainland. However, the settlement was abandoned after three years. At its southern extremity, across Ocracoke Inlet, the park is bordered by Cape Lookout National Seashore.

Graveyard of the Atlantic

Three lighthouses are positioned at strategic points on the islands. Cape Hatteras Lighthouse, built in 1870, is the tallest in the country at 208 feet (63 m). When Cape Hatteras Lighthouse was built, it was about 2,000 feet (600 m) from the breaking waves. Since then, changing ocean currents have carved away at the shoreline while depositing sand onto the southern shore of the island. As a result, the lighthouse was in grave danger of being undercut by pounding waves. In June 1999, the 4,800-ton lighthouse was moved, slowly rolled along on a bed of steel beams, 2,900 feet (884 m) from its original site to a higher position. The journey took 23 days to complete at a cost of $11.8 million. Near the lighthouse, a visitor center houses displays about the island's maritime history.

Despite the presence of the lighthouses, dangerous currents, dense fog, and severe storms have exacted their toll on ships over the centuries. Sailors refer to the area as the "Graveyard of the Atlantic." More than 600 ships have been wrecked over the past four centuries along this coast, which is one of the stormiest in America. In 1585, Sir Richard Grenville's ship *Tiger* ran aground on Ocracoke Inlet. In the early 1700s, a notorious pirate, Edward Teach (better known as Blackbeard) and his buccaneers chose Ocracoke Island, 40 minutes by ferry from Hatteras, as their land base.

Above, right: Mallard ducks are widespread in the United States.
Opposite: At Cape Hatteras, a narrow barrier island protects Pamlico Sound from the powerful currents of the Atlantic.

Above: At Cape Hatteras, the tallest lighthouse in the United States warns ships of treacherous seas.

Right: The Canada goose is an abundant waterbird that migrates in winter to the United States' southern states.

Opposite, top: Historic Chicamacomico Life Saving Station near the northern end of Hatteras Island.

Opposite, bottom: Wooden cottages and coastal villages cling tenaciously to a coast frequently battered by violent storms and hurricanes.

During the Civil War in 1863, the famous ironclad *Monitor* met a fate similar to the *Tiger* and sank in a storm. The remains of the *Laura Barnes* now rest on Coquina Beach after a storm sank the ship in 1921.

Wildfowl and Wetlands

During winter, large flocks of snow geese, Canada geese, and many species of ducks migrate to the islands. Over 300 species of birds have been recorded. For a distance of at least 3 miles (5 km) on the inland side of the islands, the water in Pamlico Sound is less than 6 feet (2 m) deep. In these shallow tidal flats, salt marshes provide an important source of food for wading birds such as sanderling, spotted sandpiper, and kildeer. The coastal marshes on the Atlantic Seaboard nurture two-thirds of the commercial fish and shellfish harvested in the United States. Twice a day, high tides wash nutrients and food items into the marshes, and shellfish scurry out of their hiding places to feed on algae and cordgrass. In the waters protected by the barrier islands, oysters, clams, mussels, and blue crabs are abundant. Submerged aquatic plants provide cover for crabs, grass shrimp, and snails. The marshes provide a nursery for many species of fish, and the spotted sea trout use them to spawn.

Visiting the Cape

From the north, Highway 12 crosses a causeway across Oregon Inlet and runs down the length of the islands. The road passes through eight coastal villages that are excluded from the park. These centers are well equipped with supply stores and accommodation options. At Hatteras, a free 40-minute ferry service bypasses Hatteras Inlet and docks on Ocracoke Island. Farther south near Ocracoke Island Lighthouse, two ferries sail to Swanquarter and Cedar Island on the mainland. The ferry trips take about two hours.

Swimming, fishing, boating, windsurfing, hiking, and relaxing on the beach are the most popular pastimes for visitors to the park. Three visitor centers are on the islands, and another is at Pea Island National Wildlife Refuge. Four campgrounds are open during summer, and there are a number of swimming beaches. Two areas have been set aside for windsurfing in the waters of Pamlico Sound. Two fishing piers are on Hatteras Island. Those who enjoy fishing are lured by catches of bluefish, sea trout, striped bass, and pompano.

MAMMOTH CAVE NATIONAL PARK

One of three national parks set aside in America primarily to protect cave systems, Mammoth Cave is the largest cave system in the world. It is at least three times longer than any other cave. Over 350 miles (560 km) of passages have been surveyed, and one room is large enough to contain a nine-story building.

The origins of this massive cave system can be traced back 350 million years when a shallow sea covered the area. Over a great period of time, marine creatures formed a thick layer of limestone on the bottom of the sea. The seafloor was later raised by movements of the continental plates. As groundwater percolated through rocks, it dissolved chemicals such as carbon dioxide and became slightly acidic. Over eons, this weak acid slowly carved giant caverns in the limestone and created dramatic curtains of flowstone and other formations.

As far back as 4,000 years ago, Native Americans mined minerals in the cave and explored the first 10 miles (16 km) of its dark passages. During the war of 1812 against Britain, saltpeter was extracted from the cave to make gunpowder. Four years later, visitors began to tour the caves. The national park was established in 1941 to protect the caves and surrounding land. Covering 82 square miles (213 sq km) of picturesque woodland and a 24-mile (38-km) stretch of the enchanting Green River, the park was declared a World Heritage Site in 1981. As many interesting and unique forms of life survive in the cave's subterranean rivers, a biosphere reserve was established in 1990 to protect the surrounding catchment.

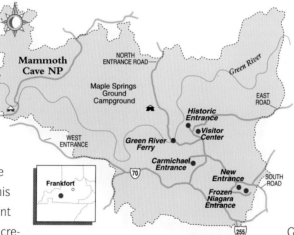

Blind Fish and Freshwater Mussels

Apart from the cave, which contains unusual creatures such as the eyeless fish and cave crayfish, the park above ground is rich in plants and wildlife. Beech trees grow on low flats, the sugar maple and tulip poplar on lower and middle slopes, and oak and hickory dominate the forests on the hillcrests. In the north, yellow birch, hemlock, and holly grow in sandstone gorges.

Great blue heron, mallard, belted kingfisher, wild turkey, wood duck, spotted sandpiper, and common yellowthroat can be seen along the banks of the Green River. This river is one of the richest in America in terms of biological diversity. It is home to 82 species of fish and over 50 types of freshwater mussel, of which 7 are listed as endangered. The park's broad-leaved forests shelter white-tailed deer, eastern chipmunk, gray fox, raccoon, gray squirrel, fox squirrel, and eastern cottontail.

Above, right: Although closely related to the pandas of China, raccoons feed on frogs, rodents, and wild fruit.

Opposite: Although the park is famous for its caves, above ground, its undulating landscape preserves a diverse temperate forest.

Location: In western Kentucky near Bowling Green.

Climate: A warm and wet climate, with most of the rain falling during spring. Winter low temperatures are moderate and average 26°F (−3°C). During summer, high temperatures of 88°F (31°C) can be expected.

When to go: The park and all campgrounds are open throughout the year. The temperature of the caves remains at around 54°F (12°C) throughout the year.

Access: Interstate 65 from Louisville to Bowling Green runs east of the park. From Exit 53, at Cave City, Highways 70 and 255 lead to the southern and eastern entrances to the park.

Facilities: Mammoth Cave Hotel and Visitor Center are situated at the historic entrance. A picnic area, campground, cottages, boat dock, and series of short walking trails have been established in the immediate vicinity. Two campgrounds are in the western half of the park, one on the Green River and another for campers on horseback.

Outstanding features: The park protects the most extensive cave system on earth with more than 350 miles (560 km) of surveyed passages. Undulating hills are clothed in broad-leaved forest. The picturesque Green River, one of the richest in America in terms of biodiversity, flows through the center of the park for 24 miles (38 km).

Visitor activities: Ranger-led guided cave tours, bus trips that begin at entrances south of the historic entrance, paddleboat cruises on the Green River from April to October, canoeing on the Green and Nolin Rivers, scenic drives, tree and wildflower identification; hiking, overnight backpacking, wildlife viewing, bird-watching, cycling, fishing, and horseback riding.

Touring the Cave System

The park is located near the town of Bowling Green in central Kentucky. The caves are situated at its center, and the six roads into the park converge at the visitor center outside the main cave entrance. About 12 miles (19 km) of the caves are open to the public. The main passage varies in width from 20 to 140 feet (6 to 45 m). At the lowest point in the cave, Echo River flows through Cascade Hall 360 feet (110 m) below the surface. The caves have a comfortable year-round temperature of 54°F (12°C) and are particularly appealing on hot summer days.

Park rangers conduct a number of tours of the caves ranging in duration from two to over four hours. One tour aimed at children involves crawling through narrow passages and climbing steep inclines. There are five alternative entrances to the caves south of the historic entrance at the visitor center. On some of the guided tours, visitors are driven to these access points.

Other Activities

The Green River meanders through the park for 24 miles (38 km). One of the park's three campgrounds is located on a bend in the river near the western boundary. In total, there are 73 miles (117 km) of trails in the park, concentrated north of the river where an extensive network can be explored by hikers and visitors on horseback. There are 12 backcountry campsites, and rangers issue free permits for their use. At the visitor center, the short Heritage Trail has been laid out for visitors in wheelchairs. In the southern section of the park, a similar trail has been laid out around Sloans Crossing Pond.

Many facilities are in the vicinity of the visitor center, including a campground, service center, hotel, restaurant, cottages, picnic area, and a 10-mile (16-km) network of trails leading down to the Green River. Along the trail to River Styx Spring, water can be seen flowing out of the cave and into the river. From April to October, one of the best ways to experience the beauty of the Green River is on a one-hour boat ride aboard the *Miss Green River II*, which resembles a Mississippi paddleboat. The Green River flows between impressive cliffs on its course through the park, and visitors can also canoe or boat down the river. Fishing is permitted—the river yields catches of muskie, white perch, bass, and catfish—and no fishing license is required.

Right: With over 350 miles (560 km) of surveyed passages, Mammoth Cave lives up to its name and is at least three times longer than any other known cave system.

THE SOUTHEAST

Heated by the equatorial sun, a warm ocean current sweeps northward across the Gulf of Mexico, carrying with it hot, humid air to the southeastern region of the United States. This is the Deep South, the land of Alabama, Mississippi, Georgia, and Florida, where extensive wetlands of moss-draped cypress trees are home to birds and alligators, and where the rare manatee feeds on underwater grass in secluded coastal inlets.

This region accounts for 6.5 percent of America's land area. In recent decades, its subtropical climate has attracted millions of Americans from the colder northern states. Twelve percent of the U.S. population now live in the southeast, and nearly half of these people live in Florida. In 1896, Miami had a population of 343 residents. Today, it is an ultramodern city that is home to approximately two million people and is one of the fastest growing cities in the United States.

Although this sun-blessed coast has become a year-round playground, wilderness areas are never far away. Much of Everglades National Park, the third largest park in the lower 48 states, is still an uncharted wilderness of flooded grasslands and mangrove swamps. North of the park, the Big Cypress National Preserve is one of the least-developed corners of America. Alligators and turtles crowd together in waterways lined by tall cypress trees festooned in Spanish moss. The last remaining Florida panthers prowl through the swamp. Apart from the three national parks that safeguard south Florida's natural treasures, national forests are scattered across all four states. In southern Georgia, the intriguing Okefenoke Swamp is protected by the largest national wildlife refuge east of the Mississippi.

From the southern tip of Florida, the turquoise waters of Florida Bay are punctuated by forested islands strung together like pearls in a 106-mile-long (170-km) chain. As a tropical paradise of coral reefs, pellucid waters, palm-fringed beaches, quaint towns, and sunken treasure, the Florida Keys are one of America's most enchanting destinations. A marine reserve surrounds the Keys, and exploitation of the abundant marine life in the surrounding shallow sea is carefully monitored by park rangers.

Left: An immense flooded grassland punctuated by tree islands, Everglades National Park preserves one of the most important wetlands in the United States.

EVERGLADES NATIONAL PARK

Location: Southern Florida, 13 miles (21 km) west of downtown Miami.

Climate: Winter temperatures average 60°F (16°C), while in summer, highs of 90°F (32°C) can be expected. Southern Florida has the highest incidence of thunderstorms in the United States, an average of 70 days each year.

When to go: Winter is the best time to visit as temperatures are more comfortable and the 60 species of mosquitoes occurring in the Everglades are less troublesome.

Access: South on U.S. Highway 1 from Miami to Homestead and then on Highway 9336 to the main entrance. The Shark River Slough, in the north of the park, can be reached on U.S. Highway 41, known as the Tamiami Trail, which heads west from central Miami.

Facilities: Three campgrounds in the eastern half of the park and a lodge overlooking Florida Bay at Flamingo. Five visitor centers, several picnic areas, and a number of self-guided interpretive trails are located along the main park roads. Canoes can be rented at Everglades City and Flamingo. There is a marina and store at Flamingo. Some facilities are closed during the hottest months of the year.

Outstanding features: An immense flooded grassland 50 miles (80 km) wide and from 6 inches (15 cm) to 3 feet (1 m) deep. Mangrove swamps, clumps of tropical forest, hundreds of islands and inlets, and a chain of coastal lakes are among the park's many attractions. Alligators are common, and many species of birds are attracted by the park's diverse habitats.

Visitor activities: Wildlife viewing, bird-watching, cycling, hiking, canoeing, boat tours, and freshwater and saltwater fishing.

This national park has been called America's subtropical wonderland, and its humid climate and high moisture levels are certainly in keeping with this definition. The Everglades' true uniqueness, though, lies in its vegetation. From the main entrance gate, the road passes through forests of slash pine (*Pinus elliottii*) that appear no different than any other coniferous forest in America. However, where the pines end, an enormous marshy grassland extends to the horizon. Dotted with white egrets, the "river of grass," as Marjorie Stoneman Douglas called it in her best-selling natural history of the Everglades, is a beautiful landscape quite unlike any other in America. It certainly would not be out of place in equatorial Africa or South America.

This immense flooded grassland is punctuated occasionally by dark clumps of tropical forest. Where slight humps occur in the land, usually no more than 3 feet (1 m) in elevation, the soil has better drainage, and thick forests of tropical hardwood concentrate. Known as hammocks, these tree islands support a dense canopy of palms and many tropical trees such as mahogany (*Swietenia mahogoni*), gumbo-limbo (*Bursera simaruba*), and willow bustic (*Dipholis salicifolia*), and provide a refuge for animals during floods.

Closer to Florida Bay, the swampy grassland gives way to a wilderness of mangrove swamp interrupted occasionally by patches of coastal prairie. In these humid swamps, alligators are abundant, while osprey and bald eagles roost in towering palms along the shore.

Everglades is the third biggest national park in the lower 48 states and was declared a World Heritage Site in 1979. Established in 1947, the park has been enlarged several times to cover 2,354 square miles (6,073 sq km) of flooded grasslands, mangrove and cypress swamps, and countless tiny islands in the shallow waters of Florida Bay. In 1974, much of the Big Cypress Swamp, encompassing 1,137 square miles (2,935 sq km), was set aside as a national preserve. Apart from preserving the moss-festooned cypress swamps, the refuge contains the last few Florida panthers, a subspecies of the mountain lion. Only 30 to 50 Florida panthers remain in the wild.

Waterbirds and Wildlife

Everglades protects 14 species that are endangered or threatened, including the American crocodile, snail kite, wood stork, and loggerhead turtle. Only 900 snail kites are found in the United States, and the entire population is restricted to Florida. In total, 350 species of birds have been recorded in the park.

Above, right: A laughing gull at the marina in Flamingo displays typical second winter plumage.

Opposite: Forests of slash pine surrender to the "river of grass," a shallow swamp 50 miles (80 km) wide.

Right: Water lilies and flooded grasses provide a sanctuary for young fish in the clear waters of a slough.

Below: An alligator displaying the high walk that is typical of this reptile family.

Some of the most common birds found in wetlands and waterways include brown pelican, anhinga, great blue heron, cattle egret, roseate spoonbill, white ibis, and mottled duck.

Over 50 species of reptiles are in the park, and the alligator is the most conspicuous. Alligators can be seen swimming around the Flamingo marina and will swim in both freshwater and salt water. Freshwater turtles are common, and four species of marine turtle are found in the marine area of the park. Seven sites have been identified along the wild west coast of the park where marine turtles come ashore to lay their eggs.

As most of the park is a wetland, aquatic mammals such as river otter and water rats occur. White-tailed deer, bobcat, gray fox, raccoon, fox squirrel, and marsh rabbit show a preference for certain habitats: the fox squirrel is restricted to mangrove swamps and the gray fox to hammocks found in the pine forests. Marine mammals such as bottle-nosed dolphin and manatee can be seen in Florida Bay. The entire national population of 1,200 manatees is restricted to Florida, and Everglades is an important refuge for this rare mammal.

River of Grass

The Everglades is often called a swamp. Actually, it is a shallow river, 50 miles (80 km) wide and 6 inches (15 cm) deep, that flows through a sea of grass. At one time, water flowed uninterrupted from Lake Okeechobee, 100 miles (160 km) north of Florida Bay, to the southern

tip of Florida. The water moved south at the rate of about 100 feet (30 m) a day and sustained about 300,000 waterbirds.

Six million people now live along the Atlantic coast of South Florida, and 1,000 new settlers arrive every day. From the 1940s onward, an elaborate system of canals, levees, and flood control gates was built to control flooding and provide water for the rapidly increasing urban population. By 1980, this network totaled 1,400 miles (2,250 km). As water was diverted from the Everglades, changes took place in its ecology. Half the wetlands in the Greater Everglades disappeared, and nesting wading birds declined by 95 percent. In the 1930s, there were 4,000 nesting pairs of wood stork in the park; now only about 250 pairs remain.

Restoring the Balance

Several attempts have been made to correct the imbalances. Congress passed a plan in the 1980s that will permit the National Park Service to purchase 168 square miles (433 sq km) of wetland adjoining the park's eastern boundary to help restore the natural water flow. It is hoped that the flow of water into the Shark River Slough will then be guaranteed.

In July 1999, a plan was presented to Congress that will require the expenditure of $7.8 billion to be shared by the federal government and the state of Florida. The plan took the U.S. Army Corps of Engineers eight years to finalize. It involves the removal of 240 miles (385 km) of canals and levees that were dredged to divert water to the Atlantic Ocean. The western 20 miles (32 km) of Highway 41, or the Tamiami Trail, will be removed and rebuilt to allow water to pass under the road. It is hoped that by supplying the park with sufficient water, many of the ecological problems caused by past human intervention will be solved.

Above: Development and water extraction beyond the park boundary poses a threat to the rare wood stork.

Below, left: The main visitor center, at the park's eastern entrance, contains informative displays and a comprehensive range of guidebooks.

Below: A young visitor examines the informative panels at the Taylor Slough.

Opposite, top: From the Royal Palm Visitor Center, pathways explore the cobalt-blue waters of the slough.

Opposite, bottom: A hammock, a slight rise in topography in the "river of grass," sustains a luxuriant jungle of tropical palms and trees.

Overleaf: Protected by the encircling arm of the Florida Keys, the calm waters of Florida Bay shelter rare loggerhead turtles and manatees.

Experiencing the Everglades

Much of the Everglades is a proclaimed wilderness area with no roads, and access is very difficult. An abundance of water attracts 60 species of mosquitoes, and it is easy to get lost in mangrove swamps and along the countless coastal inlets. Roads are limited to Highway 9336, which runs from the town of Homestead, south of Miami, to Flamingo, and a road on the northern boundary that leads to an observation tower. The main road to Flamingo includes several turnoffs. There are several stopping places where a short walking trail explores a forested hammock or leads to an elevated lookout. All stopping points along the road are worth exploring, and the turnoff to the Royal Palm Visitor Center ends at the cobalt-blue waters of a slough. A short trail follows the water's edge, and many species of fish can be easily viewed in the crystal-clear water.

There are five visitor centers in the park and a comprehensive museum forms part of the Flamingo Visitor Center, which overlooks the bay. The adjacent coastal grasslands are shaded by tall palm trees, and boats dock at the nearby marina. A large campground is situated on the extensive grassland, and there is a lodge overlooking the waters of Florida Bay. Several short hiking trails can be explored from Flamingo, and the longest, the Coastal Prairie Trail, ends at Clubhouse Beach.

At Flamingo, activities focus on the island-dotted waters of the bay. Regular cruises provide visitors with close-up views of the alligators and waterbirds. Motorboats and canoes may also be hired, and fishing is permitted in the bay. A Florida State license is required for all fishing.

One of the best ways to explore the Everglades is by canoe. Five canoe trails skirt the lakes and waterways in the vicinity of Flamingo. Some 40 backcountry campsites, built on small wooden piers, provide canoeists with ideal places to pitch a tent for the night. Most of these campsites are located along the 100-mile (160-km) Wilderness Waterway, a marked route that weaves through channels from Flamingo to Everglades City on the northwestern boundary. Others are located on the tiny islands that dot the western coastline.

BISCAYNE
NATIONAL PARK

Viewed from the surface of the sea, the waters of Biscayne Bay are a crisp turquoise. The coastline, crowded with tropical palms and trees, is a green fringe in the far distance, while ten uninhabited forested islands form a thin protective barrier 8 miles (13 km) out to sea. Below the surface, the greens and blues of sky and water are replaced by brilliant color. Schools of tropical fish in translucent displays of purple, green, white, yellow, and red dart among sheltering fingers of coral. In the shallow coastal waters, the unusual manatee, once erroneously regarded by sailors as a mermaid, feeds on the beds of sea grass that grow between the mangroves on the shore and the coral reefs in the bay. Though they resemble seals or walruses, manatee never leave their aquatic home, and babies are born underwater.

Biscayne, one of two national parks set aside to protect coral reefs and subtropical seas in Florida, covers 281 square miles (725 sq km) and is unusual in several respects. Much of the park area consists of warm, shallow water dotted with coral reefs. Its land area is limited to 14 square miles (36 sq km), and is restricted to a coastal strip running from South Miami to the park's southern boundary and the chain of forested Keys that run parallel to the coast in a thin band for 14 miles (22 km).

The park is one of only two in the country that is literally on the edge of a major city. In 1910, Miami was home to 5,000 people. Since then, Florida's year-round sunny and warm climate has attracted millions of people from elsewhere in America. Miami is now a city of two million inhabitants. As development spread along the coastline, conservationists lobbied to protect the bay's natural splendor. In 1968, a national monument was established, and in 1980 the area was redesignated as a national park.

When the park was established, it became the first American national park dedicated to the protection of coral reefs and subtropical ocean. Preservation of this biologically rich region, which includes some of the most important coral reefs in America, was extended in 1990 for 220 miles (350 km) southwest to beyond Key West. This marine sanctuary, along with the John Pennekamp Coral Reef State Park, helps to protect the fragile reefs and control aspects of human usage such as boat damage of coral and overfishing.

Visiting Biscayne

The park is best explored by boat. However, Cape Florida State Park, on the tip of Key Biscayne, is linked to central Miami by a causeway offering easy access to

Above, right: The great egret, the largest of the three species of white egret that occur in Florida, can be identified by its long, yellow bill.

Opposite: Sunrise over the mangrove-fringed waters of Biscayne Bay.

Location: In Biscayne Bay, adjoining Miami.

Climate: Winter temperatures average 59°F (15°C), while highs of 90°F (32°C) can be expected in July and August. Rain falls mostly as intense summer thunderstorms, and annual rainfall often exceeds 85 inches (2,125 mm).

When to go: Winter, especially January to March, when temperatures are not as high and mosquitoes are less troublesome.

Access: From central Miami, south on Highway 1 to Homestead and then east on SW 328 Street to the Convoy Point Visitor Center.

Facilities: At Convoy Point Visitor Center, there is a marina and picnic area, and canoes can be rented. A boat dock and picnic area can be found on Adams Key. Two backcountry campgrounds, on Boca Chita and Elliott Keys, can be reached only by boat, and only Elliott has drinking water. Snorkeling and scuba diving equipment can be rented at Convoy Point.

Outstanding features: Largely an underwater park, its centerpiece is a picturesque bay warmed by the clear, turquoise, tropical waters of the Gulf of Mexico. A chain of 10 large keys and about 40 smaller isles shelter Biscayne Bay from the ocean. An extensive coral reef is situated 2 miles (3 km) offshore from the Keys.

Visitor activities: Snorkeling, scuba diving, swimming, waterskiing, hiking, and saltwater fishing. Stone and blue crabs may be caught, but lobsters are protected within the bay. Glass-bottomed boat tours of the bay and reefs depart from Convoy Point.

Map labels:
Tallahassee
N
Biscayne NP
Boca Chita Key
Convoy Point Visitor Center
Elliott Key Ranger Station
Biscayne Bay
Adams Key

the north section of the bay by car. The ponds that carry water to cool the Turkey Point Power Station, and the nearby Crocodile Lake National Wildlife Refuge on Key Largo, protect two of the three remaining breeding populations in the United States of the American crocodile.

Glass-bottomed boats provide visitors with superb views of marine life on cruises lasting about three hours. Longer cruises cater to visitors interested in snorkeling and scuba diving to explore the beautiful coral reefs. In the shallow waters between the shore and the chain of Keys, submerged beds of sea grass provide an important nursery for crabs, lobsters, and shrimps. On Adams Key is a dock and a picnic area. Tropical hardwoods and dense vegetation crowd the island and its larger neighbor, Elliott Key. The notorious pirate, Black Caesar, once made his hideout on these islands. In 1965, a chest containing silver coins was discovered hidden on Elliott Key.

Back at the visitor center, tourists can hire canoes to paddle up creeks lined with mangroves. These trees tolerate saltwater conditions. Their dense root systems and branches help to stabilize coastal areas by trapping silt washed in by the waves. Submerged roots provide an important nursery for crabs, snails, and many species of fish. Mangroves are unusual in that most of

Above, right: The shallow, tropical waters of Biscayne Bay provide a refuge for more than 250 species of fish.

Below: Mangroves hug the shoreline at Convoy Point, the only part of the park that is accessible by road.

their roots are exposed during much of the day when the tide is out.

Two backcountry campgrounds on the Keys can be reached only by boat, while a hiking trail explores the length of Elliott. The campground and picnic area here are located at the ranger station in the northern half of Elliott Key. The second campground is situated on tiny Boca Chita Key, 10 miles (16 km) north of the dock on Adams Key.

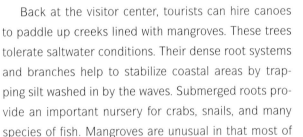

DRY TORTUGAS NATIONAL PARK

One of the newest and smallest national parks in America is Dry Tortugas. It is also one of the most interesting. The park was established in 1992. It covers 100 square miles (260 sq km) of coral reef and turquoise sea in the Gulf of Mexico, some 70 miles (110 km) west of Key West, which itself is the southernmost tract of dry land belonging to the United States. In this tropical paradise, where the park's land area totals just 85 acres (0.3 sq km) spread across five tiny islands, or Keys, the appearance of a five-story, hexagonal military fort from the 1850s is somewhat startling. Fort Jefferson, the largest fort built on the American Coast in the nineteenth century, just fits onto the tiny Key it occupies. A moat surrounds it on all sides. Where the fort was wider than the island allowed, a low wall was built in the sea to contain the water in the moat. What little remained of the island contained docks for off-loading supplies.

This remote outpost, which nowadays conjures up images of pirates and Caribbean adventures, was used as a prison for Civil War deserters and for the men accused of assassinating Abraham Lincoln. In 1858, a lighthouse was built on Loggerhead Key, which is the largest island in the park, to warn ships of the shallow seas. Shipwrecks were common. Two partially submerged wrecks lie west of Fort Jefferson along with ten submerged wrecks in shallow waters. After the fort was abandoned in 1874, the area was set aside as a refuge for the sooty tern, later as a national monument, and finally redesignated as a national park.

The park is 10 miles (17 km) wide—the boundary was determined to incorporate the coral reefs that form a broad arc in the center of the park. Coral, formed by millions of small creatures known as polyps, is the only living creature on earth visible from outer space. There is an extensive reef near Loggerhead Key and significant reefs near Fort Jefferson. The area was named Las Tortugas by the Spanish in 1513 after the four species of sea turtles that were abundant there at the time. This part of the Gulf of Mexico later became known as Dry Tortugas after sailors' maps indicated that no freshwater was present on the Keys.

Fort Jefferson

The fort occupies Garden Key, one of three small adjacent islands. Once across the bridge that spans the moat surrounding the fort, the visitor center is located inside the fortress. The remains of the officers' quarters, soldiers' barracks, and magazine are located across the

Above, right: This region was named Las Tortugas by early Spanish explorers after the abundance of turtles in the area. Turtles are still common in Dry Tortugas today.

Location: Off the coast of southern Florida, 70 miles (110 km) west of Key West.

Climate: Humid subtropical climate. Temperatures may reach 85°F (30°C) during summer. Strong winds can be experienced during winter months, and the park is located in the belt where hurricanes occur during summer.

When to go: The park is open throughout the year, but weather conditions are most favorable during spring months.

Access: Only by boat or seaplane from Key West.

Facilities: There is a dock for tour boats at Fort Jefferson and a nearby picnic area and primitive campground next to the fortress. Visitors need to be self-sufficient as there is no freshwater in the campground. A drawbridge crosses the moat surrounding the fort, where a visitor center is located inside the towering walls. Private boats and seaplanes must be moored overnight in designated areas near Fort Jefferson.

Outstanding features: Extensive patches of shallow sea have given rise to coral reefs that form a broad arc in the center of the park. Dry land is limited to six tiny Keys. Historic Fort Jefferson, a hexagonal fortress built in the mid-nineteenth century, is rich in history and the park's only significant building. The Keys protect important colonies of nesting birds and marine turtles.

Visitor activities: Swimming, sunbathing, snorkeling, scuba diving, bird-watching, and fishing. Some of the best places to snorkel include two partially submerged wrecks, the shallow waters north of Loggerhead Key and around Fort Jefferson. Barrier reefs to the south of the Keys provide superb scuba diving opportunities.

Map labels

Garden Key
Visitor Center
Bush Key
Moat
Dockhouse
Dry Tortugas NP
Hospital Key
Lighthouse
Loggerhead Key
Fort Jefferson
East Key
Tallahassee
N

Above and right: Constructed in the mid-nineteenth century, Fort Jefferson dominates Garden Key. To the left of the fort, a footbridge crosses the moat between the boat dock and the fortress, and the remains of two coal docks can be seen. Inside the historic structure, the crumbling remains of officers' quarters and soldiers' barracks once accommodated 2,000 soldiers.

grassy courtyard enclosed by the high walls. On the tiny spur of land south of the fort is a picnic area and campground. A delightful swimming beach of white sand adjoins the campground, and the shallows along the seawall are ideal for snorkeling. A limited number of goggles and snorkels can be borrowed at the visitor center for viewing some of the over 440 species of fish that have been identified on the coral reefs

Turtles and Terns

The park protects four species of marine turtle—green, hawksbill, leatherback, and loggerhead. The reefs teem with an abundance of tropical fish, lobsters, rays, crabs, and coral. In deeper water, amberjack, tarpon, barracuda, and sharks can be found. Between March and September, an estimated 100,000 sooty terns gather on Bush Key, located 200 yards (200 m) east of the fort, to nest. About 2,500 brown noddies also return here each year to nest, and the Key is closed to the public during the nesting season. The park attracts a rich diversity of bird life. Notable species include brown pelican, roseate tern, frigate bird, and peregrine falcon.

Dry Tortugas is best approached by boat and activities center on the sparkling water and its coral reefs. Diving, swimming, snorkeling, and bird-watching are the most popular outdoor activities. Camping is permitted only at the campground below the fort. Two small Keys, Hospital and Long, are closed to the public and Loggerhead Key in the west, where a 167-foot-high (51-m) lighthouse stands, can be visited only during the day. Visitors may gather shells on the beaches, but all forms of coral are strictly protected.

Below: Garden Key was not large enough to accommodate Fort Jefferson, and a seawall had to be built to contain the moat around three of its six battlements.

THE GREAT LAKES

Extending over 94,460 square miles (244,650 sq km), North America's Great Lakes of Superior, Michigan, Huron, Erie, and Ontario represent the largest reservoir of freshwater in the world. Lake Superior, with a maximum depth of 1,333 feet (406 m), is the largest of these lakes, and the largest freshwater body in the world, containing 10 percent of the earth's freshwater. Many thousands of years ago, rapid fluctuations in world temperatures and climate caused the continental ice sheet to advance and retreat over short periods of time. When the ice sheet finally melted, ice-scoured depressions filled with water to form the lakes. The lake levels dropped as water drained away, and the present shorelines of the lakes were formed as recently as 10,000 years ago.

First visited by French explorer Samuel de Champlain in 1603, the Great Lakes region was once home to Iroquois, Huron, and Algonquin Native American tribes. Although relations between these tribes and the French were friendly, disputes with the British finally led to war. By 1832, when the Black Hawk War ended, the traditional way of life in the Great Lakes was brought to an end.

Since the early 1800s, the bustling cities of Chicago, Milwaukee, Detroit, Cleveland, and Toronto have sprung up along the lakeshores of the more southerly lakes. Fifteen percent of America's population now lives in this highly industrialized and urbanized region, which accounts for 8.8 percent of America's land area. However, the northern lakes are still surrounded by immense tracts of coniferous and deciduous forests. In Wisconsin, Michigan, and Minnesota, hundreds of smaller lakes, formed by the enormous scouring and plucking power of the continental ice sheet, now dazzle like jewels scattered across vast expanses of national forest. National parks and national lakeshores conserve examples of the area's natural beauty, but protection also comes in the form of long, cold winters that help to restrict human endeavor.

Isle Royale, in Lake Superior, is the only American national park located on a Great Lake and the only one that encompasses a single island. Voyageurs, in northern Minnesota, is a wilderness of water and forest and is bounded to the north by the Rainy and Namakan Lakes, which mark the watery, invisible border between the United States and the Canadian province of Ontario.

Left: The largest freshwater lake in the world and the deepest of the Great Lakes, Lake Superior has been known to freeze during exceptionally cold winters.

SLEEPING BEAR DUNES NATIONAL LAKESHORE

On Michigan's lower peninsula, and on the eastern shore of Lake Michigan, Sleeping Bear Dunes National Lakeshore preserves two islands in the lake and a scenic 32-mile (51-km) stretch of lakeshore that includes high bluffs and sandy beaches reminiscent of an ocean island. The park consists of three blocks of land along the eastern shore of the lake, and two islands located 7 miles (11 km) offshore. It is named after an Indian legend of a bear and her two cubs who swam across Lake Michigan. The cubs drowned near the shore and became the Manitou Islands; their mother climbed to the top of a bluff and waited patiently for them, and the Sleeping Bear Dune marks the spot where she waited. The dunes cover 4 square miles (10 sq km) of the park's total area of 110 square miles (286 sq km). There are two types of dunes in the park: Beach dunes are formed when prevailing westerly winds blowing across Lake Michigan accumulate beach sand into dunes, and perched dunes, on plateaus above the lake, are formed from wind-blown glacial sands. The Sleeping Bear Dune is an example of a perched dune.

Manitou Islands

North Manitou Island is the larger of the two islands included within the park. The entire island has been designated a wilderness area of about 25 square miles (60 sq km). The island rises to a high point of 420 feet (128 m) above Lake Michigan. Lake Manitou, situated in the center of the island, is an attractive, isolated body of water. From the air the island, with the lake in its center,

appears to have been formed by volcanic activity, but its origins can be traced to the gigantic continental ice sheet that scoured the immense depression now flooded by Lake Michigan.

South Manitou Island, located 4 miles (7 km) to the southwest, has a visitor center and three backcountry campgrounds. A lighthouse was built on its southern shore in 1871 to guide ships through the Manitou Passage and into the island's harbor. Despite the presence of the lighthouse, several ships were wrecked, and rescue teams manned wooden rowboats to aid the survivors. The life-saving station and historic buildings on the island are reminders of these heroic feats.

Nowadays, ferries depart from Leland, a settlement on the narrow peninsula that leads to Cat Head Point on the mainland north of the park. Ferries operate from May to mid-October and provide visitors with a unique opportunity to explore these intriguing islands.

Visitor Activities

Apart from the picturesque islands, the land along the lakeshore offers many outdoor activities. The Platte River flows through three lakes in the southwestern corner of the park before entering Lake Michigan, and there is a campground on the river's banks. A second camp-

Above, right: Westerly winds blowing across the lake have formed beach sand into sand dunes.

Opposite: A short trail at Empire Bluffs offers panoramic views across Lake Michigan and Platte Bay.

Location: On the western edge of Michigan's lower peninsula. Traverse City is 24 miles (38 km) east of the Empire visitor center.

Climate: In summer maximum temperatures vary from 70° to 90°F (21° to 32°C). In winter, temperatures average 16° to 20°F (-9° to -7°C), but on some days temperatures may drop below 0°F (-18°C). An average of 100 inches (2,500 mm) of snow falls in winter, and cold winds blowing off Lake Michigan raise the discomfort index.

When to go: Best visited from spring through fall. The park's campgrounds are closed during winter.

Access: From Grand Rapids north on U.S. Highway 131, north to Exit 176, and then west on Highway 115 to Frankfort.

Facilities: There is a campground on the Platte River and another further north at Glen Haven. Two picnic areas are located near the Sleeping Bear Dunes. A ferry service operates from Leland to South Manitou Island from May to mid-October, and to North Manitou Island from June to August.

Outstanding features: The park's main attractions include two large islands in Lake Michigan, 32 miles (51 km) of sandy beaches along the lakeshore and a chain of inland lakes interspersed by broad-leaved forest. High bluffs rise to 440 feet (135 m) above Lake Michigan, and wind-blown dunes are elevated above the surrounding countryside.

Visitor activities: Scenic drives, hiking, overnight backpacking, beach walks, dune climbing, birdwatching, swimming, canoeing, fishing, boat tours to the islands, and tours of historic settlements on South Manitou Island.

Above: During summer, canoeing on the Platte and Crystal Rivers is a popular outdoor activity.

Right: Continental Ice Age glaciers supplied the building material for the Sleeping Bear dunes that form the center-piece of the park.

ground is located farther north in Glen Haven near Sleeping Bear Point. Apart from Lake Michigan, the park encloses or adjoins 20 smaller lakes, the largest of which, Crystal Lake, is 8 miles (13 km) wide. Canoes can be rented on the Platte and Crystal Rivers, and fishing for trout, bass, and king salmon is a popular sport. During the months of September and October, salmon return to the Platte River to spawn.

The Pierce Stocking Scenic Drive is a one-way, 7-mile (11-km) circular route that explores the country between Glen Lake and the lakeshore north of the visitor center in Empire. Two picnic areas are along the route, and the road offers panoramic views of the Sleeping Bear dunes, Lake Michigan to the west, and Glen Lake to the east.

Thirteen hiking trails, half of which meander across the central block of land around Sleeping Bear Dune, encourage visitors to explore forests of maple and beech and areas of the park away from the main road. A climb to the top of the dune at the Dune Climb provides splen-did views across Glen Lake, the second largest lake in the immediate vicinity of the park. Visitors can hike the Dune Trail, a 3.5-mile (5.6-km) route that begins at

the Dune Climb. Near the Coast Guard Station and Maritime Museum, at Glen Haven, a 3-mile (4.5-km) loop trail leads to Sleeping Bear Point.

VOYAGEURS NATIONAL PARK

A watery wilderness that embraces over 50 lakes and dozens of islands within its boundaries, Voyageurs is one of three national parks situated along the 49th parallel that marks the border with Canada. The bewildering number of lakes and waterways that connect Lake Superior to northwestern Minnesota and Manitoba, Canada—in a straight line a distance of some 280 miles (450 km)—was recognized as a major trade route in the past. The park's name commemorates the eighteenth- and nineteenth-century *voyageurs*, hardy French-Canadian canoeists who transported furs along the watery trade route that linked the Canadian northwest to the emerging cities on the Great Lakes. The voyageurs paddled canoes constructed from a cedar frame covered in birch bark and sealed with pitch, a technique taught to them by the Native Americans. These lightweight boats were easily repaired with materials found in the forests, and the fur trade rapidly grew into a lucrative enterprise. The treaty that defined America's northern border in 1783 specified that the boundary line should follow the route of the waterway.

Voyageurs, established in 1975, is one of the newest national parks in the country. The park covers 340 square miles (879 sq km). Its considerable water bodies effectively divide the park into two sections. Kabetogama Peninsula, which comprises two-thirds of the park's land surface, is completely surrounded by the Rainy, Namakan, and Kabetogama Lakes. Rainy Lake is the largest, and the park's northern border follows an invisible line through its center for 30 miles (50 km), coinciding with the national border.

Lakes of the Canadian Shield

Voyageurs is located near the southern edge of the Canadian Shield, where some of the oldest rocks on earth have been exposed by glaciation. The enormous continental ice sheets that advanced and retreated across North America during the last Ice Age have long since removed any traces of more recent rocks and have exposed the ancient bedrock. The scouring force of the ice left numerous deep recesses that have since flooded to form the countless lakes and waterways. The forests of white spruce (*Picea Glauca*) that now form the dominant plant community have colonized the land only in fairly recent geological time, since the ice sheets retreated. The extensive lakes and wetlands attract aquatic mammals such as the beaver, muskrat, and river otter. Waterbirds are well represented and include the osprey, bald eagle, great blue heron, Canada goose, green-winged teal, double-crested cormorant, mallard duck, and the exquisite loon. The forests surrounding the lakes sustain moose, white-tailed deer, black bear, chipmunk, fisher, mink, red fox, and wolf. This is one of the few places in America where naturally occurring gray wolves are still found, although seldom seen.

Above, right: The red fox relies on its keen hearing to locate the rodents and rabbits on which it preys.

Location: Northern Minnesota on the Canadian border, about 14 miles (22 km) east of International Falls.

Climate: In winter, average lows of −8°F (−22°C) are common, frequent snowstorms occur, and the lakes remain frozen for at least six months of the year. Summer temperatures are moderate, with an average high in July of 79°F (26°C).

When to go: During winter, the lakes freeze over and breaking ice can be an added hazard. Summer months are therefore best for exploring the park's many lakes.

Access: From Duluth, take U.S. Highway 53 north to International Falls.

Facilities: There are three visitor centers, but only Rainy Lake is open throughout the year. A small hotel situated at remote Kettle Falls is open in summer. There are no campgrounds within the park, but two are located on the southern border on adjoining state forests. Over 175 backcountry campsites can be reached only by water during summer. Overnight accommodations, restaurants, general stores, and other services can be found in the four towns that border the park.

Outstanding features: The park offers some of the finest wilderness canoeing experiences in the United States.

Visitor activities: Voyageurs is dominated by water. Boating, canoeing, swimming, waterskiing, fishing, bird-watching, and hiking are the main activities. During summer months, boats are essential for exploring the park, and houseboats, canoes, and motorboats can be rented. During winter, cross-country skiing, snowmobiling, ice fishing, and snowshoeing are popular outdoor activities, and a road across the frozen lakes is open as far as Cranberry Bay.

Top: The striking colors of the autumn foliage in the forests contrasts with the deep blue of the waterways.

Above: At the end of the last ice age, retreating ice sheets left deep depressions that have since filled with water to form a multitude of lakes.

Exploring Voyageurs

Voyageurs is a park that is best explored by boat. Visitor roads total a modest 5 miles (8 km) and are restricted to two access routes leading to the Ash River and Rainy Lake Visitor Centers. The major portion of the park is accessible only to hikers, canoeists, and yachting enthusiasts. The National Park Service provides 175 campsites that are accessible only by water, and these are classified as either tent, houseboat, or day-use sites, with zoning clearly indicated. For visitors who do not have access to boats, canoes can be hired, and guided boat trips depart from the visitor centers.

The many lakes and waterways offer superb fishing opportunities for smallmouth bass, muskie, lake trout, and northern pike. In winter, a snowmobile route and a cross-country ski trail allow visitors access to the Kabetogama Peninsula. Ice fishing is also popular, and a track follows the frozen surface of Rainy Lake as far east as Cranberry Bay.

Accommodations are available in several resorts bordering the park. Facilities at Kettle Falls, in the northeastern region between the Rainy and Namakan Lakes, include a lodge and portage facility for larger boats. Along almost its entire southern boundary, the park adjoins state and national forests. There are two campgrounds and several hiking trails in the forests. To

the east, canoeists can paddle over 1,000 portage-linked lakes in the Boundary Waters Canoe Area Wilderness, a specially designated area within the 5,940-square-mile (15,320-sq-km) Superior National Forest.

Above: A wilderness of water, Voyageurs preserves the memory of the intrepid French-Canadian canoeists who established a trade route across the chain of lakes.

ISLE ROYALE NATIONAL PARK

In 1671, French trappers named an island near the northern shore of Lake Superior in honor of Louis IV. An unspoiled wilderness of secluded inlets, hidden lakes, and tranquil forests inhabited by moose and wolves, the island is 45 miles (72 km) long and 8 miles (13 km) across at its widest point. Located on the border between the United States and Canada, Isle Royale is one of the most unusual national parks in the world. Because surrounded by an immense freshwater lake, the park has no vehicular access and no roads—visitors can arrive only by boat or seaplane. At the closest point, the mainland is 15 miles (24 km) away. To the south, the nearest land mass, Keweenaw Point in Michigan, is 40 miles (65 km) away. Isle Royale is open for only six months of the year, from April to October, and virtually the entire park is a designated wilderness area. Apart from two small service centers, 34 backcountry campgrounds and a network of hiking trails are the only facilities that await visitors to the heart of the island.

Isle Royale was formed about 10,000 years ago when the continental ice sheet melted and water drained away to form the Great Lakes. Its convoluted shoreline, and many jagged inlets, were carved by the mighty erosive force of the ice sheet. There are 27 named lakes on the island, formed when meltwater filled ice-scoured depressions. Siskiwit Lake in the south is the largest of these and is separated by a narrow spit from Malone Bay.

By water, there are three approaches to the park. The *Voyageur II* and *Wenonah* sail from the Grand Portage Indian Reservation, in the extreme northeastern corner of Minnesota, and the journey takes from two to three hours. The *Ranger III* and *Isle Royale Queen III* sail from Houghton and Copper Harbor, two small ports on Michigan's narrow Keweenaw Peninsula, which protrudes into the lake for 60 miles (100 km) north of the mainland. These approaches from the south across the vastness of the lake take from four to six hours.

Historic Isle Royale

The observant visitor will notice shallow pits now crowded with blueberry thickets. Nearly 1,000 of these depressions now indicate sites where Native Americans mined copper as far back as 4,500 years ago. By using beach pebbles and boulders as tools, they chipped away at the bedrock to reveal nuggets of pure copper. Mining started again during the nineteenth century, but ceased before the 895-square-mile (2,304-sq-km) national park was established in 1940.

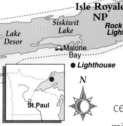

Rock Harbor Lighthouse was built in 1855 to guide ore ships. After copper mining ceased at the end of the nineteenth century, commercial fisheries were established to supply fur trappers. By the 1950s, most of the commercial fishing operations had closed. The historic Edisen Fishery, near Rock Harbor Lighthouse, has been preserved as part of the park's cultural heritage.

Above, right: The moose is the largest of the deer family.
Opposite: The road from Splitrock Lighthouse, on the northern shore of Lake Superior, ends at Grand Portage, where boats cross the vast lake to the remote island.

Location: In Lake Superior, Michigan. The nearest accessible American town is Copper Harbor, 56 miles (90 km) to the south across the lake.

Climate: Winters are harsh. In January, the average temperature range is from 4° to 24°F (–16° to –4°C). Summer temperatures are moderate; average highs range from 66° to 72°F (19° to 22°C) in July.

When to go: The park is open from mid-April to October. August and September are good months to visit, although spells of cool weather can be expected.

Access: North on Interstate 39 from Madison, Wisconsin, to Merrill. Then north on Highway 17 and U.S. Highway 45 to Rockland, and east on Highway 26 and U.S. Highway 41 to Copper Harbor. The ferry from Copper Harbor sails from May to September and can transport small boats but no vehicles. A seaplane service to the park operates from the nearby town of Houghton, on U.S. Highway 41, during summer.

Facilities: Information center, store, lodge, and marina where diesel and gasoline can be purchased at Rock Harbor. Windigo has an information center and a store but stocks only gasoline. Boats can be hired at both centers. For visitors who explore by boat, 5 day-use docks and 20 overnight docks are spaced at fairly regular intervals along the island's shoreline.

Outstanding features: This 45-mile-long (72-km) island is surrounded by the largest freshwater lake in the world. Nearly 30 island lakes are surrounded by tranquil forests.

Visitor activities: Sailing, canoeing, freshwater fishing, overnight back-packing, visits to historic buildings, wildlife viewing, and bird-watching.

Moose and Wolves

At the closest point, the Canadian shore is 15 miles (24 km) away from Isle Royale, a barrier wide enough to prevent black bear and white-tailed deer from colonizing the island. It is well-known for its populations of moose and gray wolf, though neither of these animals was present here at the beginning of the twentieth century. In the early 1900s, moose migrated to the island. Although it is not certain where they came from, it is likely that they swam across the lake from Canada. In the absence of predators, the moose population increased rapidly and, by the 1930s, had exceeded the vegetation's carrying capacity. An extensive fire in 1936 contributed to their decline but stimulated new plant growth that again encouraged the moose to increase. During the winter of 1948, the lake froze over between Canada and the island, and a small pack of gray wolves was able to cross the ice. The new arrivals helped to keep the moose population in check by preying on young, old, and sick animals. In turn, severe winters often brought about a rapid decrease in moose numbers, which then affected the wolf packs. Before the Wolf Recovery Program was launched in 1995, the wolves on Isle Royale, and other packs roaming the forests of northern Minnesota, represented the only wild wolves in the lower 48 states. Both the moose and wolves have shown great fluctuations in population depending on food availability and weather conditions. In the late 1990s, severe winters caused the moose population to plummet from 2,400 to 500. Wolves at one time increased to 50 in four separate packs and have decreased to as few as a dozen individuals on occasion. Disease also appears to be a factor in controlling wolf numbers. Research has revealed that although moose and wolf populations fluctuate considerably, often in patterns not immediately linked to each other, both species display a remarkable resilience.

Exploring the Island

Isle Royale appeals to visitors in search of a wilderness experience—the only accommodations in the park are located at Rock Harbor. Two service centers, Rock Harbor and Windigo, are located at opposite ends of the island. They are linked on land by a 165-mile (264-km) network of hiking trails that run the length of the island. The backcountry campgrounds cannot be reserved in advance; all the campgrounds are located along the shore or adjoin one of the inland lakes. The highest peak on the island, Mount Desor in the western region, at a height of 1,394 feet (425 m), offers a magnificent view of the islands and Lake Superior. A trail follows the ridge leading to the summit, and the surrounding slopes are clothed in maple and birch forests.

Another way to see the park is to sail along its shoreline. There is a marina at Rock Harbor, and boats can be hired here and at Windigo. Twenty overnight docks and five for day use only are located along the shore and on some of the smaller islands. Fishing is a popular pastime, and the island's remoteness has ensured that it sustains healthy stocks of northern pike and lake trout. No license is required for inland lakes, but a Michigan fishing license is necessary for all Lake Superior waters. Regulations also control the catching of brook trout.

Left: Twenty-five docks along the shoreline of Isle Royale, and some of the smaller adjacent islands, provide access to the wilderness heartland.

Below: Lake Superior's unfathomable vastness ensures that the island remains a remote wilderness.

THE GREAT PLAINS

The mighty Mississippi River, revered by Native Americans as "the father of waters," drains the vast, low-lying center of the United States. The river's immense drainage basin includes portions of 31 states, or one-third of the total area of America. Between the Mississippi and the Rocky Mountains, an enormous plain stretches to infinity like an endless, ochre-colored carpet rolled out between river and mountain.

The six states in this region comprise 10.4 percent of the total area of America and are home to 5 percent of the total population. The northern states of North and South Dakota are lightly populated, each with fewer than one million people. Their uncrowded prairies stretch to the distant horizon. Population increases in a southerly direction and eastward toward the Mississippi. Occasionally, the flat prairies are broken by east-flowing rivers such as the Missouri, Platte, and Arkansas. Although the center of this region is situated 1,250 miles (2,000 km) from the nearest ocean, there is no dramatic rise in topography. Across this flat plain, altitude varies from 1,500 feet (460 m) in the east to 4,450 feet (1,355 m) in the west.

Between the mountains in the west and the eastern forests, three types of prairie occur. The short-grass prairie forms a narrow band along the edge of the mountains. Mixed-grass prairie covers a larger area and is the dominant vegetation in North and South Dakota, Nebraska, and Kansas. Only relic patches remain of the tall-grass prairie in the latter three states.

Trees are scarce on the seemingly endless prairies. The ferruginous hawk, the largest of its family, often nests on the ground when no tree can be found. In the nineteenth century, the prairies were home to an estimated 60 million bison and 50 million pronghorn antelope. Now their fertile soils are devoted to the production of cattle, pigs, corn, wheat, and irrigated crops. This is America's breadbasket, and protected areas are therefore limited both in size and number. The combined acreage of the three national parks in the Great Plains region is a minute percentage of the total area, although extensive areas of national forests and grasslands, especially in South and North Dakota, significantly increase the total conserved area. Little Missouri National Grassland, in North Dakota, covers 1,605 square miles (4,145 sq km). The Badlands, Wind Cave, and Theodore Roosevelt National Parks are surrounded by extensive tracts of national grasslands and forests.

Left: Variations in rainfall produce three distinct prairie types on the Great Plains, and together they form one of the largest grasslands on earth. Poet Walt Whitman once called the prairie "North America's characteristic landscape."

BADLANDS NATIONAL PARK

To the Lakota Sioux, this region of eroded spires and gullies was known as *mako sica* (bad land). Centuries later, French fur traders named the region *mauvaises terres à traverser,* meaning "bad lands to travel across." The Badlands, a maze of eroded canyons and columns of raw sediment, presented a formidable obstacle to adventurers in previous centuries. Today, access from Interstate 90 is straightforward. From the small farming town of Wall, famous for its drugstore displaying one of the finest collections of western art in America, Highway 240 heads south for 7 miles (12 km) to the park entrance.

Badlands covers 382 square miles (990 sq km), comprising four units and two separate blocks of land. Originally a national monument approved in 1929 by Congress and established in 1939 by Presidential Proclamation, Badlands was redesignated as a national park in 1978 after the Stronghold and Palmer Creek Units were added during the 1960s. Although the park has an irregular boundary and is narrow in parts, the far larger Buffalo Gap National Grassland surrounds the North Unit and part of the Stronghold Unit.

Windswept Prairie and Castles of Sand

Situated almost in the center of the United States, Badlands is 1,125 miles (1,800 km) from the nearest source of oceanic moisture and receives just 16 inches (400 mm) of precipitation per year. Despite this low rainfall, 56 species of grass and nearly 200 species of wildflowers are present. About half the park is covered in prairie grasses. The remainder consists of barren, eroded gullies and natural sculptures carved by eons of water erosion.

The fascinating geologic features in the Badlands were formed by erosion of mudstones, claystones, and siltstones that readily disintegrate in water. This has revealed telltale parallel bands of sediment that recount 65 million years of geologic history. The Badlands are known as one of the richest fossil beds in the world. In mud now solidified as Pierre shale, evidence of an ancient sea can be seen in the form of fossilized ammonite, clams, and baculites. Yellow and red soils, deposited on top of shale, suggest that a tropical forest grew in the area once the sea had disappeared.

Many of the sediments in the area were deposited between 26 and 32 million years ago. Fossils indicate that around then, the area was covered by a fertile plain inhabited by large herds of wild animals. Some of these included oreodonts, a particularly abundant piglike creature; horses the size of large dogs; sheep-sized camels; giant pigs; many-horned antelope-like creatures; and three species of rhinoceros. Many of the fossils found in the Badlands are exhibited at the Museum of Geology in Rapid City, but careful observation in the area will reveal many fossilized bones and teeth.

Above, right: Mule deer rely on strength and horn size to deter rival males during the autumn breeding season.
Opposite: Castles of raw sediment rising in the Badlands conceal the fossilized remains of extinct mammals.

Location: In the southwestern corner of South Dakota near the town of Wall.

Climate: A dry continental climate with low humidity levels. Summers can be hot and in July average highs reach 92°F (33°C). The Badlands is situated in a semiarid region, and an average of 13 inches (325 mm) of rain falls in spring and summer. Light snow occurs in winter but seldom poses a major obstacle to travelers. In January, an average low temperature of 12°F (−11°C) can be expected.

When to go: The park is open throughout the year. Temperatures are moderate during May and September.

Access: On Interstate 90, take Exit 110 at Wall. Highway 240 provides access to the park's most visited areas, and side roads lead to the Stronghold Unit.

Facilities: Cedar Pass Lodge, which is closed in winter, and a campground are located near the Ben Reifel Visitor Center. There are picnic areas and interpretive trails along the Badlands Loop Road. White River Visitor Center in the Stronghold Unit is open during the summer.

Outstanding features: Eroded horizontal layers of mudstone, claystone, and siltstone have created a raw landscape of gullies, canyons, and spires of sediment. Within these, the remains of many extinct animals can be found, and the park protects one of the most important fossil beds in the world. Where erosion has not stripped away the surface, undulating prairie grasslands are home to many species of birds and mammals. The endangered black-footed ferret has been successfully reintroduced to the area.

Visitor activities: Scenic drives, short interpretive walks, hiking, overnight backpacking, wildlife viewing, and bird-watching.

Left: Dawn on the windswept mixed-grass prairie along the Badlands Loop Road.

Below left: Tall prairie grasses provide a home for many grassland birds, such as the red-winged blackbird and western kingbird.

Below right: Native Americans living on the prairies would boil the flowers of the gumweed to treat whooping cough, and the gum is still used in modern cough syrups.

Bottom: From the Pinnacles Overlook, the rising sun paints the Badlands' eroded spires and canyons.

Wildlife on the Prairie

Mule deer are common in the Badlands, a few white-tailed deer are present, and pronghorn can be seen between Dillon and Big Foot Passes on the loop road. Small mammals are well represented, including chipmunk, jackrabbit, and ground squirrel. Predators include coyote, swift fox, and bobcat. Bison were reintroduced in 1963 and bighorn sheep a year later. The bison are most commonly seen in the wilderness area and in the Sage Creek Unit. The bighorn sheep are descendants of 22 animals that were captured in Pikes Peak, Colorado, and currently number about 150. Research has since shown that the sheep have largely remained in the area where they were released. So in 1996, park rangers captured a herd of 16 and released them near the Ben Reifel Visitor Center.

One of the most interesting mammals in the park, the black-tailed prairie dog, is intricately tied to the most endangered mammal in America, the black-footed ferret. This ferret depends on prairie dogs for food. However, throughout the Great Plains, the range of the prairie dog has shrunk by 98 percent. As a result, the ferret was thought to have become extinct when the last one died in captivity in 1979, but a small population was later discovered in Wyoming. By 1985, only 18 ferrets remained. The U.S. Fish and Wildlife Service decided to

capture the remaining ferrets and embarked on a captive-breeding program. In 1994, the first group of 36 ferrets was released into the Badlands, with a further 300 introduced over a four-year period. The current population of black-footed ferrets in the park is the largest in America and represents a spectacular improvement in the fortunes of a highly endangered mammal. Apart from the ferret, 134 species of vertebrates benefit from prairie dog towns, which are a series of communal underground tunnels dug by the prairie dogs.

Many species of birds can be seen on the park's prairies and eroded sediments. Near the prairie dog town on the Sage Creek Road, bird-watchers will detect burrowing owl, upland sandpiper, grasshopper sparrow, sharp-tailed grouse, American kestrel, and prairie falcon. A walk along the Ciff Shelf Nature Trail, near the Ben Reifel Visitor Center, can reveal Black-billed magpie, mountain bluebird, cliff swallow, rufous-sided towhee, great horned owl, and brown thrasher.

Exploring the Badlands

Within the national park, the largest block of land, the Stronghold Unit, is not easily accessible to the general public. The North and Sage Creek Units are most accessible. The easiest way to explore some of the park's fascinating eroded pinnacles and gullies is to continue east along the Badlands Loop Road (Highway 240) for 23 miles (36 km) to the Ben Reifel Visitor Center.

Sage Creek Rim Road, a diversion from the northern Pinnacles Entrance, is a gravel 11-mile (18-km) route that skirts the Badlands Wilderness, passing a prairie dog town and then heading west to the Sage Creek Campground. The wilderness area, set aside under the Wilderness Act of 1964, encompasses 100 square miles (260 sq km) of mixed-grass prairie. Within the wilderness, no roads are permitted, and access is limited to

hikers and visitors on horseback. Horseback riding is allowed everywhere in the park except on roads and walking trails.

There are nine scenic lookouts and several short trails along the loop road leading to the visitor center. A short trail at the fossil exhibit passes several models of fossils found in the area. On the opposite side of the road, the longer 5-mile (8-km) Castle and Medicine Root Trails end at the restrooms near the visitor center. Four short trails are in the vicinity that range from 100 yards (100 m) to 1 mile (2 km). Backpackers can camp anywhere in the park, but sites must be chosen at least 0.5 mile (800 m) from any road or trail. As the Badlands water is limited and unsuitable for drinking, backpackers must carry all their own water.

The Ben Reifel Visitor Center houses a comprehensive display on the ecology of the Badlands. From June to September, park rangers arrange naturalist programs, including short walks and educational talks. The Buffalo Gap National Grassland, adjoining the North and Sage Creek Units, acts as a valuable buffer. It is managed by the U.S. Forest Service, and details can be obtained from the headquarters in Wall. Continuing south of the national park, a scenic road crosses undulating grasslands in the Pine Ridge Indian Reservation, leading to the site of the infamous massacre that took place at Wounded Knee on December 29, 1890.

Above: The Badlands Loop Road offers panoramic vistas over the park and the surrounding Buffalo Gap National Grassland.

Below, left: Along the Fossil Trail, hardy plants maintain a foothold in a dry gulch of infertile sediment.

Below: The fruit of the prairie crab apple, a native of the eastern tall-grass prairies, is eaten by rabbits, squirrels, and many species of birds. The plant is widely cultivated as an ornamental shrub for its lovely white flower heads.

WIND CAVE NATIONAL PARK & CUSTER STATE PARK

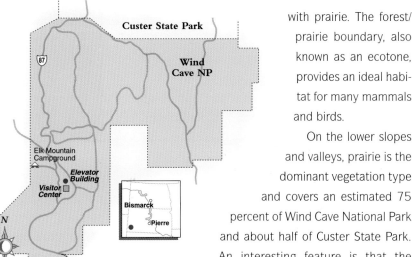

South Dakota is known for its flat prairie, which has been divided into farms that raise large herds of cattle and sheep and produce crops such as barley, rye, spring wheat, and soybeans. The major portion of this state is devoted to intensive agriculture and is not normally associated with wild America. However, in the Black Hills on its western border, two adjoining parks offer exceptional wildlife viewing and an opportunity to see remnants of the bison herds that once roamed across the prairies in the millions. Wind Cave National Park and the adjacent Custer State Park together cover 158 square miles (410 sq km) of undulating grasslands and forested hills. They adjoin the Black Hills National Forest, 1,875 square miles (4,840 sq km) of scenic mountains and canyons clothed in ponderosa pine (*Pinus ponderosa*) and spruce forests. The Black Hills attract millions of visitors each year to the giant sculptures at Mount Rushmore, the incomplete Crazy Horse Memorial, and the historic 1876 mining town of Deadwood, once home to Wild West personalities such as Wild Bill Hickock and Calamity Jane.

East Meets West

From the town of Custer, Highway 87 winds through forested mountains and gradually descends to the prairies of the lower valleys. The forests of the higher elevations contain a mixture of spruce and pine, while on the lower slopes ponderosa pine is the dominant tree. These forests grow in a patchwork interspersed with prairie. The forest/prairie boundary, also known as an ecotone, provides an ideal habitat for many mammals and birds.

On the lower slopes and valleys, prairie is the dominant vegetation type and covers an estimated 75 percent of Wind Cave National Park and about half of Custer State Park. An interesting feature is that the prairie is a composite of plant communities typical of both the east and west—eastern tall grasses and western short grasses both occur. The Black Hills represent an important convergence zone between the east and west and sustain a rich diversity of plant and animal life. Seasonal variations in climate provide the cool, moist conditions required by eastern plants and the warm, dry conditions required by plants of the west. Ponderosa pine, a western species, and American elm (*Ulmus americana*) and bur oak (*Quercus macrocarpa*), both eastern species, can be seen growing together in the forests.

The World's Oldest Cave

Wind Cave National Park was established in 1903 primarily to protect one of the most interesting cave systems in the world. Wind Cave is one of the oldest, longest, and most complex caves in the world. In total,

Above, right: Wind Cave was sculpted by rainwater percolating through the ground and dissolving limestone.

Opposite: National Park Service rangers conduct guided tours through some of Wind Cave's 83 miles (133 km) of winding passages.

Location: In the Black Hills in the southwestern corner of South Dakota, near Custer.

Climate: Total annual precipitation varies from 16 to 20 inches (400 to 500 mm), falling mainly from April to September. There is a great range in annual temperatures, from an average high of 90°F (32°C) in July to a low of 4°F (−16°C) in January.

When to go: Best visited in April to May and during the summer months. Light snow may begin to fall in early October.

Access: From Rapid City, on Interstate 90, head south on Highway 79 then west on Highway 36 and U.S. Highway 16, passing through Custer State Park. Turn south on Highway 87; the road leads to the main points of interest in Wind Cave National Park.

Facilities: An elevator descends into the cave near Wind Cave Visitor Center. Elk Mountain has a campground. In adjacent Custer State Park are two Visitor Centers, eight picnic areas, ten campgrounds, and four lodges that incorporate restaurants and general stores. Boats, mountain bikes, and horses can be rented at some of the lodges, and the State Game Lodge, on U.S. Highway 16A, offers game-viewing jeep drives.

Outstanding features: Extensive limestone cave with 83 miles (133 km) of known passages.

Visitor activities: Scenic drives, guided cave tours, short interpretive walks, hiking, overnight backpacking, cycling, wildlife viewing, and bird-watching. Custer State Park has facilities for fishing, boating, swimming, and horseback riding. In early October, the capture of surplus bison attracts many visitors. In winter, snowmobiling and ice fishing are allowed on certain lakes.

83 miles (133 km) of passages have been explored and mapped. However, by studying air flow at the entrance, researchers believe that 95 percent of the cave system has yet to be discovered.

Wind Cave was formed in Pahasapa limestone, a rock comprised mostly of seashell fragments that were deposited into a warm, shallow sea around 350 million years ago. Gypsum (calcium sulfate) crystallized from the seawater and filled cracks in the limestone. These deposits were later converted to calcite (calcium carbonate). About 65 million years ago, the Black Hills uplift created more fractures in the limestone. Water in the limestone slowly began eroding the rock and revealed the delicate fins of boxwork formations—these thin sheets of calcite, found on the ceiling and walls of the cave, resemble a car's radiator in structure and are older than the cave itself.

In 1881, two brothers, Jesse and Tom Bingham, came across a loud whistling noise on the prairie that led them to a small hole in the ground. This proved to be the cave's only known opening, and a strong wind was blowing out of the hole. The wind is caused by differences in atmospheric pressure—under certain weather conditions, the cave sucks in air.

An Abundance of Wildlife

In 1913, a herd of 14 bison was donated by the Bronx Zoo in New York. On the park's ample prairies, the animals responded well to protection. They currently number about 350. Bison are common on the picturesque undulating prairies in the southern section of Wind Cave, and Highway 385 offers superb game viewing. Mule deer are also common, and a well-known prairie dog town is located at the junction of Highways 87 and 385. Coyotes are known to patrol the vicinity in the hopes of catching an unsuspecting resident.

Approximately 1,500 bison inhabit Custer State Park. Large herds are frequently encountered, especially in the southern rangelands near the buffalo corrals. Other wildlife species include elk, white-tailed deer,

Above, right: Intricate ceiling boxwork was formed when gypsum filled cracks in limestone deposits at the bottom of a primeval sea.

Right and opposite, left: After decades of careful protection, large herds of bison once again roam across Wind Cave's undulating prairies.

bighorn sheep, and pronghorns. Mule deer are often seen along Highway 16A, where it passes through Custer State Park. Small herds of Rocky Mountain sheep are often sighted near Game Lodge.

As elevation varies from 6,800 feet (2,090 m) in the north to 3,700 feet (1,140 m) in the east, these differences in altitude produce many different habitats, which support 212 species of birds. Wild turkeys forage in the understory of the pine forests and blue jays, from the east, can be seen in the company of western and mountain bluebirds. Raptors are well represented with 17 species present, the red-tailed hawk, American kestrel, and turkey vulture being the most common.

Hikes and Outdoor Activities

From the Wind Cave Visitor Center, rangers conduct regular guided tours of the cave, beginning with a short walk leading to the elevator building. For hikers, there are three prairie trails, two canyon trails, a forest trail, a short trail at the campground, and three longer trails. Most of these hiking trails explore the terrain east of the main road that winds through the park. Rangers also arrange guided two-hour excursions into either prairie or forest during summer. A self-guided geology driving tour along the main road highlights seven points of interest, and two gravel roads, NPS 5 and 6, offer visitors the opportunity to venture into the less-visited eastern prairies of the park beyond the main road.

Custer State Park offers many outdoor activities including game viewing, fishing, boating, swimming, hiking, and horseback riding. In summer, there are gold-

panning demonstrations at the Peter Norbeck Visitor Center and guided nature walks. During winter, snowfalls are often light in comparison with much of the state. Snowmobiling is restricted to four lakes, while ice fishing on these lakes is a popular pastime. There are four interpretive trails and two shorter trails for hikers. A 22-mile (35-km) section of the Centennial Trail passes through the park. The French Creek Natural Area is a 12-mile (19-km) path that follows a stream through a scenic gorge, and the Walk-in Fishing Area Trail follows Grace Coolidge Creek from a campsite on Highway 16A to Center Lake. The park is perfect for biking and mountain bikes are permitted on most of the roads and trails.

Bison Stampede

Early in October, the annual Buffalo Roundup takes place in Custer State Park. Visitors can watch as park rangers stampede bison herds into the corrals. Once in the corrals, the animals are sorted and the majority are released back into the park. Several hundred, representing the annual increase, are retained and auctioned to private ranchers in November. Funds raised from the auction contribute 20 percent of the park's annual income. An arts festival and cooking competition take place over three days, coinciding with the roundup, making this a popular time of year for visitors.

Above: Because livestock farming dominates on the prairies, these parks preserve an important, unspoiled remnant.

Below: The bulb of the small soapweed, a species of yucca, was once used by Native Americans to make soap.

THEODORE ROOSEVELT NATIONAL PARK

Theodore "Teddy" Roosevelt, twenty-sixth president of the United States, did more for the conservation of America's natural environment than any other president, establishing 5 national parks, 16 national monuments, and 51 national wildlife refuges. In 1905, he helped to form the U.S. Forest Service, placing nearly 195,000 square miles (504,000 sq km) of land under its protection.

In 1978, portions of Roosevelt's two ranches in North Dakota, covering 110 square miles (284 sq km), were set aside as a national park. The park consists of three separate pieces of land surrounded by the extensive 1,606-square-mile (4,143-sq-km) Little Missouri National Grassland.

Vegetation and Wildlife

Vegetation consists of prairie grasslands and includes significant areas of arid badlands. Winters are long and very cold, while summers are hot, if fleeting.

Woodlands of willow, cottonwood, green ash (*Fraxinus pennsylvanica*), box elder (*Sambucus melanocarpa*), and juniper grow along the banks of the Little Missouri. Of the 54 bird species that breed in the park, 39 nest only in the riverine woodlands. Wildlife includes prairie dogs, mule deer, pronghorn, bison, and bighorn sheep. The Park Service maintains a herd of wild horses in the South Unit and a herd of longhorn steers in the North Unit as symbols of the Old West.

Visiting the Park

The park's headquarters in the historic settlement of Medora include a visitor center and the Maltese Cross Cabin, Roosevelt's 1884 home. The South Unit covers two-thirds of the park. A scenic, circular drive of 36 miles (58 km) passes five viewpoints and a picnic area. A number of hiking and horseback trails explore the country away from the scenic drive. The land west of the Little Missouri River has been set aside as a wilderness area, and a trail explores its Petrified Forest Plateau.

The Little Missouri flows through the center of the North Unit, and from the North Unit Visitor Center, a 13-mile (21-km) road provides panoramic views over the river and the extensive badlands on either side, ending at a viewpoint. The 11-mile (18-km) Buckhorn Trail passes two prairie dog towns, and the Achenbach Trail explores the country on both banks of the river.

Above, right: Black-tailed prairie dogs are gregarious animals that live in large colonies in underground burrows.
Opposite, top left: Roosevelt's Maltese Cross Cabin is situated at the southern entrance to the park in Medora.
Opposite, top right: Coyote are often sighted in the park.
Opposite, bottom: Framed by a flowering yucca, the Little Missouri River meanders through the park's separate units.

Location: North Dakota. The park is separated into three separate blocks, and the southern block is situated near Belfield on Interstate 94.

Climate: In July, an average high temperature of 84°F (29°C) can be expected. Rain falls mainly between April and September. From October to April, the minimum temperature can drop below freezing, and the average minimum temperature in January is 0°F (–18°C).

When to go: Best visited in summer. During winter, some roads in the park are closed.

Access: Interstate 94 follows the southern boundary of the South Unit. Exit 24 or 27 to Medora provides access to historic buildings and the Scenic Loop Drive. To visit the North Unit, continue east on the Interstate and at Belfield, take U.S. Highway 85 north until the turnoff to the North Unit Visitor Center.

Facilities: The Medora and the Painted Desert Visitor Centers, open only in summer, are easily accessed from Interstate 94. The North Unit Visitor Center is open in summer and for a limited period in winter. Two campgrounds overlook the Little Missouri River. A number of motels are in Medora on the southern boundary.

Outstanding features: Undulating prairie grasslands, eroded features, and badlands crossed by the Little Missouri River. The Maltese Cross Cabin was once the home of President Theodore Roosevelt.

Visitor activities: Scenic drives, hiking, overnight backpacking, fishing, horseback riding, wildlife viewing, bird-watching, and wildflower identification. If sufficient water is in the Little Missouri River, canoeing and raft trips are possible.

TEXAS AND THE SOUTH

As the second largest of the 50 states that make up the United States, Texas accounts for two-thirds of the South. At one time, Texas was an independent republic. Its history is interwoven with battles between Spaniards and Native Americans, and later Texans against Mexicans, best remembered in the Battle of the Alamo. European influences can be traced back to the sixteenth century. In 1519, the Spanish governor of Jamaica sent a captain to map the coast of Texas. In 1528, a group of 600 Spaniards landed in Florida in search of the mythical wealthy Seven Cities. After storms and disease killed most of the party, their treasurer, Alvar de Vaca, led the survivors on an eight-year march from Florida across Texas to Mexico. Only four men finally reached Mexico.

This region covers 8.6 percent of the United States and accounts for 9 percent of the population. Its vegetation is especially diverse, ranging from rugged desert to moss-draped cypress swamps. Before the arrival of settlers, prairie grasses covered most of Oklahoma and half of Texas. Although large areas have been replaced by croplands, extensive areas of prairie still remain in central and northern Texas. At the edge of the prairie, a vast deciduous forest once stretched eastward as far as the Atlantic Ocean. Tall broad-leaved trees characterize these forests. The most common trees include oak, beech, birch, walnut, hickory, holly, elm, and maple. In upland regions where soils are better drained, the deciduous forest is dominated by oak, hickory, and holly. In low-lying areas along the Gulf of Mexico, where the water table is often high, forests of cypress, live oak, and magnolia form a vegetation type best described as temperate rain forest. Where extensive areas of swamp and flood plain occur, especially in the vicinity of the Mississippi delta, the bald cypress is the dominant tree. As moisture and humidity levels are high throughout the year, many of the trees are festooned in Spanish moss.

This region has three national parks. The rugged Big Bend in west Texas is the largest and conserves deserts and mountains bordered by a broad bend of the Rio Grande. National grasslands and wildlife refuges protect remnants of the prairie in Oklahoma and northern Texas. The broad-leaved forest is preserved in national forests scattered across Arkansas, Louisiana, and eastern Texas.

Left: El Capitan's jagged peak rises above the rugged mountain wilderness of the Guadalupe Mountains, western Texas.

HOT SPRINGS NATIONAL PARK

Hot Springs is an unusual national park in many respects. Covering a modest 8 square miles (22 sq km), it is the smallest of America's 55 national parks. It is the only national park in the country to be included within city limits—it adjoins the city of Hot Springs in Arkansas in a circular block of land that surrounds part of the city and protects the hills above its residential areas. The hot springs were formed by rainwater soaking into the hills, being heated deep below the earth's surface, and eventually emerging along a fault at the base of the hills some 4,000 years later. The water cascades down a tufa terrace, a fascinating rock formation formed by minerals dissolved in the water.

In the late nineteenth and early twentieth ceturies, the springs were well-known. The National Park Service's first director, Stephen Mather, persuaded Congress to set the area aside as a national park in 1921. A total of 47 springs occur within the park. The water gushes to the surface at the rate of 100,000 gallons (300,000–400,000 L) per day. The water contains dissolved elements such as calcium, bicarbonate, and silica and has an average temperature of 143°F (62°C) at the surface. As the resort developed, most of the springs were covered over. Hot water was then piped to a reservoir and distributed to bathhouses.

Historic Bathhouses

Central Avenue, which drew large crowds to its "Bathhouse Row" in the late nineteenth century, follows a narrow gap in the hills. The road is lined with cast-iron lampposts. The historic buildings on the right-hand side have been included within the park and their exteriors carefully restored. The third building on the right, Buckstaff, is an active bathhouse. The visitor center is located further up the road, and thermal fountains and hot springs can be viewed on the paths behind the building. In its prime, Bathhouse Row was known for its elegant buildings, which included marble floors, stained-glass windows, decorative tiles, statues, and fountains. In the 1950s the bathhouses began to lose popularity and gradually closed. During the 1980s, private grant money assisted the Park Service in restoring the buildings. The Fordyce Bathhouse, which houses the visitor center, has been meticulously restored, and 23 of its rooms have been furnished in period furnishings. A visit to the building recalls its heyday in the 1920s when people traveled across the country by train to enjoy the therapeutic power of the hot springs. The springs still attract devotees, and several nearby hotels offer bathhouse facilities.

Above, right: Visitors can fill containers with mineral water at the thermal fountains along Bathhouse Row.

Opposite: The Hot Springs Mountains are the source of several creeks and the thermal springs that supply the pools on the carefully restored Bathhouse Row.

Location: Central Arkansas, surrounding the city of Hot Springs.

Climate: Humid subtropical climate with moderate variation in temperature extremes. January is the only month of the year where the average low dips below freezing. Summers are hot. In July, an average high temperature of 93°F (34°C) can be expected. Rainfall is plentiful, and the region receives an average of 54 inches (1,350 mm) per year.

When to go: Summers can be hot and humid, but winters are mild. The water in the springs is hot and gushes out at a constant temperature of 143°F (62°C).

Access: South from Little Rock on Interstate 30 to Exit 111, then west on U.S. Highway 70 to Hot Springs.

Facilities: Hot Springs Visitor Center is located in the historic Fordyce Building on Central Avenue, where 23 rooms have been restored to their former glory. On the same street, Buckstaff is an active bathhouse. There is a campground to the east at Gulpha Gorge and picnic areas on the summits on either side of the valley. There are no other accommodations in the park, but the city of Hot Springs has many hotels and motels.

Outstanding features: A range of forested hills gives rise to 47 springs of mineral water. A row of historic buildings along the Grand Promenade has been beautifully restored.

Visitor activities: Scenic drives, relaxing in mineral baths, tours of historic buildings, short walks, hiking, cycling, horseback riding, birdwatching, and tree and wildflower identification.

Above: Apart from preserving hot springs and historic buildings, much of the park consists of the forested slopes of the Hotspring and Sugarloaf Mountains.

Above, right: In its heyday in the 1920s, Bathhouse Row attracted large crowds of devotees.

Right: Between the historic buildings in Bathhouse Row and the forested hillside, several short trails and the Grand Promenade pass by many hidden springs.

Other Activities

Two scenic drives allow visitors to enjoy the beauty of the hills bordering Central Avenue. The West Mountain Drive ends at a car park on the crest of the mountain. From this point, the circular 9-mile (14-km) Sunset Trail follows the summit of the hills and then traverses the Sugarloaf Mountains across the valley before ending at the Gulpha Gorge Campground, located on Highway 70B, a short distance to the east of Central Avenue.

From Central Avenue, the Grand Promenade behind the historic bathhouses takes in attractions such as the tufa terrace and Hot Water Cascade. The one-way Hot Springs Mountain Drive, which includes three loops, leads to an observation tower on the summit of Hot Springs Mountain. The 216-foot-high (65-m) tower provides panoramic views over the hills and the adjacent city. The mountain's delightful forests of white oak (*Quercus alba*), red maple (*Acer rubrum*), and hickory are best observed from the extensive network of interconnected hiking trails.

GUADALUPE MOUNTAINS NATIONAL PARK

Situated on the border of New Mexico in western Texas is this remote national park that protects the scenic Guadalupe Mountains, four canyons, dunes of white gypsum sand, and surrounding tracts of semiarid scrub. Established in 1972, the park extends over 135 square miles (348 sq km) of the mountains and deserts to the west. Guadalupe Peak, at 8,749 feet (2,667 m) the tallest mountain in the state of Texas, and 8,085-foot (2,464-m) El Capitan form a dramatic gateway to the park.

Apart from Highway 62 from El Paso, which crosses the park for 3 miles (5 km), park roads are restricted to three short access routes to the Dog Canyon and Pine Springs Campgrounds and to the Frijole Ranch History Museum. Few people live in the region, and the nearest gasoline station is 35 miles (56 km) away in any direction. The Butterfield Stage Route, the first transcontinental mail route from the mid-1800s, passes through the park, and the ruins of a stagecoach station can still be seen. Half of the park has been set aside as a wilderness area. Modern-day visitors to Guadalupe need to explore its mountains and canyons on foot. They are drawn by its remoteness and the untamed landscapes that have changed little since the frontier days of the Wild West. There are several popular walks through the park, taking visitors through a landscape that changes from bare desert to verdant mountain forest.

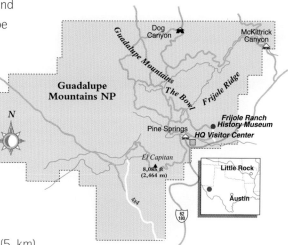

Relic Forests and Desert

The Guadalupe Mountains are unusual in that their towering cliffs are formed from limestone that was deposited by marine creatures in a primordial ocean about 200 million years ago. The reef formed a horseshoe for 400 miles (650 km) along the shores of the ocean that once flooded the areas now known as western Texas and southeastern New Mexico. When uplifting of the earth's crust later occurred, parts of the reef were left exposed by erosion of the surrounding sediments.

Forests of ponderosa pine (*Pinus ponderosa*), near the eastern limits of their distribution, grow on the high mountains in the company of aspen (*Populus tremuloides*), Douglas fir (*Pseudotsuga menziesii*), and southwestern white pine (*Pinus strobiformis*). These forests are botanical relics from a period some 15,000 years ago when a cooler, wetter climate allowed the forests to spread over a large region. Elk were reintroduced in the 1920s, and small herds inhabit the high mountain forests. Other mammals occurring in the park include mule deer, jackrabbit, desert cottontail, gray fox, kit fox, coyote, black bear, and mountain lion.

Above, right: The yucca, state flower of neighboring New Mexico, depends on only one group of male moths for pollination.

Location: Western Texas, on the border of New Mexico. The nearest town, Whites City in New Mexico, is 35 miles (55 km) from the main entrance.

Climate: A dry steppe climate with an annual average of less than 16 inches (400 mm) of rain. In July, an average high of 92°F (33°C) can be expected. Average lows in January range from 22° to 30°F (−6° to −1°C) and snowstorms can occur during winter.

When to go: Best visited from September to November when trees in the canyons display fall foliage.

Access: From Interstate 10, take U.S. Highway 62/180 in El Paso and head east to the park entrance. The northern campground at Dog Canyon can be reached from Highway 137, which turns off U.S. Highway 285 north of Carlsbad.

Facilities: The campground at Pine Springs is situated near the Headquarters Visitor Center. McKittrick Canyon Visitor Center is located near the eastern boundary of the park, and there is another campground on the northern boundary at Dog Canyon. A picnic area near the Frijole Ranch History Museum includes a homestead, schoolhouse, and barn.

Outstanding features: The highest peak in Texas and an imposing ridge of the Guadalupe Mountains. Much of the park is designated wilderness area with deep canyons, rugged peaks, and remnant forests of pine and fir.

Visitor activities: Four-wheel-drive excursions, hiking, short walks to natural springs, visits to cultural history museum, overnight backpacking, horseback riding, wildlife viewing, and bird-watching.

Above: Rainfall varies considerably on the parched Chihuahuan Desert Plains.

Below, right: Manzanita Spring, near the Frijole Ranch Museum, is an excellent spot for bird-watching.

Opposite, top: The ruins of The Pinery, a station along the Butterfield Stage Route, date back to 1858 when horse-drawn stagecoaches carried mail across the country.

Opposite, bottom right: Pine Springs Campground is situated at the foot of the Guadalupe Mountains near the park headquarters.

The Chihuahuan Desert surrounds the mountains. This sun-baked arid plain receives an annual rainfall varying from 10 to 16 inches (250 to 400 mm). Agave, yucca, and prickly pear are well adapted to the desert's harsh conditions. Many rodents and reptiles are active only at night and spend the heat of the day hidden in burrows to conserve moisture.

Hiking in the Guadalupes

An 80-mile (130-km) network of hiking trails ventures into the wilderness area north of the visitor center at park headquarters. There are ten backcountry campgrounds in the mountains, and hikers need to carry their own water. The ascent to Guadalupe Peak is a 9-mile (15-km) round-trip hike that requires a full day. To the north of the visitor center, the Tejas Trail climbs the mountain slope to The Bowl, a secluded forest of ponderosa pine and Douglas fir. The shortest return hike from The Bowl is 9 miles (15 km) in length, and several loops offer alternative routes. Bush Mountain Trail, leading from The Bowl to Dog Canyon Campground on the northern boundary, is a long hike that passes two backcountry campgrounds along the route. The

2-mile (3-km) Smith Spring Trail at the Frijole Ranch Museum passes two springs at the foot of the mountain that attract a wealth of birds and wildlife. Two-thirds of the hiking trails in the mountains can also be used by visitors on horseback.

A hike along the 4-mile-long (7-km) McKittrick Canyon, in the northeastern corner of the park, takes

visitors through some of the Guadalupe Mountains' most beautiful scenery. The canyon is watered by the park's only perennial stream, and its sheltered banks are lined with oak, maple, ash, walnut, and Texas madrona (*Arbutus texana*). During fall months, the changing pallet of leaf colors adds to the park's rugged beauty.

BIG BEND NATIONAL PARK

The seventh largest national park in the lower 48 states, Big Bend safeguards a diverse landscape that includes 118 miles (189 km) of the convoluted channel of the Rio Grande. While marking the border with Mexico, the river sustains plants that attract a rich diversity of birds. On the arid plains of the Chihuahuan Desert, 60 species of cacti occur, plants well adapted to storing moisture from the brief showers that fall during summer. In the center of the park, the rugged peaks of the Chisos Mountains rise to 7,825 feet (2,384 m), and provide a refuge for plants and animals that have become isolated by the aridity of the surrounding desert.

Proclaimed in 1944, Big Bend covers 1,250 square miles (3,230 sq km). The park is named after a great bend in the Rio Grande, which flows along its boundary for 118 miles (189 km). Over eons, the erosive sediments of the Rio Grande have carved a course across the sedimentary rocks of the region. Along its passage through the desert, the Rio Grande flows through three impressive canyons, where cliffs of limestone and sandstone tower up to 1,500 feet (450 m) above the river's muddy waters. In the southwestern corner of the park, the river first enters the Santa Elena Canyon, then turns and flows north to enter Mariscal Canyon, and finally passes through Boquillas Canyon near the eastern boundary of the park. Although Apache and Comanche tribes and Spanish explorers established crossing points on the Rio Grande, the canyons were explored in detail only toward the end of the nine-

teenth century. In 1889, Robert Hill, of the U.S. Geological Survey, and five others paddled down the length of the river for the first time.

The National Park Service administers a 127-mile (203-km) stretch of the Rio Grande on the east of the park. Big Bend adjoins the Santa Elena Canyon and Maderas Del Carmen protected areas in Mexico to the south. On the American side of the river, the Black Gap Wildlife Management Area borders the park to the east. In 1989, a bilateral agreement between the United States and Mexico was signed to protect the natural resources along the international border.

Desert Wildlife

Big Bend is located on an important bird migration route. Many tropical bird species are found here at the northern extreme of their distribution. A total of 434 bird species have been recorded, more than in any other American park and undoubtedly one of the highest bird counts for a national park anywhere in the world. The bird list includes bird species such as the peregrine falcon and the Colima warbler, a bird found nowhere else in the United States.

Above, right: The peccary is restricted to the deserts in the extreme south of the United States.
Opposite: Santa Elena Canyon is the first of three canyons carved by the silt-laden Rio Grande.

Location: Western Texas, south of the town of Alpine.

Climate: In July, an average high of 98° F (36°C) is reached in the desert, with a maximum of 110°F (43°C). Winters are mild. In January, average temperatures range from 30°F (–1°C) to a high of around 67°F (19°C).

When to go: From March to May when temperatures are milder and bird-watching can be particularly rewarding.

Access: From Interstate 10, take U.S. Highway 385 south past Marathon to the main entrance. The western entrance near Maverick Junction is 80 miles (127 km) south of Alpine on Highway 118.

Facilities: Several visitor centers, five picnic areas, and a number of short interpretive trails. There is a lodge at Chisos Basin and three campgrounds in the park, two of which border the Rio Grande. Groceries can be purchased at Panther Junction, Chisos Basin, Rio Grande Village, and Castolon. In this arid region, it is advisable to carry drinking water in the car at all times. Many four-wheel-drive roads explore the rugged terrain between Castolon and Rio Grande Village.

Outstanding features: Three major gorges carved by the Rio Grande flowing along the park's southern boundary for 118 miles (189 km); rugged peaks of the Chisos Mountains dominate the center of the park, surrounded by the arid plains of the Chihuahuan Desert.

Visitor activities: Scenic drives, hiking, short walks, overnight trails, four-wheel-drive excursions, cycling, fishing, river raft trips, horseback riding, and bird-watching.

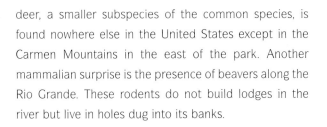

Below: River rafting is one of the best ways to explore the wilderness of the park.

Bottom: Sotol Vista Overlook, on the road from Santa Elena Canyon to Castolon.

The Chihuahuan Desert covers much of Big Bend. Its typical wildlife includes mule deer, pronghorn antelope, coyote, desert cottontail, and jackrabbit. The kit fox, which preys primarily on kangaroo rats, and the peccary, one of only two wild pigs found in the Western Hemisphere, are two unusual desert mammals. Mountain lion and Mexican black bear roam across the mountains, while the Carmen Mountains white-tailed deer, a smaller subspecies of the common species, is found nowhere else in the United States except in the Carmen Mountains in the east of the park. Another mammalian surprise is the presence of beavers along the Rio Grande. These rodents do not build lodges in the river but live in holes dug into its banks.

Discovering the Desert

There are two entrances to the park, four visitor centers, and three major campgrounds. The visitor center in Rio Grande Village is closed during the summer. A 161-mile (258-km) network of paved and gravel roads provides access to the northern, western, and central regions of the park. However, the remainder of the park is accessible only by four-wheel-drive vehicle or on foot.

From the northern entrance gate on Highway 385, a paved road crosses the desert to Panther Junction and then climbs through woodlands of Mexican pinyon pine (*Pinus cembroides*) and oneseed juniper (*Juniperus monosperma*) to the Chisos Basin, where there is a campground and lodge accommodations. From the Chisos Basin Visitor Center, hikers can follow routes to the summit of Emory Peak, the highest point in the park, or follow four other trails through the mountains.

Starting at Panther Junction, to the east another road heads 21 miles (34 km) to Rio Grande Village on the sun-baked banks of the river. A side road off this ends at the Boquillas Canyon Overlook where there is a short trail.

West of the Chisos Basin, the Ross Maxwell Scenic Drive crosses desert dominated by impressive mesas and reaches Castolon on the Rio Grande after 22 miles (35 km). Castolon served as an American army post during the Mexican Revolution of 1916, and many of the old buildings still remain. The road west of Castolon follows the course of the river for 8 miles (13 km) to the Santa Elena Canyon Overlook. A little further along, a short trail leads to the entrance to the canyon, and a gravel road heads back north to the western entrance at Maverick Mountain.

There are 40 backcountry campgrounds in the park. These are accessible from the main roads or from the four-wheel-drive tracks.

Visitors may also fish in the Rio Grande. They can obtain permits from rangers for canoe or raft trips in inflatable dinghies down the river, a unique means of viewing the park's attractions.

Above: From Lajitas, on the park's western boundary, the Rio Grande flows for 118 miles (189 km) through a rugged desert landscape.

Left: The Window in the Chisos Mountains, the southernmost range in the United States, is accessible by hiking trail from the Chisos Basin Campground.

THE MOUNTAIN STATES

North America's most impressive and awe-inspiring mountain range, the Rocky Mountains, stretches in a rugged, snow-crowned spine for 3,000 miles (4,800 km) from Alaska to northern New Mexico. Named after these jagged peaks, the Mountain States of Colorado, Wyoming, Montana, and Idaho occupy a vast and beautiful territory covering 432,142 square miles (1,114,926 sq km), or 11.7 percent of the United States. This region of formidable summits, extensive forests, and wide-open spaces is home to fewer than 6 million people, just 2 percent of the nation's population. It still evokes images of the America of the intrepid explorer, the hardy pioneer, and the hopeful gold miner.

Yellowstone, the world's first national park, was proclaimed in 1872 in northwestern Wyoming. The establishment of Yellowstone signified a fundamental change in approach to the natural environment: plants, scenery, and wild animals would from now on be regarded as the property of the nation and not merely economic resources for individual gain. The concept of a national park, "a pleasuring ground for the benefit and enjoyment of the people," as distinct from a preserve where wildlife was protected for the elite, was accepted with enthusiasm and adopted by almost every nation on earth.

Yellowstone and its adjacent southern neighbor, Grand Teton, protect one of the most intricate and fascinating ecosystems in North America. Among the region's many natural treasures are the world's largest active geothermal area, North America's largest mountain lake (Yellowstone Lake), spectacular river gorges, impressive waterfalls, untamed rivers, and quiet forest glades that are home to bison, elk, and grizzly bear.

The Mountain States' other parks include Glacier in Montana and Rocky Mountain in Colorado, both well-known for their glacial and mountainous features; Mesa Verde in southern Colorado, where stone ruins of Anasazi Native American settlements are complemented by spectacular scenery; and the untamed grandeur of the Black Canyon of the Gunnison.

Much of the land in Idaho and Wyoming, and about half of all land in Montana and Colorado, remains the property of the federal government. The United States Forest Service controls extensive tracts of forest surrounding many national parks, in particular the Yellowstone, Grand Teton, Glacier, and Rocky Mountain parks. In this region, wilderness areas established primarily on national forest lands cover an area seven times larger than Yellowstone. While untouched and free of any roads, wilderness areas extend protected areas for considerable distances beyond the official park boundaries.

Left: For a few months in summer, the snow melts and mountain goats feed on moss and alpine grasses on the upper slopes of the mountains in Glacier National Park.

GLACIER NATIONAL PARK

Jagged mountain peaks, ice-scoured valleys, 30 large glacial lakes, more than 50 glaciers, and a spectacular array of wildlife are among the attractions of two adjacent national parks, shared between the United States and Canada. Glacier National Park was established in 1910. It encompasses 1,584 square miles (4,086 sq km) of the Livingston and Lewis Mountains, which give rise to numerous lakes and rivers. This park is sometimes confused with Glacier Bay National Park in southeastern Alaska. The adjoining Waterton Lakes National Park, in the Canadian province of Alberta, is marked by the 49th parallel (or line of latitude), the borderline agreed to between the United States and Canada in 1818. It was established in 1895 and covers 201 square miles (519 sq km). This park is well-known for its rugged mountain peaks and three picturesque glacial lakes.

The watershed formed by the Rocky Mountains, known as the Continental Divide, follows a line drawn through the center of Glacier. Snow falling on the high peaks ends up in three separate oceans. West of the divide, tributaries course down mountain slopes to join the Flathead River, which flows northwest to the Pacific Ocean. To the east, the Saint Mary River flows north across Canada to Hudson Bay. The Two Medicine River meanders east across the prairies to meet the Missouri River and eventually becomes a small part of the mighty Mississippi.

In 1932, the governments of both countries established the world's first transfrontier peace park, a concept that has since been adopted in other parts of the world, particularly in southern Africa. Waterton-Glacier International Peace Park was declared a World Heritage Site in 1995. Three contiguous wilderness areas extend 95 miles (150 km) south of Glacier to safeguard an area nearly twice the size of the park. Forest reserves form an unbroken corridor that stretches north from Waterton to the enormous Banff and Jasper National Parks in western Alberta.

Mountain Forests and Wildlife

Several types of coniferous forests occur in the park, while alpine vegetation replaces forest above the tree line. On the western slopes of the mountains, a moist forest of red cedar (*Thuja plicata*) and western hemlock (*Tsuga heterophylla*) is the dominant vegetation type. Above the valleys, these trees are replaced by Douglas fir (*Pseudotsuga menziesii*), lodgepole pine (*Pinus contorta*), and western larch (*Larix occidentalis*). Higher up the slopes, a subalpine forest of Engelmann spruce (*Picea engelmannii*), subalpine fir (*Abies lasiocarpa*), and alpine larch (*Larix lyallii*) can be found to an altitude of

Above, right: Glacier is home to a significant population of grizzly bears, and visitors are warned to take precautions.

Opposite: The summit of 8,760-foot-high (2,670-m) Clements Mountain straddles the Continental Divide.

Location: Northwestern Montana, on the Canadian border, near Kalispell.

Climate: From September to May, minimum temperatures drop below freezing. In January, the average low is 0°F (−18°C) and heavy snowfalls occur, and in July the average high is a moderate 72°F (22°C).

When to go: The only road through the park is open from mid-June to mid-October, depending on weather conditions. July and August are the best months to visit.

Access: From Interstate 90, take U.S. Highway 93 at Exit 90 near Missoula and head north to Kalispell. Then head east on U.S. Highway 2 to the entrance at West Glacier.

Facilities: Three visitor centers along Going-to-the-Sun Road are open from early May until October. Apgar Visitor Center is open on weekends during winter. Eight campgrounds and six lodges are open during summer, the majority located along Going-to-the-Sun Road. Picnic areas, stables, food outlets, boat rentals, and interpretive trails are located on the shores of the two large lakes along this route.

Outstanding features: Many peaks rise above 9,850 feet (3,000 m), with 32 large glaciers on the high summits and 30 lakes flooding the deep ice-scoured valleys.

Visitor activities: Hiking, overnight backpacking, mountain climbing, cycling, fishing, boating, guided cruises, horseback riding, and wildlife viewing. Waterton offers the above activities as well as golf and swimming. During winter, cross-country skiing and snowshoeing are added attractions. However, snow accumulation poses a danger to mountain climbers and special precautions need to be taken.

Map labels: ALBERTA · Waterton Lakes NP · BRITISH COLUMBIA · MONTANA · Waterton Park · Belly River · Kintla Lake · Goat Haunt · Bowman Lake · Livingston Range · Many Glacier · Quartz Creek · Logan Pass Visitor Center · Saint Mary Visitor Center · Logging Creek · GOING—TO—THE—SUN ROAD · Rising Sun · Lake McDonald · Lewis Range · Glacier NP · Apgar Visitor Center · Two Medicine · Helena · N

deer. The smaller, less-conspicuous mammals include the beaver, porcupine, northern flying squirrel, golden-mantled ground squirrel, yellow-pine chipmunk, hoary marmot, and pika. The park and its surrounding national forests provide an important habitat for 300 grizzly bears, one-third of the total population of the lower 48 states. In the past, the bears used to gather along streams to catch spawning kokanee salmon, but a decline in fish stocks has forced them to find other sources of food. Visitors are warned to keep their own food stocks well protected. Predators are well represented, although most are secretive and nocturnal. They include pine marten, fisher, mink, short-tailed weasel, lynx, mountain lion, and wolverine.

Birds of prey include the northern goshawk, bald eagle, golden eagle, osprey, merlin, short-eared owl, and snowy owl. On the park's glacial lakes, waterbirds such as the northern pintail, redhead, harlequin duck, and hooded merganser can be seen. Birds that favor high mountains or coniferous forests include Clark's nutcracker, mountain chickadee, marbled godwit, white-tailed ptarmigan, mountain bluebird, spotted towhee, and Cassin's finch.

Return of the Wolf

In 1979, a female gray wolf appeared on the western edge of the park. Two years later, the tracks of a male wolf were found, but the newcomer was accidentally killed soon afterwards. The female was later seen with seven pups, and the wolf and her offspring soon became known as the magic pack. Since then, a further eight packs have become established in Montana, most of them descendants of the original pack. Several packs of wolves range through Glacier National Park and the Flathead and Lolo National Forests to the west and south. Some have wandered as far south as the

Above: The Trail of the Cedars explores a delightful forest near the Avalanche Creek Campground.

Above, right: During the brief summer, the high mountain meadows are ablaze with bright displays of glacier lilies.

around 7,500 feet (2,300 m). At the upper limits of the forest, near the tree line where the growing season is too short and temperatures too low in summer to permit trees to grow, twisted specimens of whitebark pine (*Pinus albicaulis*) struggle to survive. On exposed slopes where strong winds dry out the soil, or in sheltered depressions where deep snow accumulates, trees are unable to grow even at lower altitudes.

Glacier is one of the few places in the lower 48 states where the full complement of mammals that occurred historically in the area can still be seen; it is one of the best parks in America for extensive wildlife viewing. Large mammals include the grizzly bear, black bear, elk, moose, mountain goat, bighorn sheep, and white-tailed

Bitterroot Range near Missoula. By removing weak deer, the returning wolves are once again playing an important role in the ecosystem. Grizzly bears scavenge on the carcasses of deer killed by wolves. Coyotes have declined since wolves reappeared, which in turn allows ground birds such as the sage grouse to prosper. In the 1990s, the U.S. Fish and Wildlife Service began reintroducing wolves to Yellowstone and to wilderness areas in Idaho. At least 25 packs now roam the mountains and forests of this region.

A Winter Park

Glacier's location on the 49th parallel and its high mountains with many peaks towering about 9,000 feet (2,700 m) ensure that large areas of the park are blanketed by snow for most of the year, making it a popular destination with visitors who enjoy winter sports.

Mountain climbers, however, are often hindered by the heavy snows. When approaching from the south or west, Highway 2 enters the park at the western entrance and the 50-mile (80-km) Going-to-the-Sun Road across the center of the park is the only road through the mountains. The road is open only from mid-June to mid-October. For the remainder of the year, only the first 10 miles (16 km) from the western entrance are open, and the first 6 miles (10 km) from the eastern entrance as far as Rising Sun. Three visitor centers are usually open from May to October, and lodges at four locations within the park are open from June to mid-September. Of the 730 miles (1,150 km) of hiking trails, many are accessible only during the summer from July onward when sufficient snow has melted. Aside from this brief summer, cross-country skiing offers the means of exploring this expanse of white wilderness.

Below: Going-to-the-Sun Road ascends the high mountains and offers sweeping vistas across the peaks of the Lewis and Livingston Mountain Ranges.

Right: McDonald Creek rushes down the eastern slopes of Mount Geduhn in the Livingstone Range and flows into Lake McDonald.

Opposite, top: Logan Pass Visitor Center, at an altitude of 6,646 feet (2,025 m), is an ideal departure point for hikers and mountaineers.

Opposite, center: An ancient glacier abraded the deep valley that is now flooded by Lake McDonald, the largest lake in the park.

Opposite, bottom right: In midsummer, when temperatures remain moderate, snow still lingers on the high mountain slopes near Clements Mountain.

Apgar Visitor Center is located near the western entrance and overlooks the southern shore of Lake McDonald. This 427-foot-deep (130-m) lake is the largest in the park. A lodge, restaurant, campground, picnic area, horse stable, and boat jetty cater to visitors. Leaving Apgar, the road passes another lodge and campground after hugging the lake's eastern shore for 8 miles (13 km).

At the end of the lake is a view site overlooking a waterfall and the glaciated valley. The road passes Avalanche Creek Campground and Picnic Area in a forest of hemlocks and red cedars. The road then bends sharply to follow the base of the Garden Wall, a narrow jagged ridge formed by glaciers scouring away the land on either side. Rugged peaks tower above Logan Pass Visitor Center, which is situated at an altitude of 6,646 feet (2,025 m) at the point where the road crosses the Continental Divide. The road then begins to descend and skirts the base of Going-to-the-Sun Mountain, following the northern shore of Saint Mary Lake. At Rising Sun on the lakeshore is a lodge along with a campground, picnic area, and boat trips. Saint Mary Visitor Center is located at the east entrance and accommodations are available.

From Saint Mary, the road heads north for 9 miles (14 km) across the Blackfoot Indian Reservation to Babb, where a side road heads back into the park to end at Many Glacier after 12 miles (19 km). Many Glacier Hotel, the largest lodge in the park, was built in 1915 by a railway company. Other facilities include a campground, horse stable, and picnic area, and boat trips are available on Swiftcurrent Lake. Several hiking trails

depart from this point. One of the most interesting involves an 11-mile (18-km) guided walk to Grinnell Glacier, the largest in the park, on the north face of the Garden Wall.

Returning to Babb, Chief Mountain International Highway begins 4 miles (6 km) north and provides access to the Waterton Lakes section. This 30-mile (47-km) road is open only in summer. A customs post is at the Canadian border of Waterton Park, situated on a peninsula overlooking Upper Waterton Lake. There are several lodges in the small town, along with the Prince of Wales Hotel. Outdoor activities include golf, horseback riding, fishing, and boating. The International Peace Park Hike is held on Saturdays. It leaves from the town of Waterton Park, ending at Goat Haunt in the United States—hikers return to Waterton by boat.

YELLOWSTONE NATIONAL PARK

The world's first national park, proclaimed in 1872—just two years after the government had sent in the first survey team, and the first American park to be declared a World Heritage Site (1978), Yellowstone protects 300 geysers and 10,000 geothermal features. The park was initially established to prevent commercial exploitation of the region's hot springs and geysers. One-quarter of the world's geysers can be found in the immediate vicinity of Old Faithful. Apart from its many geothermal features, Yellowstone, the adjacent Grand Teton National Park, and seven surrounding national forests safeguard the largest temperate ecosystem and one of only two unspoiled geyser basins in the world.

In recent years, emphasis has shifted to managing the Greater Yellowstone Ecosystem, an area six times larger than Yellowstone park itself, as a single unit. Yellowstone is one of only two parks in the lower 48 states where the full complement of animals that occurred historically in the area can still be seen today. It contains vital habitats for rare species such as grizzly bear, bald eagle, peregrine falcon, and trumpeter swan. The park's name is derived from the Yellowstone River, translated in 1798 from the Minnetaree Native American name *Mi tsi a-da-zi* (rock yellow river), a reference to the ocher-colored sandstone bluffs that line the lower course of the river.

Hot Spot

Yellowstone covers 3,384 square miles (8,764 sq km), consisting mainly of a high, volcanic basin ringed by mountains. Around most of the earth, the crust overlying its molten center ranges in thickness from 15 to 30 miles (25 to 50 km). However, in the Yellowstone region, the presence of a hot spot below the crust forces magma upward to within 1 mile (2 km) of the surface. The great heat generated produces the geysers and hot springs that can be seen throughout Yellowstone National Park.

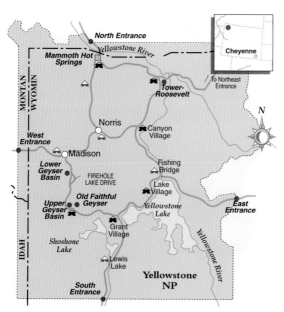

Yellowstone's world-famous geyser, Old Faithful, so named because it consistently erupted every 65 minutes until earthquakes in 1959 and 1983 altered the pattern, now directs a spout of water and steam into the air once every 69 to 76 minutes. Over three million people visit the park each year to observe this, one of the most intriguing geyser basins in the world. Geysers form when water seeps into deep rocky fissures and comes into contact with molten rock or magma. Unable to boil at normal

Above, right: Heat rising from the terraces at Mammoth Hot Springs attracts a variety of animals in winter.
Opposite: Iron Spring Creek, in the Black Sand Basin near Old Faithful, is warmed by geysers and hot springs.

Location: Northwestern Wyoming. The nearest town is West Yellowstone in Idaho.

Climate: Temperatures are below freezing for nine months of the year, with high snowfall. In July, the average high ranges from 70° to 80°F (21° to 27°C).

When to go: Although the weather can be unreliable, the park is best visited in spring and fall, when leaf colors are at their best and roads are less crowded.

Access: From the south, take Exit 189 on Interstate 25 and follow U.S. Highway 20/26 west to Riverton. Then head north on U.S. Highway 26/287 to Moran, and continue to the South Entrance. If approaching from the west, take Interstate 15 north from Salt Lake City to Idaho Falls, then U.S. Highway 20 north to the West Entrance.

Facilities: Four visitor centers; only the Albright Visitor Center in Mammoth Hot Springs is open throughout the year. Lodges in several areas. Twelve campgrounds, most open from mid-May until September or October. Picnic areas and short trails throughout the park. Boating is allowed on some lakes.

Outstanding features: 300 geysers and thousands of geothermal features. Yellowstone Lake, the largest mountain lake in North America; spectacular gorges of yellow rock; fast-flowing rivers and impressive waterfalls.

Visitor activities: Scenic drives, hiking, short walks to waterfalls and geothermal features, overnight backpacking, stagecoach rides, cycling, canoeing, boating, guided cruises, fishing, horseback riding, wildlife viewing, and bird-watching.

Right: Old Faithful, the most famous and predictable of the more than 70 geysers in the Upper Geyser Basin, expels more than 10,000 gallons (40,000 L) of water with each eruption.

Below, left: Heat-sensitive algae produce the bright colors of Beauty Pool in the Upper Geyser Basin.

Below, center: A small hot spring at Artist Paint Pots, north of Firehole Lake. Brown algae grows on the cooler edges of the pond, while blue algae favors the deeper, hotter water.

temperatures because of the pressure caused by the weight of water above, water is then superheated to temperatures as high as 400°F (190°C).This water is then converted into steam. Pressure builds until eventually a column of water and vapor is forced to the surface to form a tall, gushing spout. A type of silica called siliceous sinter, or geyserite, is deposited around these geysers at a rate of about 1 inch (2 cm) every hundred years.

In the northwest region of the park, at Mammoth Hot Springs, the hot waters deposit travertine, a softer white substance. The springs add two tons of material each day to the terraces, some of which, at Mammoth, are up to 200 feet (60 m) high. Another interesting phenomenon is caused by algae and bacteria. At temperatures of 130°F (54°C), orange-brown growths occur; at 160°F (71°C), the water appears blue; and at 167°F (75°C), the pools are colored yellow.

The area between Old Faithful and Madison offers some of the finest geothermal features in the park. There are 24 geysers along the bicycle trail that leads for 1 mile (2.2 km) north of Old Faithful. The road heading north closely follows the Firehole River, where the exploratory expedition of 1870 camped and there are turnoffs to the numerous geothermal attractions along the way. The first stop is the Black Sand Basin where fascinating, multicolored pools shrouded in clouds of steam can be seen along the Iron Spring Creek. The dark blue water of the creek is framed by spouts of steam gushing from the bank.

The Firehole Lake Drive, 7 miles (12 km) from Old Faithful, passes the massive cone of the White Dome Geyser and Firehole Lake, the largest hot spring in the area with a temperature of 158°F (70°C). The nearby Fountain Paint Pot is an intriguing region of brightly colored pools, boiling mud, fumaroles, and geysers that is easily explored along a 0.5-mile (800-m) trail. Steam and other gases rising to the surface have converted the surrounding rocks into clay. Minerals in the clay dye the mud a variety of colors. The effect is spectacular. From the air, the pools resemble paints on an artist's palette.

Right: A hot spot below Yellowstone produces 30 times more heat than is normal in the United States and gives birth to an unrivaled concentration of geysers, hot springs, and fumaroles.

Below, right: An aerial view of Grand Prismatic Spring, which is Yellowstone Park's largest hot spring and the second largest in the world.

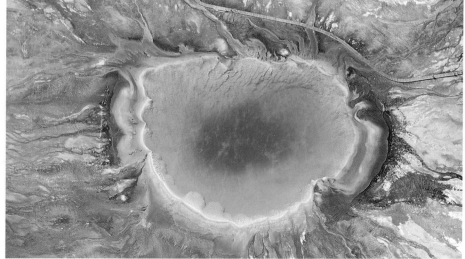

Yellow Rocks and "Piney Woods"

As Yellowstone was covered by ice as recently as 8,500 years ago and has been subject to several violent volcanic eruptions, the area is not especially rich in plants. Only 13 tree species and 1,000 species of flowering plants occur. Early travelers referred to the vegetation as "big piney woods," and the lodgepole pine is exceptionally common. About 80 percent of the park is clothed in forests dominated by the lodgepole pine. Other trees present include the aspen (*Populus tremuloides*) and Douglas fir. In summer, the green meadows are splashed with wildflowers such as the Indian paintbrush, mountain bluebell, and fringed gentian.

Situated in the southeastern region of the park is Yellowstone Lake. At 7,733 feet (2,357 m) in elevation, it is the largest mountain lake in North America. Its convoluted shoreline encompasses 100 miles (160 km) of quiet bays and isolated beaches. This beautiful lake, framed by pine trees and backed by snow-covered mountains, measures 14 miles (23 km) across and is 320 feet (98 m) deep in parts. Boating on the lake, and on nearby Lewis and Shoshone Lakes, is permitted but is not on the park's rivers. Along its northern shore, the lake discharges into the Yellowstone River.

After flowing for 16 miles (25 km) along the Hayden Valley, where bison are often seen, the river enters the Grand Canyon of the Yellowstone. This narrow canyon yields some of the park's most impressive scenery and reaches depths of 1,500 feet (450 m) in places. The rock lining the canyon is volcanic rhyolite that has been chemically altered by geothermal activity from its original dark color to striking yellow and orange hues. The vistas over the canyon are some of the most spectacular in the park. In early summer, river flow increases to 64,000 gallons (256,000 L) per second. Two spectacular waterfalls mark the entrance to the rugged gorge. The spectacular Lower Falls, twice as high as Niagara, plunge 308 feet (94 m) into the canyon. A circular drive hugs the northern edge of the canyon, and observation points offer grand views. Careful observation will reveal the nests of between six and ten osprey pairs on the rocky pinnacles.

Left: After cascading down the Upper and Lower Waterfalls, the Yellowstone River flows through the chemically stained cliffs of the Grand Canyon of the Yellowstone.

Above: Conifers are well suited to cold climates with a short growing season, and forests of lodgepole pine and Douglas fir cover much of the park.

Left: Resembling miniature battlements, the terraces of Mammoth Hot Springs are constantly changing as limestone dissolved in hot water is deposited at the rate of two tons per day.

Below: As recently, in geologic terms, as 12,000 years ago, Yellowstone Lake was hidden beneath a 3,000-foot-thick (1,000-m) glacier. Today it is the largest mountain lake in North America.

Elk, Bison, and Grizzly Bears

Yellowstone is home to six species of wild herbivores as well as black and grizzly bears and many species of predators including coyote, gray wolf, red fox, lynx, bobcat, mountain lion, and river otter. Of the large mammals present, visitors are most likely to see elk: Yellowstone supports about 35,000, which is the largest population in the world. Three main herds are in the park. The northern herd, numbering about 19,000, occupies the northern range between Mammoth Hot Springs and the Lamar Valley. In summer, elk herds congregate in Yellowstone and in Grand Teton to the south. However, during winter some of the elk leave the park in search of food. Yellowstone's bison number around 3,500, one of the largest herds in the country and the only population that is not carefully managed. Because bison carry brucellosis, a disease dangerous to cattle, every year some animals are shot by ranchers north of the park. This is a controversial action that is vehemently opposed by animal rights groups. In 1999, a ranch north of the park was purchased to provide a refuge for migrating bison.

The park's other wild herbivores include moose, some 2,300 mule deer, 600 pronghorn antelope, and 300 bighorn sheep. The latter can be seen north of Mammoth and on Mount

Washburn, but the population is not thriving. Competition from elk herds in the park is believed to be the primary reason.

Yellowstone protects between 500 and 650 black bears and one of the few remaining grizzly bear popula-

Left: Elk from the northern Yellowstone herd migrate into the Lamar and Yellowstone River valleys as winter approaches.

Below, left: An adult bison bull can weigh 2,000 pounds (900 kg). Its formidable head and thick coat are perfectly adapted for survival in the cold climate of the northern states.

tions in the lower 48 states. Grizzly bears number about 250 and appear to be benefiting from the reintroduction of wolves. In the past, when garbage dumps were open to bears, conflicts between visitors and bears were common. An average of 48 bear-related human injuries were

reported each year. Rangers removed troublesome bears to remote areas, fined visitors for feeding bears, and installed bear-proof garbage cans. Bear-related injuries have decreased to one per year. Although experts disagree on the exact number of grizzly bears in the park, a comprehensive management plan has been compiled to guarantee the survival of the species.

Between 1914 and 1926, when early conservationists saw their job as increasing the number of "game animals," a total of 136 wolves were killed and the species disappeared from Yellowstone. In 1995, a pack of 14 wolves from Canada was released in the park, followed by a further 17 in January 1996. The introductions were successful, and several packs now roam the Yellowstone ecosystem. The return of the wolf has corrected imbalances. Coyotes have declined, and natural predation of elk has increased. In extreme winters, up to one-fifth of the elk die from lack of food. As wolves must also compete with other prey animals, the wolf population will stabilize around the availability of prey.

The Fire of 1988

Parts of Yellowstone, especially the northwestern quarter of the park, stand as stark evidence of the fire of 1988. An exceptionally dry summer, strong winds, human carelessness, and lightning strikes produced 249 fires in the Yellowstone region, some of which burned into the park. Although most fires affected very small areas, the largest burned 504,025 acres (195,400 ha). On August 20, a fire burned 150,000 acres (60,000 ha) in a single day. Within Yellowstone itself, 45 percent of the park was burned, although many of the burns were superficial and only 1 percent of the area was consumed by intense fire. In total, $120 million was spent on combating the fires. At one point, 10,000 firefighters were involved and over 800 miles (1,200 km) of firebreaks were cut. However, little could stop the blaze. Sparks driven by wind were even able to leap the Grand Canyon of the Yellowstone. It was only when snow began to fall that the fires were extinguished.

In many areas, the fires killed the mature stands of lodgepole pine and cleared the way for plant succession to take place—sedges, wildflowers, and grasses provided food for animals, and the whole process of forest regeneration began again. Evidence suggests that massive fires affect Yellowstone once every 200 years.

Below: Yellowstone Lake is an important spawning area for cutthroat trout. Fishing enthusiasts are encouraged to catch lake trout, an accidentally introduced species that competes with the cutthroat for available food.

Access and Visitor Facilities

There are five entrance gates to Yellowstone, 12 camping sites, and lodges situated in six service centers. A 142-mile (227-km) road network, designed in 1905 by the U.S. Army Corps of Engineers, forms a figure eight in the center of the park. It was carefully designed to allow easy, unobtrusive access to Yellowstone's natural wonders. Five access roads, totaling 94 miles (150 km), connect the entrance gates to the road network, and allow visitors from any direction access to the major attractions. Information for visitors is presented in nine information centers that include museum displays, regular informative videos, and a comprehensive range of guidebooks. These provide an introduction to the park's history and point out some of its major attractions. Apart from the tourist roads, which experience considerable volumes of traffic during busy summer months, visitors can experience the true Yellowstone wilderness along 1,000 miles (1,600 km) of backcountry trails. In some areas, such as the plateau between Old Faithful and Canyon, hiking trails are limited due to the presence of grizzly bears. A permit is necessary for all backcountry hiking, available from rangers or from the visitor centers. Adopting precautionary measures while trekking in bear country is essential.

Walks and Trails

Apart from the backcountry trails and the extensive system of trails and boardwalks that explore the geothermal features, there are many short walks in the park that can be attempted by reasonably fit visitors. The Tower Falls Trail departs from the Hamilton store and leads downhill to a delightful valley on the Yellowstone River and the waterfall on a side tributary. This 1-mile (1.6-km) trail passes the crossing used by the Bannock tribe between 1840 and 1878, en route to their summer hunting grounds.

In the Grand Canyon of the Yellowstone, a short but steep walk leads to a splendid view site overlooking the Lower Falls. A series of switchbacks descends through a silent forest and then down a wooden staircase to the lookout. In the center of the park, in the vicinity of Fishing Bridge on Yellowstone Lake, several short walks provide panoramic views of the lake.

Above: Old Faithful Inn boasts a central lobby that is 84 feet (26m) high. The eight-story structure, built in 1904, accommodates visitors in 325 rooms.

Above: A 0.5-mile (800-m) boardwalk at the Fountain Paint Pot in the Lower Geyser Basin passes seven erupting geysers, boiling pools of mud, fumaroles, and algae-dyed hot springs.

GRAND TETON NATIONAL PARK

The awe-inspiring peaks of the Grand Tetons were set aside as a national park in 1929. Over the years, John D. Rockefeller Jr. gradually bought up land in Jackson Hole, the valley below the mountains. In 1950, an additional 52 square miles (133 sq km) was added to the park as a gift to the American people. Grand Teton now extends over 484 square miles (1,248 sq km), and includes the highest mountains in Wyoming and some of the most beautiful country in the United States. There are seven natural lakes in the park and a chain of cirques on the high peaks. Jackson Lake, the park's largest body of water and a natural glacial lake, was increased in size by the construction of a dam on the Snake River in 1959. Two lodges and a marina are situated along the eastern lakeshore. At dawn, the sun's rays strike Mount Moran, towering 5,780 feet (1,778 m) above the still waters of the lake. The mountain was named after Thomas Moran, a landscape painter and member of the 1870 expedition to Yellowstone. Moran's superb paintings helped to persuade Congress to set Yellowstone aside as the world's first national park. Decades later, Theodore Roosevelt referred to the Tetons as "the most beautiful country in the world."

The Tetons were formed in the distant geologic past when a major fault caused a large block of land to sink to the east while the western block rose and tilted. Subsequent erosion and Ice Age glaciers then removed much of the material and shaped the moun-

tains. This produced the abrupt eastern side of the Tetons that rise up to 6,600 feet (2,000 m) above the valley floor. These geologic processes have created some of the most accessible alpine mountains in the world.

Plants and Animals

The park includes eight summits of the Tetons that are higher than 11,400 feet (3,500 m). The high peaks consist of alpine meadows, ice, and rock, and Engelmann spruce grow in some of the valleys above the 6,800-foot (2,100-m) contour. About 100 bighorn sheep are found on the high slopes. Below the jagged pinnacles, the eastern half of the park consists mainly of a dry sagebrush steppe. Single specimens of limber pine (*Pinus flexilis*) can be seen growing on the steppe. The blue spruce (*Picea pungens*), aspen, and whiplash willow (*Salix lasiandra*) grow along the banks of the picturesque Snake River.

There is a herd of 400 bison in the park, often visible from Highway 191 between Jackson and Moran Junction. Moose can be seen along the Snake River, particularly at Oxbow Bend and Willow Flats. Mule deer, however, favor the edge of forests and are often seen at Jackson Lake. Oxbow Bend is also a good place to see beavers and muskrats, while

Above, right: Both sexes of bighorn sheep have horns.

Opposite: The awe-inspiring Tetons tower above the surprisingly flat valley known as Jackson Hole.

Location: Northwestern Wyoming, near the town of Jackson.

Climate: In January the average low is −8°F (−22°C), but temperatures can plummet to −25°F (−31°C) during the night. Summers are mild with an average of 80°F (27°C) in July.

When to go: June to September; days are warm and nights are cool. Teton Park Road and almost all accommodations are closed to visitors in winter.

Access: From Interstate 80, take U.S. Highway 189 north to Jackson from Exit 18. The park adjoins Yellowstone and can also be approached from Casper, Wyoming, and Salt Lake City, Utah. If approaching from Salt Lake City, follow Interstate 15 to Idaho Falls and then take U.S. Highway 26 east to Jackson.

Facilities: Jenny Lake and Colter Bay Visitor Centers are open during summer; Moose Visitor Center is open year-round. The four campgrounds close for winter and reopen in May or June. Only Dornan's at Moose is open for accommodations throughout the year. Moose, Signal Mountain, Jackson Lake Lodge, and Colter Bay Village offer a wide range of facilities. Jackson Hole airport is located near the southern boundary.

Outstanding features: Grand Teton dominates the mountain range. Seven glacial lakes and a dozen glaciers cling to the high peaks.

Visitor activities: Hiking, overnight backpacking, mountain climbing, cycling, canoeing, boating, river float trips, cruises, fishing, horseback riding, wildlife viewing, and bird-watching. Cross-country skiing, ice fishing, ice skating, snowshoeing, and snowmobiling can be enjoyed during winter.

bird life includes bald eagles, ospreys, and white pelicans. The Teton Park Road crosses the sagebrush steppe at the foot of the high peaks, where pronghorn can usually be seen feeding near the road. Both black and grizzly bears also occur in the park. In recent years, three packs of wolves have moved into the park in winter from Yellowstone. At Colter Bay, a short trail to Swan Lake and Heron Pond offers sightings of moose, beavers, and the rare trumpeter swan.

The Jackson Hole elk herd numbers around 15,000 and migrates with the change in seasons. In winter, about half of the herd congregates on the adjacent National Elk Refuge, which was established in 1913. In summer about 4,000 elk are present in the national park. At the southern end of the elk refuge is an extensive wetland that attracts large flocks of waterfowl such as Canada geese, cinnamon teal, coots, and mallard ducks. The road to Jackson passes the wetlands, where there are several viewing sites and informative displays.

The Snake River cutthroat is the only species of trout native to the park, although rainbow, lake, and brown trout are also present. The Snake River cutthroat is a recognized subspecies, and park rangers carefully monitor the population because it is an important food source for ospreys, eagles, otters, and bears. Anglers are permitted to catch cutthroat trout and other fish species along the Snake River, but the National Park Service issues guidelines for the safe release of small trout.

Mountain Glaciers

At extreme heights, climatic conditions favor the formation of glaciers. About a dozen glaciers are found in shaded east- or north-facing aspects on the high peaks. The highest pinnacle in the range, Grand Teton, rises to 13,770 feet (4,197 m), and the Teton Glacier is clearly visible from the Teton Park Road. This glacier was formed 500 to 1,000 years ago during the so-called Little Ice Age rather than during the Ice Age proper. Jenny Lake, a

Above: Canada geese are among the bird species in the National Elk Refuge.

Above, right: The Snake River flows south through the valley known as Jackson Hole.

Right: The still waters of Jenny Lake, formed by a natural moraine dam, were named after Jenny Leigh, the Shoshone wife of trapper Dick Leigh.

Opposite: At the end of summer, snow still clings to the peaks of Grand Teton and Mount Owen, the highest summits in the range.

natural lake formed behind a moraine ridge, offers superb views of the towering peaks reflected in its tranquil waters. On Mount Moran, which overshadows Jackson Lake, the Falling Ice and Skillet Glaciers are easily visible on the mountain's east-facing slopes.

Outdoor Activities

Grand Teton is a paradise for outdoor enthusiasts. Apart from its scenery and wildlife, activities include mountain climbing, overnight hiking, self-guided walks, fishing, canoeing, horseback riding, and raft trips down the Snake River. Waterskiing, yachting, and motorboating are allowed on Jackson Lake. Mountaineers regard the Tetons as offering some of the best climbing in North America. The crystalline rock is very hard, and cracks and ledges provide ample handholds and footholds. Just south of the park boundary, at Teton Village, a cableway ferries skiers up the mountain slope. Downhill skiing is a popular sport, and the area attracts many visitors in winter. The Triangle X Ranch on Highway 191 offers western ranch activities including cookouts, dancing, and horseback riding.

During the long winter months, when an average of 4 feet (1.2 m) of snow covers the valley, only the main thoroughfares remain open and the Teton Park Road is closed. Visitors can take part in a variety of activities including cross-country skiing, ice skating, snowshoeing, and ice fishing.

A Superb Setting

Visitor facilities have been planned to maximize the park's scenic beauty. Visitor centers at Moose, Colter Bay, and Jenny Lake house informative displays and are stocked with a good range of park maps and guidebooks. Colter Bay Village, on the shores of Jackson Lake, includes cabins, a tent village, a camping area, restaurants, and a marina. Nearby, Jackson Lake Lodge offers luxury accommodations, and the rooms at Signal Mountain Lodge all offer splendid views of the lake and Mount Moran. The campsite at Signal Mountain occupies a wooded hillside and provides panoramic views of the high peaks rising above the lake. Farther south, Jenny Lake has a lodge and camping area, while Dornan's at Moose has restaurants, stores, and accommodations overlooking the Snake River. Because the Grand Teton area receives heavy snowfalls in winter, the lodges are closed from October to May.

The town of Jackson, at the southern boundary of the National Elk Refuge, is a popular destination that has many western-style stores catering to tourists. The square in the center of the town is well-known for the arches made from elk antlers marking each of its four corners.

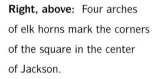

Right, above: Four arches of elk horns mark the corners of the square in the center of Jackson.

Right: Kayaking across Jenny Lake to the foot of the Teton range provides access to a short trail leading to Hidden Falls.

Left: The small settlement of Moose, at the southern entrance to the park, is situated on the banks of the Snake River.

Below: Signal Mountain Lodge and Campground, on the eastern shore of Jackson Lake, affords panoramic views of the lake and magnificent Mount Moran.

ROCKY MOUNTAIN NATIONAL PARK

In 1884, Enos Mills, a sickly 14-year-old boy from Kansas, settled in the town of Estes Park in Colorado. Mills began guiding visitors into the surrounding mountains. At the age of 17, he completed a solo climb of Longs Peak. Altogether, Mills ascended the peak on 296 occasions, and his great affection for the mountains motivated him to campaign for national park status. After years of negotiations, one of America's most beautiful national parks was established by Congress in 1915. The park incorporates nearly 40 miles (65 km) of the Continental Divide and conserves 415 square miles (1,070 sq km) of hidden valleys, rugged mountain peaks, glacial lakes, and extensive areas of alpine tundra. Much of the park is located above the timberline—altitude ranges from 7,630 feet (2,325 m) to 14,255 feet (4,345 m)—and alpine tundra accounts for one-third of the total surface area.

Ice-Sculpted Peaks

The Continental Divide meanders through the center of the park. It diverts water flowing east into the South Platte River, which in turn flows into the Mississippi, eventually reaching the Atlantic. West-flowing water carried by the Colorado River reaches the Pacific Ocean in the Gulf of California. Of the 113 named peaks within the park, the highest point, Longs Peak in the southeastern corner, rises to 14,255 feet (4,345 m).

Evidence of glaciation can be seen throughout the park in features such as U-shaped valleys, rugged ridges, horns, glacial lakes (tarns), and moraine deposits in the lower valleys. Five small glaciers cling to east-facing valleys along the Divide. These glaciers were formed about 3,800 years ago but have retreated as global temperatures have increased. On the highest slopes, blue tarns fill ice-abraded hollows. A total of 156 lakes are dotted across the park. The delightful Kawuneeche Valley, on the park's western boundary, gives rise to the headwaters of the Colorado River.

Map labels

Rocky Mountains NP
Denver
Alpine Visitor Center
Lava Cliffs
Timber Creek
TRAIL RIDGE ROAD
The Rockies
Aspenglen
Beaver Meadows Visitor Center
Estes Park
Lily Lake Visitor Center
Kawuneeche Visitor Center
Chiefs Head ▲ 13,579 ft (4,139 m)
Long Peak ▲ 14,255 ft (4,345 m)
Lake Granb
N

Four Vegetation Zones

As visitors travel through the park, four distinct vegetation communities are visible. Each zone is determined by an increase in altitude that brings about a rapid decrease in moisture and temperature. In the Rocky Mountains, an increase in elevation of 1,000 feet (300 m) is equivalent to traveling 300 miles (480 km) north, exposing visitors to wide biological diversity.

On the lower slopes, below 10,000 feet (3,000 m), dense forests of ponderosa pine (*Pinus ponderosa*), particularly on drier slopes, and Douglas fir form the

Above, right: Coyotes scavenge in the park's lower valleys.
Opposite: As altitude increases in the Rocky Mountains, forests of spruce and pine are replaced by alpine tundra.

Location: Northern Colorado, near Estes Park.

Climate: In the lower valleys temperatures can reach 85°F (29°C) in July. In the mountains, the air will be 50°F (10°C) cooler. A fall high of 75°F (24°C) can be expected during the day, but the windchill factor on the higher slopes causes temperatures to plunge below freezing.

When to go: Because the park has a limited road network, during summer it can be very crowded and is best visited during the autumn months of September and October.

Access: From Interstate 25 take Exit 257 and head west on U.S. Highway 34 to Estes Park.

Facilities: Beaver Meadows Visitor Center, located on U.S. Highway 36 near Estes Park. Lily Lake Visitor Center, open from May to September, is located south of the town. Kawuneeche Visitor Center is situated on the western side of the mountains. Alpine Visitor Center, located at an altitude of 11,796 feet (3,595 m), is open from June to September once sufficient snow has melted. Five campgrounds are located in the valleys, but there are no stores, restaurants, lodges, or service stations in the park. There are 16 picnic areas along park roads and a number of interpretive trails.

Outstanding features: The road across the park reaches an altitude of 12,183 feet (3,713 m) and offers panoramic vistas across the high, snow-capped mountains.

Visitor activities: Short walks to historic sites, overnight backpacking, mountain climbing, cycling, fishing, horseback riding, wildlife viewing, bird-watching, cross-country skiing, ice fishing, snowshoeing, and snowmobiling.

Right: Elk cross the road through the park, near the Beaver Meadows Entrance.

Center, below: Snow lingers throughout summer on the frigid, windswept slopes near the Alpine Visitor Center.

Below: Trail Ridge Road offers breathtaking views of Mounts Julian and Ida and the deep, glacier-carved Forest Canyon.

Opposite, top: At high altitudes, tiny tundra plants grow close to the ground for protection from frost.

Opposite, bottom right: West of the Continental Divide (the Rocky Range), which runs through the center of the park, melting snow feeds streams that join together to form the mighty Colorado River.

dominant plant community. These forests are occasionally interrupted by aspen groves, grassy meadows, and stream-bank communities. Because the forests on north-facing slopes are cooler, moisture levels are higher and forests of Douglas fir occur. The aspen has the greatest distribution of any tree in America. Aspen forests are rich in bird life because they support a denser understory in comparison with pine forests. Woodpeckers drill nests in the trees, and abandoned homes are later colonized by wrens, bluebirds, and swallows. Mammals such as elk, black bears, least chipmunks, red squirrels, cottontail rabbits, and porcupines feed on the understory shrubs.

Between 10,000 feet (3,000 m) and 11,000 feet (3,350 m), the subalpine zone contains dense stands of Engelmann spruce and lodgepole pine, which are closely related to Canadian boreal forest. Snow accumulating in this zone helps to water lower elevations.

Before reaching the alpine zone, cold, wind, and ice on the upper slopes combine to produce the *krummholz* ("crooked wood"), clumps of stunted and twisted spruce and fir trees that are shaped by strong winds. This plant community grows on the tree line. In these harsh conditions, trees grow extremely slowly. A tree of 3 feet (1 m) in height may be hundreds of years old; 1 inch (2 cm) added to its trunk's diameter represents 100 years of growth.

Alpine tundra occupies all the land above the *krummholz*, where the slopes are too cold and dry for trees. Strong, dry winds blowing across the tundra carry away much of the snow before it has a chance to melt

Above: Elk show a marked preference for the pine and fir forests of the warmer, lower-lying valleys.

Below: On the western slopes of the mountains, a picnic area overlooks the beaver ponds on a tributary of the Colorado River.

several seasons. The alpine sunflower (*Rydbergia grandiflora*) is restricted to the Rocky Mountains and flowers once in ten years before dying. Above 14,000 feet (4,250 m), plant life is limited to lichens.

Many raptors can be seen soaring above the mountains. However, the white-tailed ptarmigan (a type of grouse) is the only bird that can survive winter on the tundra. Superbly camouflaged, it grows feathers under its feet, which serve as protection from winter temperatures.

Mountain Wildlife

The most commonly sighted wild animals include elk, bighorn sheep, moose, mule deer, coyote, yellow-bellied marmot, and pika. The elk population varies with the seasons, and in summer, up to 3,000 of them congregate in the park. About 800 bighorn sheep inhabit the high mountains. During spring and summer, park rangers control traffic to allow the sheep to move to their favorite feeding grounds. Moose feed on aquatic plants and prefer the wetlands on the western side of the park. An estimated 25 to 30 black bears are present, though sightings are infrequent. Other seldom-seen predators include mountain lion, bobcat, badger, pine marten, long-tailed weasel, striped skunk, and river otter. The dams and lodges of the nocturnal beaver can be seen throughout the lower valleys.

and produce what is, in effect, a high-altitude desert. About 300 species of plants occur on the tundra. On the high slopes, frost-free days are limited to 40 per year. Temperatures remain below freezing for five months, so most tundra plants are perennials, relying on a short growing season of six to ten weeks. These plants grow near the ground, their tiny waxy or hairy leaves offering protection and helping to reduce water loss. Most of each plant is hidden beneath the surface. As the plants store energy in their roots, they may flower only after

Exploring the Park

From the town of Estes Park, Trail Ridge Road climbs steeply to reach its highest point at 12,183 feet (3,713 m) before descending into the Kawuneeche valley. The road offers some of the most dramatic scenery in the entire mountain range and for 4 miles (7 km) runs above the 12,000-foot (3,660-m) contour. The highest point is passed between Lava Cliffs and the Gore Range. From the Forest Canyon Overlook to the Alpine Visitor Center, the scenery is breathtaking, and several short trails explore the surrounding tundra. On these high exposed slopes, icy winds blow at speeds of up to 200 miles (320 km) per hour, and warm, protective clothing is essential.

In total, 355 miles (570 km) of trails allow hikers and mountaineers to explore the park. There are 46 trails on the eastern side of the park and 11 on the western side, ranging in length from 500 yards (500 m) to 9 miles (14 km). In summer, lightning storms are common, while in winter, severe weather conditions require special precautions. Some of the trails can be traveled on horse-

back. Horses and guides can be hired at a number of locations both inside the park and on the boundary, and 260 miles (420 km) of trails are open to visitors on horseback. Although fishing is permitted in the park, certain streams and lakes are closed to anglers to protect Colorado River cutthroat and greenback cutthroat trout.

Climbing Longs Peak is popular in summer, but the easiest route, Keyhole, requires a high degree of fitness. The trip from the ranger station to the summit is 15 miles (24 km) long, and the altitude gain is 4,850 feet (1,478 m). Climbers are advised to begin the climb at 3:00 A.M., which allows sufficient time to climb the peak and avoid the chance of an afternoon thunderstorm on the high slopes.

There are four visitor centers and a museum in the park, providing a quick introduction to the park's history and major attractions. Boating is permitted on three beautiful lakes—Grand, Shadow Mountain, and Granby, which fall within the Arapaho National Recreational Area bordering the park's southwestern corner.

Above: At Beaver Meadows Visitor Center, a topographical model helps visitors identify the mountain's many peaks.

BLACK CANYON OF THE GUNNISON NATIONAL PARK

The Gunnison River rises in the forested mountains above Aspen and flows west to meet the Colorado River. On its westward journey, the Gunnison flows through a spectacular gorge 50 miles (80 km) in length. Formed over millions of years by water slowly eating away at the hard underlying rock, the Black Canyon is an awe-inspiring sight. Its sheer walls of dark rock, interspersed with white bands of gneiss, rise 2,000 feet (600 m) above the river, which meanders like a silver thread between dark, towering walls.

In this remote, semiarid corner of Colorado where scrub oak woodlands splash the hillsides in brilliant reds and oranges and place names such as Poison Spring Ridge and Deadhorse Gulch are indicative of the harsh environment, this former national monument became America's 55th national park on October 21, 1999. The park covers 47 square miles (122 sq km), and protects the deepest and most spectacular 13-mile (21-km) section of the Black Canyon.

The park's eastern boundary adjoins the Curecanti National Recreation Area, land surrounding three dams in the canyon that is also administered by the National Park Service. The western boundary borders the Gunnison Gorge National Conservation Area, administered by the Bureau of Land Management, which includes a wilderness area. Although the dams have flooded the upper reaches of the canyon, the most dramatic stretch is protected within the national park.

Awesome Silence

The majority of the canyons in America's Southwest were formed when rivers eroded soft sedimentary rocks. These canyons are usually wide and descend in a series of steps caused by differing layers of rock hardness. However, when rivers flow across hard igneous rock, steep gorges result over eons. The Black Canyon was formed by water cutting through dark volcanic schist. Although it requires a road journey of 80 miles (130 km) to travel from the North Rim to the South Rim Campgrounds, the canyon is, for the most part, only 1,500 feet (460 m) wide. Between the access roads and view sites on the North and South Rims, the cliffs plunge vertically to the river below. At The Narrows the canyon is only 1,150 feet (350 m) wide. The steepness of the cliffs prevents sunlight from illuminating much of the canyon, confirming the aptness of the name Black Canyon. Although this is one of the smallest national parks in America, its modest size in no way detracts from visitors' enjoyment. Many of the popular national parks receive several million visitors per year, the majority crowded into the summer months. The Black Canyon receives about 230,000 visitors, mostly

Above, right: The desert cottontail rabbit is abundant in the Gambel Oak woodlands of the less-visited North Rim.
Opposite: Dwarfed by the black walls of the canyon it created, the Gunnison River flows west toward the Colorado.

Location: Western Colorado, near Montrose.

Climate: Average annual precipitation is less than 12 inches (300 mm). The high altitude and low levels of humidity reduce the effect of summer temperatures. In July average highs vary from 72° to 84°F (22° to 29°C), and January temperatures can drop to 8°F (−13°C).

When to go: In September and October when the leaves of oak trees on the edge of the canyon turn a fiery orange.

Access: From Interstate 6, take Exit 26 at Grand Junction and head south on U.S. Highway 50 to Delta. For the North Rim, head east on Highway 92 to Crawford; visitors to the South Rim continue south to Montrose and follow U.S. Highway 50 east to the turnoff to Highway 347.

Facilities: The visitor center is situated on the South Rim near Gunnison Point. There are campgrounds on either side of the canyon, though both are closed in winter. During summer, light lunches are served at Rim House, but there are no lodges, restaurants, stores, or service stations in the park. The road along the South Rim is paved and ends at a picnic area. The gravel road to the North Rim is closed in winter.

Outstanding features: An immense, narrow canyon with sheer walls rising 2,000 feet (600 m) above the Gunnison River. In some places, the opposite walls are just 1,150 feet (350 m) apart, and much of the canyon floor remains in shadow throughout the day.

Visitor activities: Scenic drives, hiking, short walks, overnight backpacking, rock climbing, cycling, and bird-watching.

Above: Attractive woodlands of gambel oak add bright colors to a semiarid region.

Below: From a view site on the North Rim, the canyon is a wild, formidable chasm.

to the South Rim. Visitors seeking solitude will delight in the unspoiled beauty of the North Rim. Attractive woodlands of scrubby gambel oak (*Quercus gambelii*) crowd the canyon's edge, guardrails run perilously close to vertigo-inducing precipitous cliffs, and, apart from the river echoing through the canyon below, silence prevails.

Exploring the Canyon

When approaching the South Rim, the road climbs through scrub-covered hills to an elevation of 8,500 feet (2,600 m) at the visitor center and campground, but there is no indication of the canyon until the first view site is reached. Twelve named view sites are located along the main road that hugs the canyon for 8 miles (13 km). These are very popular with day visitors hoping for a quick canyon experience. At the end of the road is a fine view west across a proclaimed wilderness area of rugged ridges and canyons.

The visitor center is open throughout the year. Rangers conduct walks and evening programs during summer. In winter, moonlight ski tours and snowshoe hikes are offered on weekends.

When approaching from the north, a gravel road turns off Highway 92 after the Crawford Reservoir, leading to a small campsite located on the canyon rim. A side road follows the rim for 5 miles (8 km) and there are six view sites. During winter, the road and ranger station are closed. Both campgrounds are often visited by deer, and rabbits are common in the surrounding woodlands.

A number of marked trails on both sides explore the flat land bordering the canyon, while three demanding trails descend to the river. Free permits are issued for inner-canyon exploration. One of the three demanding inner-canyon hikes, the Gunnison Route, descends 1,800 feet (550 m) over 1 mile (1.6 km) and requires a high level of physical fitness.

MESA VERDE NATIONAL PARK

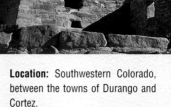

In the southwestern corner of Colorado, an impressive plateau rises 2,000 feet (600 m) above the Montezuma Valley. This is Mesa Verde, or "green table" in Spanish, a scenic highland dissected by rugged gorges and offering magnificent views across the surrounding countryside. Extending over 81 square miles (209 sq km), Mesa Verde is the only national park in America established primarily to preserve ancient Anasazi Native American settlements. Apart from its many fascinating stone ruins, the park protects scenic canyons, gambel oak woodlands, and untamed, broken terrain surveyed by raptors soaring overhead.

Mesa Verde's intriguing archaeological treasures were first documented as late as 1888 when two cowboys in search of lost cattle stumbled upon the fascinating Cliff Palace. They discovered pottery and tools in the stone houses but did not realize that the settlement had been abandoned for 600 years. Later investigations revealed many pueblos, or stone villages, tucked into the sandstone caves—a common feature of the mesa. In 1906, the high plateau with its impressive stone ruins, adjoining the northern boundary of the Ute Mountain Indian Reservation, was set aside as a national park. Mesa Verde was declared a World Heritage Site in 1978.

From the entrance gate on Highway 160, the 21-mile (34-km) access road climbs a steep pass, closely follows the craggy edge of the mesa, then passes the park's visitor center and Far View Lodge before reaching the stone-walled museum built to resemble the ancient structures. Five cliff settlements are open to the public,

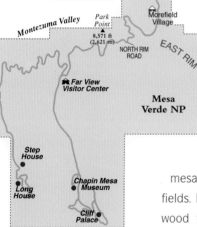

two on guided trails, offering visitors a glimpse into a long-lost culture.

People of the Mesa

In Mesa Verde, nearly 600 cliff dwellings have been documented, though the vast majority contain less than five rooms. The extensive stone villages for which the park is famous are restricted to a few localities representing a process of architectural development that occurred between the sixth and the thirteenth centuries.

From archaeological discoveries, the Anasazi, or Ancestral Puebloans, apparently settled the region early in the sixth century. They lived in pit houses clustered in villages on the crest of the mesas and grew corn and squash in small fields. Forests of pine and juniper provided wood for fires and construction. Domesticated dogs and turkeys were also part of the village scene. Game was plentiful, and the people also ate wild plants such as pinyon pine (*Pinus edulis*) seeds and Mormon tea. The spiny yucca plant was extremely important: Its fibers were used for making baskets, ropes, nets, and sandals, while its fruit and flower stalk were eaten.

Above, right: The compact settlement of Cliff Palace was constructed during the twelfth century but has not been inhabited for some 700 years.

Location: Southwestern Colorado, between the towns of Durango and Cortez.

Climate: Average temperatures in July range from 84° to 96°F (29° to 36°C). In January, an average low temperature of 12°F (−11°C) can be expected.

When to go: The western section of the park and many of the cliff dwellings are closed during winter. All the ruins are open from the end of May to early October.

Access: From Interstate 6, take U.S. Highways 50 and 550 south to Durango. Then head west on U.S. Highway 160 to the park entrance.

Facilities: Far View Visitor Center, situated on the main road, is open from late spring to midautumn. Far View Lodge includes a restaurant, cafeteria, and gas station. The lodge is open from mid-April to the last week of October. The campground at Morefield Village, open during spring and summer, has food stores, a laundry, and a gas station. Picnic areas and view sites are along the main roads, and several short trails explore some of the ruins. The archaeological museum at Chapin Mesa remains open throughout the year.

Outstanding features: This park is best known for the intriguing Anasazi cliff dwellings that were built from the sixth to the thirteenth centuries. Tucked into sandstone caves, these well-preserved stone villages stand as silent monuments to a vanished civilization.

Visitor activities: Guided tours of cliff dwellings, visits to the archaeological museum, scenic drives, hiking, short walks to lookout points, cycling, and bird-watching. During winter, cross-country skiing and snowshoeing are permitted on certain roads if sufficient snow has fallen.

Right: The largest of the cave villages, Cliff Palace, was built facing southwest to maximize seasonal climate changes. Winter sun provided warmth, but in summer the lip of the cave restricted the sun's rays.

Baskets were used for carrying food and water. The Anasazi waterproofed baskets by lining them with pitch and even cooked food in them by dropping heated rocks into water. When they mastered the ability, in the middle of the sixth century, to make pottery, their basket-weaving skills soon declined. The Native Americans quickly became skilled potters, producing decorative pots, mugs, and jars. Black paint was made from roots, and distinctive artistic designs were passed from mother to daughter.

The Anasazi traded produce and other items with passing traders. After 200 years, they acquired the bow and arrow and also began to cultivate beans. Around 750 A.D. they began to live in large settlements, and started building pueblos. Timber and adobe were replaced by stone for building houses. To encourage crop production, dams were built to store water and canals were built to lead water to these reservoirs.

From Stone Houses to the Sandstone

Success with farming and a settled lifestyle encouraged a population increase. By 1100, about 2,500 people lived on the mesa. For reasons yet unexplained, the people then moved from the mesa crests to the spacious caves that commonly occur in the sandstone band overlying the shales of the region. Over a span of 70 years, they built extensive stone villages tucked into these sandstone caves. Most of these settlements were located at an altitude of 7,000 feet (2,100 m).

Archaeologists believe that from 1276 onward, a severe drought affected the region for 23 years. At the time, the resident population had increased to about 5,000 and natural resources had become scarce. The prolonged drought worsened this scarcity. The people abandoned the cliff dwellings and moved to more fertile regions. By 1300, Mesa Verde was deserted.

Left: The Anasazi began living in large settlements from the middle of the eighth century and built an economy based on farming, hunting, and trading. There are interesting dioramas of all the stages of Anasazi development in the museum at Chapin Mesa.

Right: Displays of Anasazi pottery in the museum.

Below: Semiarid Soda Canyon offers few clues to the landscape that the Anasazi knew before the drought that drove them away.

Below, right: The museum at Chapin Mesa is built from natural stone in keeping with the park's many cliff dwellings.

Visiting the Pueblos

Chapin Mesa, in the southern part of the park, can be explored along three circular one-way roads. The Chapin Mesa Museum is located on the edge of the canyon overlooking Spruce Tree House and contains many artifacts as well as detailed models depicting life in the pueblos. From the museum, the Spruce Canyon Trail explores just over 2 miles (3 km) of the adjacent canyon. Petroglyph Point Trail follows the rim of the canyon in a southerly direction for 3 miles (4.5 km). A short, steep, self-guided trail descends into the canyon to Spruce Tree House, where 114 rooms and eight kivas (sunken circular group meeting places) occupy a sandstone cave.

Continuing along the loop roads, there are many ruins on the crest of the mesa, including the Sun Temple and pit houses, that can be explored along short walking trails. The route provides access to 600 years of cultural

development, beginning with the mesa-top ruins and ending with the later cliff dwellings. On the eastern loop road, guided tours are led by rangers to the Cliff Palace and Balcony House. Tickets must be purchased at the museum or visitor center. The ruins are closed during winter. Cliff Palace, the largest cliff dwelling in America and the most famous of the park's ruins, contains 217 rooms and 23 kivas, once home to a population of about 200 people.

Bicycles are permitted on all park roads with the exception of the road to Wetherhill Mesa. Three hiking trails explore the countryside in the vicinity of Morefield Campground. Along the main road, the short walk to the lookout tower at Park Point, the highest point in the park at 8,571 feet (2,621 m), offers a spectacular vista over the North Rim, the Montezuma Valley, the La Plata Mountains, and westward to Utah and Arizona.

In the western corner of the park, the 12-mile (19-km) road to Wetherhill Mesa, open only in summer, offers access to Long House, Step House, and Badger House. Visitors park at the kiosk, and a minitrain follows a circular route passing several ruins. Long House is the second largest pueblo in the park, containing 150 rooms. The minitrain continues to the Badger House Community, the ruins of a village built on top of the mesa, before returning to the kiosk where a short trail leads to Step House.

Right: A path descends from the museum to the Spruce Tree House ruins. The Anasazi built their cliff dwellings in shallow overhangs in the softer sandstone band that caps the mesas.

THE SOUTH-WESTERN DESERT

A sun-baked land of desert plains, immense canyons, and inhospitable mountains, this region covers 11.6 percent of America. Less than 15 inches (300 mm) of rain falls over the lower areas of Nevada, Utah, and New Mexico. In the deserts of southern Arizona, annual rainfall can be as low as 2 inches (50 mm). Much of Nevada and Utah form part of the Great Basin, a barren upland broken by parallel mountains, where the rain that falls never reaches the ocean but is carried by streams that flow inland into the desert. Summer temperatures often soar to 105°F (41°C) in Las Vegas and in Parker, Arizona, a temperature of 127°F (53°C) has been recorded.

Despite the harshness of much of the landscape, human history here can be traced back many centuries. The oldest continuously inhabited settlement in America, Oraibi, was built by the Hopi in northern Arizona in the twelfth century. Spanish explorers searched for gold in the region in 1540, and the road between Santa Fe and Chihuahua was first opened in 1581. The desert canyons were later the home of Geronimo and his famous Apache warriors. Western legends included Kit Carson, Jim Bridger, Billy the Kid, Pat Garrett, and Butch Cassidy. The promise of gold brought many settlers to the region.

While gold did not always last, water proved to be the true lifeblood. In 1936, Hoover Dam, one of the largest dams in the world, was completed on the Colorado River. Farther upstream, Glen Canyon Dam was completed in 1964, creating a lake 186 miles (298 km) long. These enormous dams have transformed the desert into a popular destination for water sports enthusiasts, and help to sustain the region's reputation as America's sunbelt. Three-quarters of this land is owned by the federal government, and one-fifth of America's national parks are located here. Utah has five national parks, the third largest number for any state. Grand Canyon, in northern Arizona, is a showcase of superlatives. Parks in Arizona and Nevada conserve examples of desert landscapes. In 1996, the largest national monument outside Alaska was proclaimed in southern Utah; Grand Staircase–Escalante protects 2,970 square miles (7,660 sq km) of rugged desert. It links three national parks and Glen Canyon National Recreation Area into an enormous contiguous conservation area covering 5,877 square miles (15,162 sq km).

Left: Dixie National Forest in southwestern Utah adjoins two national parks and the recently proclaimed Grand Staircase–Escalante National Monument.

GREAT BASIN
NATIONAL PARK

Location: Eastern Nevada, near Ely.

Climate: Moderate summer temperatures of around 70°F (21°C) can be expected. Winters are long and cold.

When to go: The park is open throughout the year, but snow closes most of the visitor roads in winter. The park is best visited from June to August.

Access: Best approached from Salt Lake City. From Interstate 15, take U.S. Highway 50 at Exit 178 and head west to Nevada. Once across the state line, Highway 487 heads south to Baker and the only paved road leading to the park.

Facilities: The visitor center is located at the end of the approach road from Baker. A gift shop and food outlet are open from April to October. Tours of the adjacent Lehman Caves are offered throughout the year. Three of the four campgrounds are located along Wheeler Peak Scenic Drive. Only Lower Lehman Creek Campground is open during winter, but no water is available during this season. The other campgrounds open in mid-May, but Wheeler Peak Campground, at 9,886 feet (3,013 m), opens in mid-June and closes at the end of September.

Outstanding features: This park's central features include four groves of rare bristlecone pines, an intriguing cave, and a 13,063-foot-high (3,982-m) peak that shelters three glacial lakes and a remnant glacier. Mountain peaks and valleys offer hikers and climbers a true wilderness experience.

Visitor activities: Scenic drives, cave tours, hiking, short walks, overnight backpacking, mountain climbing, four-wheel-drive excursions, cycling, fishing, horseback riding, wildlife viewing, and birdwatching. Cross-country skiing and snowshoeing in winter.

The federal government owns almost all of the state of Nevada. In this largely uninhabited desert area, most of the land falls under the control of the Bureau of Land Management. It is surprising, then, that Nevada's first national park was established as recently as the 1980s. Conservationists began campaigning in 1958 for a national park in the unique Great Basin area, an arid upland with no inland drainage trapped between the Rocky and the Sierra Nevada Mountains. The area's varied topography and wildlife were worthy of protection, but four groves of bristlecone pines (*Pinus aristata*) presented the strongest argument. Bristlecone pines can live for 3,000 years (needles are known to live for 30 years), and the tree is restricted to a few localities in the west. After years of political wrangling, 120 square miles (311 sq km) of land in eastern Nevada was proclaimed a national park in 1986. The mountain slopes within the park protect the largest grove of bristlecone pines in the world. Other attractions include the second highest peak in Nevada, a glacier, and a limestone cave.

Wheeler Peak and Lehman Cave

Access to the park is along Highway 487 from the town of Baker, which is situated 10 miles (16 km) south of Highway 50. From the entrance, a scenic 12-mile (19-km) drive winds up the mountain slopes to Wheeler Peak Campground, situated at 9,886 feet (3,013 m). The road is open only during summer. Hikers can explore the park's mountain peaks and valleys along 65 miles (104 km) of hiking trails. At the end

of the road, a trail heads south to the mountain's summit and glacier at 13,063 feet (3,982 m). Another 3-mile (5-km) trail passes glacial tarns, including Stella and Teresa Lakes, while a side loop explores a bristlecone forest.

Lehman Cave, known for its large number of intricate stalagmites and stalactites, is situated near the visitor center, which is open throughout the year. Tickets for 90-minute guided tours can be purchased at the visitor center. In summer, park rangers offer candlelight tours of the cave.

There are four campgrounds in the north of the park and two primitive campgrounds in the south near Shoshone Creek. Lexington Arch, in the southeast corner of the park, is a natural limestone arch that can be reached only along a four-wheel-drive track that follows the Lexington Creek. Apart from the network of backpacking trails that crosses the mountains, access to the undeveloped southern region of the park is restricted to rough roads that traverse the adjoining Humboldt-Toiyabe National Forest.

Above, right: Bristlecone pines grow on exposed, dry mountain slopes and occur mainly in Nevada, Utah, and Colorado. As the oldest known living tree, some specimens are more than 4,500 years old.

Opposite: Hikers pause to admire the scenic grandeur of Wheeler Peak, the highest summit in the Snake Range.

Map labels: N; Wheeler Peak; Lehman Cave; Salt Lake City; Wheeler Peak 13,063 ft (3,982 m); Bristlecone Pines; Visitor Center; Baker Creek; Snake Range; Shoshone; Great Basin NP; Lexington 8,720 ft (2,658 m)

On the return journey to the entrance gate, a 6-mile (10-km) road to the right heads northwest to the Fiery Furnace; at sunset, narrow rocky passages that tower 200 feet (60 m) high are ablaze in color. Between March and October, rangers organize guided walks through this Fiery Furnace.

The park's Devils Garden Campground is located near the trailhead, and nightly campfire talks are presented during summer. From the trailhead, a 5-mile (8-km) circular trail leads to the Landscape, Partition, Navajo, Wall, Double-O, and Private Arches.

Backcountry camping is permitted in parts of the park, but there are no marked trails and visitors must obtain a free permit from the visitor center, where a series of exhibits explains the process by which arches are formed. There are photographs of some of the more stunning examples in the park.

South of the park entrance and just before the tourist town of Moab, Highway 128 hugs the banks of the Colorado River and heads north to join Interstate 70. The Bureau of Land Management operates a campground on the banks of the river. There are three sites for launching boats, and the river is popular for kayaking, canoeing, and river trips in inflatable rafts.

CANYONLANDS NATIONAL PARK

A scorched desert, wide open spaces, sheer rocky cliffs reflecting the sun's shifting rays, and the almost unfathomable power that rivers wield as architects of the landscape are among the attractions of this 527-square-mile (1,360-sq-km) park. Established in 1964, the park preserves the land surrounding the meandering beds of the Green and Colorado Rivers and a sizable piece of land south of their confluence. Evidence suggests that the two rivers have carved through a vertical distance of over 1 mile (1.6 km) of sedimentary rock in the region. Erosion has left no trace of more recent rocks. From elevated view sites located 2,300 feet (700 m) above the rivers, an enormous eroded landscape of mesas, buttes, canyons, fins, and spires stretches to the horizon.

This park lies at the apex of the eastern leg of an enormous contiguous conservation area that covers an area nearly twice the size of Yellowstone. The establishment of the Grand Staircase–Escalante National Monument in 1996, connecting the Glen Canyon National Recreation Area to Bryce Canyon, Capitol Reef, and Canyonlands National Parks, doubled in size the area under permanent protection in southern Utah. Adjacent to the northeastern corner of Canyonlands, Dead Horsepoint State Park offers a superb panoramic view of a tight bend in the Colorado River. Some 9 miles (15 km) south of the park, the Dark Canyon Wilderness and Primitive Area encompasses the rugged country bordering the Colorado River.

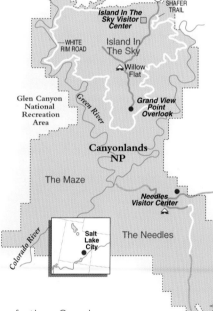

Early Inhabitants and Explorers

Archaic hunter-gatherers living in the region left petroglyphs in Horseshoe Canyon, now an isolated unit of the park located 8 miles (13 km) west. Many centuries later, the Anasazi and Fremont peoples settled in the area, and ruins of their dwellings can still be seen in the park. They cultivated the canyon floors, but a severe drought in the late thirteenth century caused an exodus from the area. The Navajo and Ute tribes later settled in the region.

In 1869, John Wesley Powell led a crew of nine men on an exploration of the Green and Colorado Rivers. The men spent 98 days exploring 1,048 miles (1,677 km) of the rivers that appeared as a great open space on maps of the time. Powell kept a detailed diary. He wrote of their passage down the river, "We glide along through a strange, weird, grand region. The landscape everywhere, away from the river, is of rock."

Above, right: Miniature caves and canyons are sculpted from sandstone by the forces of erosion.

Opposite, top: The view east across Shafer Canyon.

Opposite, bottom left: Parallel bands in the sandstone suggest that an enormous desert once covered the region.

Opposite, bottom right: On the shallow soil of Island in the Sky, tufts of desert grasses grow among a stunted woodland of pinyon pine and juniper.

Location: Southeastern Utah, near Moab.

Climate: Total annual precipitation is less than 8 inches (200 mm), and rain falls mostly in the form of thunderstorms, which occur on an average of 45 days in late summer and early autumn. In midsummer, this is one of the hottest regions of Utah. An average high of 100°F (38°C) can be expected, with an absolute maximum of 110°F (43°C). Winter days are cool and light snow falls. Temperatures drop below freezing overnight. The average low in January ranges from 8° to 16° F (–4 to –9°C).

When to go: Summer is very hot and hikers need to guard against heat exhaustion. Best visited during spring and autumn.

Access: From Interstate 70, at Exit 180 take U.S. Highway 191 south to Moab.

Facilities: Island in the Sky Visitor Center is situated near the northern entrance and The Needles Visitor Center can be approached on Highway 211 south of Moab. Both sections have a campground and picnic areas, and there is a small store at The Needles. There are no restaurants, lodges, or gasoline supplies in the park. The third section, The Maze, is totally undeveloped and can be approached only along four-wheel-drive tracks.

Outstanding features: Over a considerable passage of time, the combined energy of the Green and Colorado Rivers has cut through 1 mile (1.6 km) of vertical rock, leaving behind a bewildering maze of canyons and side gullies.

Visitor activities: Scenic drives, hiking, short walks, overnight backpacking, four-wheel-drive excursions, cycling, fishing, river rafting, and bird-watching.

Exploring the Canyonlands

The two large rivers and their deeply incised canyons divide the park into three distinct regions. Because the rugged topography prevents any direct road access between each region, a long circuitous drive is necessary to visit the different areas of the park.

Island in the Sky, the northern section of the park, is an elevated mesa that rises 2,300 feet (700 m) above the river below and is easily accessible from Moab. The name for this section of the park is most appropriate because the plateau is isolated from the surrounding canyons by vertical cliffs and there is no other access route apart from the road crossing a narrow neck. The road into the park ends at a cul de sac at Grand View Point Overlook after 12 miles (20 km). Along the road are five view sites, and a side road leads to Upheaval Dome and Whale Rock. Hikers can explore areas away from the main road along 15 trails ranging in length from 1 mile (1.5 km) to 20 miles (36 km). A small campground is situated at Willow Flat, and there are two picnic areas at view sites.

The 100-mile (160-km) White Rim Road is a four-wheel-drive trail that follows a route mirroring the meanders in the rivers and requires at least two days. This route follows the White Rim, 1,000 feet (300 m) above the inner gorge, and passes through prime habitat for desert bighorn sheep. Near the entrance, Shafer Trail Road provides access to this track, descending in sharp hairpin bends down an immense rocky basin.

South of the Colorado River, The Needles region can be reached from Highway 191 south of Moab. There is a visitor center, along with two picnic sites and two campgrounds. The Needles consists of weathered spires of red and white sandstone that rise 400 feet (120 m) above the surroundings. A network of asphalt and four-wheel-drive roads explores the area, and a number of hiking trails traverse smaller canyons or lead to the banks of the Colorado. Cataract Canyon, downstream of the confluence of the two rivers, is the best known in the region. There are 26 rapids in this 14-mile (22-km) section of the river, rivaling any in the Grand Canyon and ranging in difficulty up to Class V. Canoes, motorboats, and inflatable rafts are permitted on the upper waters of the Green and Colorado Rivers. Backcountry permits can be

Below: Island in the Sky is a high desert plateau surrounded by deep canyons engraved into the landscape.

obtained from the visitor centers. Advance booking is needed for white-water rafting because the number of available permits is limited.

The land west of the Green and Colorado rivers, known as The Maze, offers visitors a true wilderness experience. There are eight primitive campgrounds, and several four-wheel-drive tracks cross this inhospitable wilderness. The area is regarded as one of the most remote and inaccessible corners of the United States. The Maze is a confusing jumble of sandstone canyons that has been described as "a 30-square-mile puzzle in sandstone." Though few people visit the area, there is access through the adjoining Glen Canyon National Recreation Area. Permits for travel in this area must first be obtained from the rangers in Canyonlands.

Below: From Grand View Point, the immense power of water over eons is evident in the maze of canyons cut by the Colorado and Green Rivers.

CAPITOL REEF
NATIONAL PARK

In a remote corner of southern Utah, where barely 4 inches (100 mm) of rain falls on average, a prominent fold stretches in a north-south direction between the Cedar and Escalante Mountains and the Colorado River. The Waterpocket Fold, so named for its many eroded depressions that fill with water after rain, is a dramatic rugged wall of eroded sandstone spires and twisted canyons carved by erosion. The fold is comprised of layers of sedimentary rock formed from deposits of sand and silt in ancient seas and deserts. About 65 million years ago, tectonic forces off the California Coast bent the earth's crust to form a large monocline, or fold, and later caused the uplift of the Colorado Plateau. Subsequent erosion has stripped away much of the fold, revealing eroded cliffs and spires compiled of different bands of sandstone.

South of the Fremont River, a rugged section of rocky pinnacles reminded early explorers of an imposing ocean reef. Rounded domes were reminiscent of a capitol building, and this section of the fold was named Capitol Reef. The Paiute tribe had an equally descriptive name for the many different rock hues and multilayered strata, calling the region "Land of the Sleeping Rainbow." In 1937, a large section of the fold, which is the largest exposed monocline in North America, was declared a national monument. In 1971, Congress redesignated the area as a national park. Covering 378 square miles (975 sq km) of towering cliffs, rocky pinnacles, stark desert, and narrow canyons, this hostile landscape contrasts with the green splendor of Fruita, a historic 1880 Mormon settlement on the banks of the Fremont River that has been incorporated into the park.

Fruita and the Fremont

From its source in the mountains to the west, the Fremont River flows through a gap in the rugged fold. It is bordered by Fremont cottonwood (*Populus fremontii*) and box elder (*Sambucus melanocarpa*) trees. They create a verdant corridor that contrasts vividly with the harshness of the surrounding desert.

In about the year 700, Native Americans settled along the river. Archaeologists have named these people the Fremont because their customs differed from the nearby Anasazi. They lived in pit houses and built stone granaries in caves to store corn. Apart from hunting and gathering food from the surrounding country, the Fremont tribe grew corn, beans, and squash with the help of irrigation from the river. They are most famous for the petroglyphs that can be seen in the area. Carefully chipped into the rock are panels of animal and human figures that are a monument to a culture that has long since vanished. In about 1275, around the same time that Mesa Verde was abandoned, the Fremont people moved away, never to return.

Above, right: Most of the 1,700 cactus species in the world are confined to the deserts of North and South America.

Opposite: The Waterpocket Fold was formed 65 million years ago by the same potent forces that later uplifted the Colorado Plateau.

Location: Southern Utah. Richfield on the interstate is the nearest medium-sized town.

Climate: In July, an average high of 92°F (33°C) can be expected, with a record high of 104°F (40°C). Snow can be expected from November to March, and the average low temperature in January is 22°F (–5°C).

When to go: The park is open throughout the year. Snowstorms in winter may close some roads. The fruit orchards are open from June to October.

Access: From Interstate 70, take Highway 24 south. This road forms a broad loop and passes through the center of the park before returning to the interstate. For visitors approaching from either the west or the east, this is the recommended route.

Facilities: The visitor center is situated in the historic Fruita district. A picnic area with extensive lawns borders the Fremont River, and short walks lead to historic farm buildings and a campground. There are no stores, restaurants, lodges, or service stations in the park. The north and south regions can be reached only on rough gravel roads.

Outstanding features: The Waterpocket Fold, centerpiece of the park, encompasses impressive rock formations and hidden canyons. The historic settlement of Fruita is a delightful oasis where fresh fruit may be picked during summer in orchards established by Mormon pioneers in the nineteenth century.

Visitor activities: Scenic drives, hiking, short walks to historic sites, overnight backpacking, cycling, fruit picking, horseback riding, wildlife viewing, and bird-watching.

The Fremont Valley was not settled permanently for another six centuries when Mormons founded the settlement of Junction (later renamed Fruita) in 1880. Farther south, in Capitol Gorge, the names of explorers who passed through the area from 1871 onward are inscribed on the canyon wall.

Discovering the Park

Although the desert appears stark, over 900 species of plants have been identified in the park; six species of flowers are restricted to the Waterpocket Fold. Birds such as the mountain bluebird and ducks can be seen along the river. However, away from water, desert life is not always immediately apparent. Many desert mammals, like the bobcat, coyote, and ringtail cat, are largely nocturnal, while reptiles and rodents can often be observed. Desert bighorn sheep were reintroduced in 1984. The depressions in the rock that hold water after rain are home to fairy shrimp and spadefoot toad tadpoles. Those tadpoles that are able to reach maturity before the pools dry up ensure this species' survival.

The paved Highway 24 provides easy access to Capitol Dome, Fruita, and the Fremont River Valley. From the visitor center, the 9-mile (13-km) Scenic Drive follows the jagged western edge of the fold, with side roads leading into Grand Wash and Capitol Gorge. A rough track continues west, but most visitors retrace their route to the Fremont Valley. Hikers can explore 30 miles (48 km) of trails in the Fruita area and nearly 120 miles (200 km) of backcountry routes. Trailheads for 15 hiking trails, ranging in length from 1 mile (1.6 km) to 4 miles (7 km), are situated along Highway 24 and the Scenic Drive. Mountain bikes are permitted on park roads only, while horses are permitted on certain trails.

There is a campground in the Fruita area along with a delightful picnic area alongside the Fremont River. Ranger-led programs are arranged from May to September. The Gifford Homestead in the Fruita district, built in 1908, is a typical Utah farmhouse that has been preserved. A novel attraction in the park is the opportunity to pick and weigh fruit in the original orchards from June to October.

Farther down the valley, the humble Behunin Cabin was once home to a family of ten. The parents and the two youngest children slept in the cabin, the boys in a nearby cave, and the girls in a wagon outside. In the nearby Fremont River, a delightful cascade offers relief from the relentless desert.

Off the Beaten Track

Highway 24, built in 1962, provides easy entry to the Fremont Valley, but access to the north and south areas of the park is more difficult. The gravel road leading to Cathedral Valley in the north section requires a four-wheel-drive vehicle. To explore the remote south section, the gravel Norton-Bullfrog Road enters Strike Valley after 29 miles (47 km). This route permits visitors to explore the Muley Twist Canyon, so named because its sharp bends and sheer walls supposedly forced mules to twist around the corners. From the canyon, Burr Trail Road crosses the Grand Staircase–Escalante National Monument for 36 miles (58 km) before reaching the isolated town of Boulder. Anasazi State Park, in the town, preserves the ruins of a settlement that was occupied from 1050 to 1200. The return journey of 37 miles (60 km) passes through the Dixie National Forest, climbing to a height of 9,400 feet (2,866 m) and offering a panoramic view of the 1,000-foot-high (300-m) fold to the east.

Opposite, top: The Castle, a spire of jagged sandstone, towers above the visitor center in the historic Fruita district.

Opposite, center: Near the Behunin Cabin, the Fremont River forms a refreshing cascade in the desert landscape.

Opposite, bottom left: The green oasis of the picnic area in Fruita contrasts with the surrounding parched desert.

Opposite, bottom right: From Fruita, the road east closely follows the Fremont River and passes imposing formations such as the Capitol Dome (center).

Below: The humble Behunin Cabin was once home to two Mormon pioneers and their eight children. Mormons settled in the Fremont Valley area from 1880 onward.

Bottom: Miniature caves, excavated by wind and water erosion, punctuate the sandstone cliffs near the cabin. A larger cave provided a natural bedroom for the boys of the Behunin family.

BRYCE CANYON NATIONAL PARK

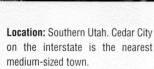

At the edge of the Paunsaugunt Plateau in southern Utah, the forests of ponderosa pine (*Pinus ponderosa*) end abruptly and a jagged, brightly colored rent in the earth's surface plunges 2,000 feet (600 m) in thousands of rocky spires, steps, and spurs into the valley below. These strange, other-worldly columns of compressed sand, and ragged eroded canyons of sediment colored white, pink, yellow, and orange, are so out of the ordinary that they resemble the toxic, chemical-stained sands of a mine dump. Bryce is not actually a canyon but 14 eroded amphitheaters set in a chain along the edge of the plateau. This spectacular example of water erosion forms the centerpiece of a 56-square-mile (144-sq-km) national park.

In 1875, Scottish immigrant Ebenezer Bryce and his wife Mary settled in the area and raised cattle. The Bryces built a ranch at the bottom of the canyon, once describing it as "a hell of a place to lose a cow." Although the Bryces moved away in 1880, the canyon retained their name. In 1923, a national monument was proclaimed, mainly to protect the canyon and its spectacular cliffs. In 1928, the monument was redesignated as a national park.

Bryce Canyon is the smallest national park in Utah yet also one of the most popular. The adjoining Dixie National Forest and the Grand Staircase–Escalante National Monument help to convey an impression of unspoiled vastness. From the many view sites along the edge of the plateau, there are spectacular vistas across the immense, untamed landscapes of southern Utah.

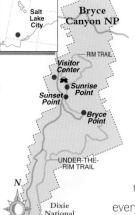

Ancient Oceans

During the Cretaceous Period, much of the central part of America was covered by an ocean. The sediments deposited here formed the brown and gray marine rocks visible at low elevations. Later, a large inland lake replaced the sea, and rivers deposited a deep layer of iron-rich sediment onto the lake bed. About 13 million years ago, warping occurred that bent the crust. Along fault lines, some blocks subsided while others rose. Stresses caused by geologic forces produced a crisscross pattern of countless cracks that were later widened and worn down by water. Subsequent erosion produced the spires and eroded cliffs of the amphitheaters. The cliff face continues to retreat by approximately 12 inches (30 cm) every 50 years.

Vegetation and Wildlife

The three distinct biogeographic zones in the park rely on altitude and moisture. Much of the plateau is blanketed in forests of ponderosa pine. In low-lying regions, pinyon pines (*Pinus edulis*) and the Utah juniper (*Juniperus osteosperma*) can be seen. Where the plateau rises to 9,115 feet (2,778 m) in the south, these forests are replaced by Douglas fir (*Pseudotsuga menziesii*), aspen (*Populus tremuloides*), and blue spruce (*Picea pungens*).

Above, right: Blue spruce grows on cool, north-facing slopes at altitudes above 6,000 feet (1,800 m).

Opposite: Bryce Canyon's countless spires and minarets were fashioned from ancient sediments deposited in a long-forgotten sea.

Location: Southern Utah. Cedar City on the interstate is the nearest medium-sized town.

Climate: The plateau's high altitude reduces temperatures and highs of around 80°F (26°C) can be expected in summer. From April to October, the days are moderate and the nights cool. During winter, heavy snowfalls are common on the plateau.

When to go: The park is accessible throughout the year. For exploring the canyons on foot, May through October is recommended.

Access: From Interstate 15, take Highway 14 at Cedar City and head east to the junction of U.S. Highway 89. Head north on this road, and then turn right onto Highway 12, which leads to the park entrance.

Facilities: The visitor center is located near the entrance. The north campground, a store, laundry, and two picnic areas are nearby. There is a lodge and restaurant between Sunrise and Sunset Points and another campground near Sunset Point. Several short interpretive trails enter the canyon from these view sites. There are two picnic areas farther south along the scenic drive. During winter, some of the spur roads to view sites are closed to allow for cross-country skiing.

Outstanding features: A brightly colored escarpment of eroded canyons and spires. Depending on the time of day, the barren sediments of the canyons glow in shades of yellow, orange, and red.

Visitor activities: Scenic drives, hiking, short walks into the canyon, overnight backpacking, cycling, horseback riding, wildlife viewing, and bird-watching. During winter, cross-country skiing and snowshoeing are popular activities.

Additionally, the rare bristlecone pine can be found in exposed, windblown locations.

Several birds and mammals feed on pine nuts and juniper berries. The western kingbird catches insects in the forests. The red-breasted nuthatch also feeds on insects but, in winter, depends on conifer seeds. The evening grosbeak has a stout bill that pries open pine cones to get to the seeds. Ground squirrels and Colorado chipmunks feed on pine nuts, and mule deer can often be seen feeding in the understory. Predators include bobcat and mountain lion, although they are seldom seen. The endangered Utah prairie dog occurs in the park meadows. During summer, rangers conduct tours to a prairie dog town.

Above: The Queen's Garden from Sunrise Point.

Above, center: Between Fairyland Point and Sunset Point, short circular trails explore the canyon.

Above, right: Guided horse trails venture into the canyon from Sunrise Point.

Right: Approaching from the west, Dixie National Forest offers the first hint of the strange formations that occur along the edge of the Paunsaugunt Plateau.

Outdoor Activities

Approaching the park from Interstate 15, the road passes a replica of a cowboy town in Bryce, while horse trails into the rugged canyon encourage visitors to recall the West's frontier days. A concessionaire operates these popular horse trails from a venue near the lodge. Guides descend into the canyon at Sunrise Point on guided trails of either two hours or half a day.

The main park road passes 13 view sites and meanders for 18 miles (28 km) along the crest of the plateau before ending at Rainbow Point. A number of trails are in the vicinity of Bryce Canyon Lodge and the park's two campgrounds. From Sunrise Point, the 11-mile (18-km) Rim Trail passes Sunset Point and Inspiration Point to end at Bryce Point. Four shorter trails, including the Navajo Loop and the Fairyland Loop, descend into the canyon. A detailed brochure describes points of interest on the Queens Garden Trail, which begins at Sunrise Point and explores the canyon for 2 miles (3 km). This one-way trail can be made into a circular route by following the Navajo Loop Trail, which climbs back up to Sunset Point.

Overnight backpacking is restricted to the Under-the-Rim Trail from Bryce Point to Rainbow Point in the southern corner of the park. This 20-mile (30-km) trail meanders along the base of the cliffs—there are seven primitive campsites along the trail, and four short branches lead back to the scenic drive. At Rainbow Point, the circular Riggs Spring Loop Trail passes The Promontory and descends into Corral Hollow and Mutton Hollow. The campsite at Riggs Spring is located near the southern boundary of the park.

Snow falls from November to March and cross-country skiing and snowshoeing are popular winter sports. The main park road is open throughout the year, but certain side roads are closed in winter to accommodate cross-country skiers. The visitor center has a number of snowshoes that are available free of charge.

Above: Desert scenery near Panguitch, a small service town catering to people visiting Bryce Canyon.

Below: A main approach road to the park from the west passes a replica of an old western town in the neighboring town of Bryce.

ZION NATIONAL PARK

A geologic showpiece that contains some of the highest sandstone cliffs in the world, which rise up to 3,700 feet (1,130 m) above the canyon floor, Zion is the oldest and most popular of Utah's five national parks, receiving 2.5 million visitors a year. In the nineteenth century, Mormon settlers saw the rocky cliffs and spires as natural renditions of temples. They named the valley Little Zion, after the Hebrew word referring to an idyllic haven of sanctuary and solace. One early visitor was Methodist minister Frederick Fisher, who was so enchanted by the splendor of the canyon that he named many of the surrounding peaks after biblical images. Among them are Great White Throne, Altar of Sacrifice, The Pulpit, Three Patriarchs, and Angel's Landing.

In many of the canyons of the Southwest, visitors gaze into the depths from elevated view sites. At Zion, visitors enter through the bottom of the canyon, dwarfed by the banded cliffs lining the river. Deep layers of red and white Navajo sandstone are a feature of the imposing cliffs, averaging 2,500 feet (760 m) in height, that flank the bed of the North Folk Virgin River. Although originally established in 1909 as the Mukuntuweap National Monument, in 1919 the protected area was expanded to its current 229 square miles (590 sq km) and redesignated a national park.

Formation of the Canyon

Kaibab limestone, which caps the rim of the Grand Canyon, forms the lowest rock strata at Zion, while the top layers of Dakota formation sandstone at Zion form the bottom strata at Bryce Canyon. Zion's rock layers were formed when sediments deposited into a shallow sea or inland lake were compressed into bands of limestone, shale, and sandstone. The thick deposits of Navajo sandstone were laid when the desert extended over 150,000 square miles (400,000 sq km). Wind-blown sand dunes were solidified into sandstone. Later, tilting of the earth's crust increased the speed of river flow, hastening the forces of erosion. Over the past 13 million years, the North Folk Virgin River has carved a narrow gorge through the layers of sandstone, exposing seven horizontal layers of sedimentary rock.

Wildlife in the Canyon

Differences in elevation and moisture create a range of habitats. Zion contains the richest diversity of plants in Utah. Along riverbanks, box elder, cottonwood, and ash trees offer shelter for wildlife. Pinyon pines and junipers grow at low elevations while, on the higher slopes, forests of ponderosa pine occur. A total of 271 bird, 75 mammal, and 32 reptile and amphibian species have been recorded here.

Above, right: In winter, snow dusts the crest of the canyon.

Opposite: Cliffs of sandstone tower above Pine Creek Valley along the scenic Zion–Mount Carmel Highway.

Location: Southwestern Utah, between the towns of Cedar City and St. George.

Climate: July and August are the hottest months, with an average high of 100°F (38°C). However, in this dry climate, nights are comfortable. Winters are mild and drop below freezing only during mid-winter. Light snow falls in the canyon, but on higher elevations, heavier snowfalls occur.

When to go: Best visited from April to October. Spring weather is often unpredictable, and leaf colors are at their best during September and October.

Access: From Interstate 15, take Highway 9 at Exit 16 and head east to the south entrance at Springdale. The north entrance at Kolob Canyon borders the interstate and can be reached from Exit 40.

Facilities: The new Zion Canyon Visitor Center has been completed in the Watchman Campground, and the original building now houses a cultural history museum. Kolob Canyon Visitor Center and a picnic area are situated in the northwest corner of the park. The park's north and south regions are connected only by hiking trails. Two campgrounds border the North Folk Virgin River at the south entrance. Zion Lodge has a restaurant and fast food outlet and offers tram tours of the valley. There is a picnic area at the Grotto.

Outstanding features: The park's centerpiece is a narrow, secluded canyon formed by the erosive power of the North Folk Virgin River. Vertical cliffs tower 2,500 feet (760 m) above the riverbed.

Visitor activities: Shuttle bus and tram rides, hiking, overnight backpacking, rock climbing, cycling, horseback riding, river tubing, wildlife viewing, and bird-watching.

Above: Checkerboard Mesa, so named for its cross-hatched cracks and joints, is a prominent landmark near the east entrance to the park.

Below: Although flash floods pose a danger, the Narrows Route offers wilderness hiking to more energetic walkers.

Mule deer and antelope, ground, and rock squirrels are often seen. Predators include gray fox, ringtail cat, bobcat, and coyote. Mountain lions are well represented, though these secretive cats are seldom spotted. Along the river, signs of beaver activity are evident. Birds include black-headed grosbeak, Gambel's quail, American kestrel, mountain chickadee, American flicker, pinyon jay, and golden eagle. At least 15 pairs of the rare peregrine falcon have been recorded in the park. When these birds are nesting, certain trails and climbing routes may be closed.

Visiting Zion

The main focus of the park is Zion Canyon, created through the erosive forces of the North Folk Virgin River. Approaching from Interstate 15, Highway 9 passes through towns like Hurricane and Virgin. In Springdale, an IMAX theater shows *Treasure of the Gods*—a fascinating documentary of Zion's main attractions—on a screen that is six stories high.

A new visitor center has been completed in Watchman Campground and the old center now houses a museum. The canyon extends into the mountains for 15 miles (24 km), and the first 8 miles (13 km) are accessible by road. The Scenic Drive follows the east bank of the river, passes Zion Lodge and the Grotto Picnic Area and ends at the parking area below the Temple of Sinawava. From the parking area, the route into the

VISITOR
CENTER

Narrows can be followed by adventurous visitors. In places, the canyon is only 20 feet (6 m) wide, with sheer walls towering 2,000 feet (600 m) above the hiker. Flash floods can occur. Because hikers have been drowned in the past, permits must be obtained before proceeding along the route.

On the return journey, from the bridge, the Zion–Mount Carmel Highway follows the southern slope of the Pine Creek Valley and scales the steep cliff face, providing spectacular views. After rounding six sharp bends, the road passes through a 1-mile-long (1.6-km) tunnel. Work on the tunnel began in 1927 and took three years to complete. At the time, the project was regarded as a feat of engineering. The road provides superb views of Checkerboard Mesa, East Temple, and the steep sides of the canyon.

Visitors who engage in rock climbing and backpacking are able to explore the wilderness heart of the park. The 12 trails in the canyon range in length from a short, easy stroll to 10 miles (17 km). During summer, horseback trails are offered by a concessionaire and can be booked at Zion Lodge. Cyclists are permitted along the Pa'rus Trail following the river and on the main roads, though they may not ride through the tunnel.

In the northwestern corner of the park, approached by a separate entrance off Interstate 15, the La Verkin Creek Trail leads to the magnificent Kolob Arch. With a gigantic span of 310 feet (94 m), this is one of the largest arches in the world. From the arch, the Wildcat Canyon and West Rim Trails lead hikers through wild country to enter the northern end of Zion Canyon after some 17 miles (27 km).

Above: At the south entrance, sheer sandstone cliffs rise 3,600 feet (1,100 m) above the valley carved by the North Folk Virgin River.

GRAND CANYON NATIONAL PARK

The Grand Canyon, an immense abyss 277 miles (446 km) long, up to 18 miles (29 km) wide, and an average of 4,700 feet (1,440 m) deep on the South Rim and 5,700 feet (1,740 m) on the North Rim, is one of the natural wonders of the world. From view sites along the canyon's rim, the Colorado River is barely visible 4 miles (6 km) away across eroded ridges and spires that plunge in rough, gigantic steps to the canyon floor. If America's man-made icons include the Statue of Liberty, Golden Gate Bridge, and the New York skyline, then the Grand Canyon is its most enduring and unchallenged natural symbol among a list of contenders that includes the Great Lakes, the Rocky Mountains, and the Mississippi River.

As one of the most popular national parks in America, the canyon receives nearly five million visitors per year, of which 30 percent are foreign tourists. Nearly one million visitors view the canyon from the air. The airport apron in Tusayan, on the park's southern border, with its fleet of 25 helicopters, could almost be mistaken for a military base. While the canyon is undeniably popular today, early visitors often failed to comprehend its magnitude or potential to attract visitors.

In 1540, Garcia Lopez de Cardenas, part of a Spanish army in search of gold, led a party of 25 men into the canyon hoping to find a great river. After arriving at the edge of the canyon and finding neither gold nor access to the river, they returned disappointed. In 1858, the federal government sent surveyor Joseph Ives to explore the region. Ives wrote, "Ours has been the first, and will doubtless be the last, party of whites to visit this profitless locality. It seems intended that the Colorado River, along the greater portion of its lonely and majestic way, shall be forever unvisited and undisturbed." A decade later, Major John Wesley Powell and nine boat crew members became the first expedition to explore the entire length of the canyon. In May 1869, the men departed in four boats of white oak and pine on a 1,000-mile (1,600-km) journey down the Colorado River that took 98 days to complete.

In 1908, President Theodore Roosevelt established a national monument to protect the canyon. In 1919, the canyon was placed under the control of the National Park Service. Subsequent land additions have increased the park to its present size of 1,904 square miles (4,911 sq km), making it the fourth largest park in the lower 48 states. In 1979, the Grand Canyon was declared a World Heritage Site. Apart from the extensive land area included within the park, three wilderness areas and a forest reserve border its northern boundary. The Secretary of the Interior has proposed setting aside the Arizona Strip National Monument bordering the North Rim. Thirteen presidents have used national monuments legislation to protect some of America's most significant landscapes, including the Grand Canyon.

Above, right: A ground squirrel surveys the chasm.

Opposite: A lone hiker is dwarfed by the sheer cliffs in the inner canyon of the Grand Canyon National Park.

Location: Northern Arizona. Williams on the interstate is the nearest large town.

Climate: The inner canyon has average summer highs of 100°F (38°C) and a maximum of 118°F (48°C). Temperatures can drop far below freezing in winter, but the inner canyon is on average 30°F (16°C) warmer than the South Rim.

When to go: Hiking is best undertaken in spring and autumn. Heavy snowfalls close the approach road to the North Rim from November to mid-May.

Access: From Interstate 40, at Exit 165 take Highway 64 north to Grand Canyon Village. To access the North Rim, continue east on Highway 64 and then north on U.S. Highway 89. After crossing the Colorado River, head south on Highway 67 through the Kaibab National Forest to the North Rim.

Facilities: Campground, restaurant, general store, and bookshop at Desert View and four picnic areas along East Rim Drive. Turnoffs lead to several view sites and a museum at the Tusayan Ruin. At Grand Canyon Village are six lodges, four situated on the canyon rim. Many other facilities are available in the village, including a railway station. On the North Rim are five picnic areas, a visitor center, campground, and the Grand Canyon Lodge, which has a restaurant, coffee shop, post office, general store, laundry, and service station.

Outstanding features: Four geologic eras are clearly visible on the high canyon walls, and the inner canyon provides superb opportunities for white-water rafting.

Visitor activities: Scenic drives, hiking, short walks, overnight backpacking, mule trips into the canyon, cycling, fishing, river rafting, helicopter tours, horseback riding, wildlife viewing, bird-watching, and cross-country skiing during winter.

The Canyon's Origins

The canyon represents a cross section of the processes that formed the earth over millions of years. At the bottom of the canyon, ancient rocks are visible. Basement rocks of schist and granite form the inner gorge. Even the Kaibab limestone on the canyon crest is estimated to be 225 million years old. Although younger rocks have been stripped away by erosion to reveal the earth's deep foundations, the formation of the canyon is a recent event in geologic time. On the canyon walls, four geologic eras are visible in the sedimentary rocks. Nowhere else in the world can such a clear view of geologic processes be obtained. About 65 million years ago, a massive uplift formed the Colorado Plateau (see p. 141). The Colorado River flowed sluggishly across the level plateau, but the earth's tilting gradually caused the land to slope upward, forming an enormous hill. The river then began to erode this massive rent in the earth over a relatively short period (in geologic terms) of six million years, though other theories suggest that the Colorado's erosive action was not solely responsible for the formation of the canyon.

Life Zones and Wildlife

The South Rim receives about 15 inches (380 mm) of precipitation on average in the form of thunderstorms in late summer or heavy winter snows. The bottom of the canyon

Above: From Lipan Point on the South Rim, the enormous rent in the earth's crust is 9 miles (14 km) wide and nearly 4,900 feet (1,500 m) deep.

ranges from 2,720 feet (829 m) to 1,200 feet (370 m) in elevation, and on average receives less than 8 inches (200 mm) of rain each year. Summer temperatures on the canyon floor can reach 118°F (48°C), and these differences in altitude, rainfall, and temperature produce the four distinct life zones that exist in the park. At the bottom of the canyon, the Lower Sonoran Zone is characterized by desert grass, creosote bush, mesquite, and cacti. The Upper Sonoran Zone extends to a height of about 7,000 feet (2,100 m) and the most common plants include pinyon pine, Utah juniper, Gambel oak (*Quercus gambelii*), and sagebrush. The Transition Zone is dominated by ponderosa pine, while forests of Douglas fir, spruce, and aspen demarcate the Canadian zone on the higher, cooler North Rim. Within these zones, subdivisions such as grassland and mountain shrub can be identified. The river creates a further aquatic habitat supporting stream bank vegetation in contrast with the surrounding arid desert.

A total of 88 species of mammals occur in the park. Some of the most common species that visitors can encounter in the pinyon–juniper woodland include rock squirrel, white-tailed antelope squirrel, Uinta chipmunk, Abert squirrel, ringtail cat, bobcat, and mule deer. Other mammals present but less often seen include mountain lion, gray fox, river otter, whitetail prairie dog, elk, desert bighorn, and black bear.

A total of 315 bird species have been recorded. Of these, 136 species are known to nest in the park. The most common resident birds in the pinyon–juniper woodlands of the South Rim include red-tailed hawk, Gambel's quail, great horned owl, hairy woodpecker, pinyon jay, canyon wren, and mountain chickadee.

Constraining the Colorado

From the rim edge, the Colorado appears sluggish and flat. However, the river drops 560 feet (170 m) over a distance of 50 miles (80 km) through the canyon between Chuar Butte and Mount Huethawali. When the Glen Canyon Dam was completed upstream in 1964, it altered the 292-mile (467-km) stretch of the Colorado between the dam and Lake Mead. The 710-foot-high (216-m) concrete wall at Glen Canyon releases clear, cold, 49°F (9°C) water from the bottom of the dam. Sunlight penetrates the water and algae bloom, which attracts tiny organisms fed on by rainbow trout; these, in turn, attract bald eagles.

Before the dam was completed, spring floods frequently washed away stream-bank vegetation and formed new sand banks and rapids. The 255-square-mile (658-sq-km) Glen Canyon Lake curtailed these annual floods along the river. Willows and exotic tamarisk trees soon became established on banks that were once bare of vegetation. These trees are fed on by many insects, which attract birds preyed on by peregrine falcons. Grand Canyon now has the largest nesting population of rare peregrines in the continental United States.

Some conservationists and river-running organizations who annually guide 25,000 visitors down the river object to some of the changes. River-running groups dislike the fluctuations in river level produced by the dam's hydroelectric turbines.

As the endangered humpback chub is found here, some interest groups want the dam to release warmer water into the cold river to prevent the fish's extinction. However, this would allow the predatory striped

Above: Mule deer inhabit the pine and juniper forests on the crest of the canyon.

Below, left and right: The Colorado River drops 560 feet (170 m) in the middle section of the canyon, and river running is a popular adventure sport here.

bass from Lake Mead to move upriver, endangering the chub.

The management of the river is complex, as opposing interests need to be reconciled. The Department of the Interior has responded to criticism. It has appointed a team of scientists to monitor and study the river. At the same time, new guidelines now regulate outflow from the dam and simulate occasional floods.

Exploring the Canyon

Approaching from the east, there are eight view sites along the South Rim and five picnic areas. The Watchtower at Desert View, designed in 1932, provides superb panoramic views over the canyon. After 25 miles (40 km), the road reaches the visitor center and Grand Canyon Village. West Rim Drive continues for another 8 miles (11 km) along the canyon rim.

The visitor center offers a dozen ranger-led activities, and there is a museum and an art studio nearby. El Tovar Hotel, built in 1905, is the first in line of six lodges. A shuttle bus service follows three loops from the village. Visiting the canyon by steam train is possible on the Grand Canyon Railway from Williams, Arizona, which is located on Interstate 40. Grand Canyon Village contains many services including campgrounds, stores, restaurants, a bank, a post office, and a clinic.

Hikers can enter the canyon along the Bright Angel or South Kaibab Trail. At least two days are necessary to complete the trails and a fee is payable. Phantom Ranch

Lodge, the only accommodation within the canyon apart from backcountry campgrounds, accommodates hikers and visitors arriving on two-day mule trips. White-water rafting trips lasting from three days to two weeks are offered by many operators.

Grand Canyon Village is separated from Grand Canyon Lodge on the North Rim by the 10-mile-wide (16-km) chasm, but it requires a 215-mile (344-km) drive to circumvent the immense gully and visit the other side. Point Imperial, on the North Rim, at 8,803 feet (2,683 m) is the highest view site overlooking the canyon. Walhalla Overlook, also on the North Rim, provides a panoramic view. The North Rim is open from mid-May to mid-October.

Below: The narrow Bright Angel Trail descends into the inner canyon to Phantom Ranch, where a suspension bridge crosses the Colorado.

Top: The Watchtower at Desert View affords awe-inspiring vistas of the canyon and beyond.
Above: Regular aerial sightseeing tours depart from Tusayan, affording visitors the best views of the canyon.
Opposite: Havasupai Native Americans ride through Havasu Canyon in the wild, western region of the park.

CANYON DE CHELLY NATIONAL MONUMENT

In northern Arizona, the level terrain of the Defiance Plateau suddenly yields to sheer cliffs of red sandstone that plunge 1,000 feet (300 m) down to the narrow, cottonwood-crowded course of the Rio de Chelly. Canyon De Chelly is situated on the Navajo Indian Reservation. In 1931, a national monument covering 130 square miles (338 sq km) was established to protect this four-branched canyon and its ancient Native American ruins.

The name De Chelly is derived from the Navajo word *tsegi*, meaning "rock canyon." Apart from its attractive red sandstone walls and sheer cliffs, ruins set in alcoves in the canyon walls represent 2,000 years of Native American occupation. A total of 700 ruins have been identified, including pit houses and south-facing pueblos that date back to the 1100s.

Canyon Geology and History

De Chelly sandstone is an old rock that was formed in a primordial desert. Sloping lines in the rock strata indicate the direction in which winds blew over the desert dunes. In recent geologic times, less than three million years ago, the Defiance Plateau rose and the uplift encouraged erosion, leading to the formation of the canyon.

Set in sheltered alcoves in the canyon walls are the pueblo ruins that can be seen from the canyon's edge. Researchers have concluded that the first buildings were erected in the year 1060. The Anasazi who lived here grew crops on the canyon floor and hunted game. The canyon was abandoned by the Anasazi near the end of the thirteenth century, at a time when similar settlements were abandoned in the Southwest, and was later occupied by the Hopi and Navajo. When the Spanish introduced horses and sheep in the seventeenth century, these domesticated animals were soon acquired by the Navajo. They settled in the vicinity of the canyon about 300 years ago. This area became well-known in the region for its fields of corn and peach orchards. The Navajo fought several wars against the Spanish, and the canyon provided a refuge until the United States took control of the land after a war against Mexico. In 1864, soldiers under command of Colonel Kit Carson entered the eastern end of the canyon and drove the Navajo out. The captured Navajo were forced to walk to a reservation at Fort Sumner, New Mexico. In 1868, the army admitted that the policy had been a mistake and the Navajo were allowed to return.

Exploring Canyon De Chelly

A Navajo circular hogan (homestead), built from wood and earth, can be seen at the visitor center, located at the junction of Highways 7 and 64. Inside the center,

Above, right: The Navajo are known throughout the world as accomplished silversmiths.
Opposite: Canyon De Chelly is situated in the heart of the Navajo Indian Reservation.

Location: Northeastern Arizona, not far from the town of Chinle.

Climate: Annual precipitation averages 12 inches (300 mm), and thunderstorms can be expected on an average of 40 days. In July, the average high ranges from 84° to 96°F (29° to 36°C) and occasionally temperatures may rise to 100°F (38°C). In January, the average low is 12°F (−11°C) and light snow falls in winter.

When to go: The Cottonwood Campground is open throughout the year. In midsummer, the inner canyon can be very hot; avoid hiking it in July and August.

Access: From Interstate 40, at Exit 333 take U.S. Highway 191 north to Chinle. From the north, take U.S. Highway 160 to the Four Corners and then head south on U.S. Highway 191.

Facilities: The visitor center, campground, picnic area and the Thunderbird Lodge are all situated at the western entrance to the park. A short trail leads to the White House Ruin, but the rest of the park is undeveloped.

Outstanding features: Situated in the heart of Navajo territory, the park preserves a spectacular four-branched sandstone canyon and the ruins of Native American cliff dwellings.

Visitor activities: Scenic drives and short walks to view sites. Guided hikes, horseback riding, and four-wheel-drive tours can be booked with Navajo guides at Thunderbird Lodge.

Top: Cottonwoods and willows line the banks of the shallow Chinle Wash.

Above: Juniper berries on the canyon's south rim.

Right, top: Sheer cliffs of colorful De Chelly sandstone line the narrow canyon.

Right, bottom: A Navajo guide outside a traditional circular hogan at the visitor center.

local craftspeople demonstrate their skills in manufacturing turquoise and silver jewelry. Because the surrounding land is owned by the Navajo people, this national monument is jointly managed by the National Park Service and the Navajo Tribal Authority.

On the canyon rim, Utah juniper, pinyon pines, Gambel oak, and prickly pear grow in cracks in the red rocks. Cottonwoods and willows crowd the sandy banks of the river at the valley bottom. A scenic road follows the north rim for 17 miles (27 km) and the south rim for 22 miles (35 km), where many view sites provide grand views of the canyon. The northern drive passes Massacre Cave, where the Navajo attempted to hide in 1805 while the Spanish fired on them from the canyon rim, killing a total of 115 people. The southern drive passes several view sites and ends at Spider Rock, a stone pinnacle 800 feet (240 m) in height that marks the junction of the De Chelly and Monument Canyons.

Guided canyon tours are available through Thunderbird Lodge, situated near the visitor center. Apart from guided walks, horseback trails, and four-wheel-drive trips provided by authorized Navajo guides, the only public access into the canyon is the 2.5-mile

(4-km) trail that leads to White House Ruin. The parking area for this trail is situated 6 miles (10 km) along the southern drive, from where the trail descends 500 feet (150 m) to the valley bottom.

PETRIFIED FOREST NATIONAL PARK

In the Painted Desert of eastern Arizona, the world's largest collection of petrified wood lies scattered across a barren and eroded landscape. In this dry region where the natural vegetation consists of a few gnarled junipers, low shrubs, cacti, tufts of grass, and seasonal wildflowers, the remains of trees that once towered 100 feet (30 m) into the air seem a little out of place. Paiute Native Americans offered what seemed a perfectly plausible explanation for the presence of such enormous logs in the middle of a desert. They believed that the petrified trees were the arrow shafts of Shinauv, their thunder god. The Navajo offered an alternative explanation, regarding the logs as the bones of Yietso, a mythological giant.

Toward the end of the nineteenth century, gem collectors began dynamiting the logs in search of quartz crystals. To prevent further destruction, a national monument was proclaimed in 1906, and this was redesignated a national park in 1962. Extending over 146 square miles (377 sq km), the park includes a large expanse of the remarkable solidified sand dunes of the Painted Desert to the north of Interstate 40. This highway passes through the narrow 1-mile-wide (1.6-km) corridor linking the northern and southern regions of the park, and provides easy access to its attractions. The park's two visitor centers are located at the north and south entrances. The major portion of the land north of the Interstate has been set aside as a wilderness area. A smaller wilderness area encompasses Puerco Ridge in the park's extreme southeastern corner.

Origins of the Petrified Logs

About 200 million years ago, tall conifers grew on the edge of a floodplain. The most common tree was a relative of the Norfolk Island pine, now classified as *Araucarioxylon arizonicum*. This tree grew to 100 feet (30 m) in height. As the trees were killed by old age, disease, or fire, they fell over in the primeval forests and were carried away by rivers to be deposited onto the floodplain. The fallen trees came to rest on mud and on sandbars and were later covered by further depositions of sediment. Eventually, the trees were buried by these sediments, which were later compressed into shale and sandstone. Water carried silica molecules from volcanic ash (created by earlier volcanic activity) into the wood, and they crystallized to form quartz. Over time, all traces of the wood disappeared, but the rock that was left behind formed a perfect cast, even reproducing details such as growth rings and knots. Although they mirror the trees they replaced, these solid stone replicas weigh six times more than a hefty hardwood.

About 70 million years ago, the land rose in a great upheaval that produced the Rocky Mountains. The Colorado Plateau was uplifted by at least 1 mile (1.6 km), which set in motion the forces of erosion. Over time, removal of sedimentary rocks gradually exposed the ancient trees. On Blue Mesa, neatly cut petrified

Above, right: Over millions of years, silica dissolved in water replaced the original wood of the trees and duplicated their cell structure to the finest detail.

Location: Northeastern Arizona, near the town of Holbrook.

Climate: Annual precipitation can be as low as 9 inches (225 mm) and falls mainly during summer in the form of thunderstorms that occur on an average of 35 days. In summer, an average high of 90°F (32°C) can be expected, but low levels of humidity reduce the discomfort index. Light snow may fall in winter in higher elevations, and the average low in January ranges from 12° to 24°F (–11° to –4°C).

When to go: The park is open throughout the year. Winter is often mild, and snow does not pose a major hazard to travelers.

Access: Interstate 40 passes through the park, and Exit 311 provides access to the park's only road, which joins U.S. Highway 180 southeast of Holbrook.

Facilities: Painted Desert Visitor Center is located just north of Interstate 40 on the 28-mile (45-km) road that winds through the park. A number of interpretive trails and two picnic areas are along the road. The Rainbow Forest Museum is situated near the southern entrance. Painted Desert has a restaurant and service station; Rainbow Forest has a snack bar.

Outstanding features: The park contains the world's largest collection of petrified wood, the remains of forests of the conifer *Araucarioxylon arizonicum*, a wilderness of desert badlands, and the remains of two ancient Native American settlements.

Visitor activities: Scenic drives, hiking, short walks to petrified logs, overnight backpacking, horseback riding, and bird-watching.

Right: The ruins of the twelfth-century Agate House, beside the fossilized remains of trees that grew on a fertile plain millions of years ago, provide evidence of dramatic changes in the earth's climate.

logs have tumbled down an eroded canyon, while other logs lie on the crest. It is a strange scene, reminiscent of a logging camp. Yet the trees that produced this timber became extinct many millions of years ago.

Pueblos and Petrified Forests

From Interstate 40, the park road passes the Painted Desert Visitor Center and nine view sites in the Painted Desert before it crosses over the highway and heads south. The first point of interest along this 28-mile (45-km) road is Puerco Pueblo, a fifteenth-century pueblo that was once home to about 70 people. At Blue Mesa, a 1-mile (1.6-km) trail allows visitors to explore the eroded landscape. The road passes Agate Bridge and Jasper Forest, and there is a short trail at Crystal Forest. After another 5 miles (8 km), a turnoff leads to Long Logs where a short trail explores the largest concentration of petrified wood. From this point, a 0.5-mile (1-km) trail heads south to Agate House, an eight-room pueblo built from petrified wood. Returning to the main road, the Rainbow Forest Museum houses dioramas depicting primeval scenes and skeletons of dinosaurs found in the park. Behind the museum, the short Giant Logs Trail passes Old Faithful, a fossil log with a diameter of 10 feet (3 m).

Right: The Paiute Native Americans believed that the colossal logs, scattered across the sunburned desert, were the arrow shafts of their thunder god, Shinauv.

Left: Erosion of the surrounding sedimentary rocks has exposed the remains of the pine forest that grew on the once fertile plain.

Below: The petrified remains of the tree *Araucarioxylon arizonicum*, a relative of the Norfolk Island pine, seem out of place in the hot, dry desert of eastern Arizona.

SAGUARO NATIONAL PARK

Where strong high pressure systems are produced when warm air from the equator descends in subtropical latitudes (particularly on the western edges of the continents), some of the driest places on earth can be found. The Sonoran Desert encircles the Gulf of California and extends over 120,000 square miles (310,000 sq km) of California, Arizona, and Mexico. This is the hottest region in America. Summer temperatures can soar to 115°F (46°C). Annual rainfall can be as low as 2 inches (50 mm), yet this arid desert is home to 300 types of cacti including the saguaro (*Carnegiea gigantea*). It also supports more than 2,500 species of plants, the richest variety found in any desert in the world.

In 1933, land containing an impressive grove of the saguaro cactus was set aside as a national monument in the Santa Catalina Mountains east of Tucson. A further 34 square miles (88 sq km) was added to the west of the city in 1961. In 1994, the two units, covering 142 square miles (368 sq km) and separated by the city of Tucson, were redesignated a national park. The western section covers the low desert situated below 3,000 feet (900 m), while three-quarters of the park falls within the higher desert of the eastern section. Adjoining Coronado National Forest, in the east the cooler mountain slopes rise to 8,666 feet (2,640 m) and the vegetation changes from saguaro stands to forests of ponderosa pine and oak.

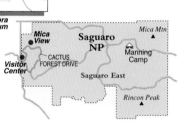

Towering Saguaro

The saguaro is the largest cactus found in North America, providing shelter and food for a wide variety of animals ranging from lizards and snakes to birds. Costa's and the black-chinned hummingbird feed on its white flowers, and the Gila woodpecker, gilded flicker, and elf owl nest in cavities in the cactus. The burrowing owl shares the burrows of desert animals and lives in colonies below the cacti. The Gila monster, one of only two poisonous lizards in the world, seeks refuge in rocky crannies nearby.

The saguaro cactus can reach an impressive height of 50 feet (15 m) and weighs up to 10 tons, of which 90 percent consists of water. A tall saguaro may be as old as 150 years. Growth in this harsh environment occurs very slowly. When rain falls in the desert, it is often in the form of an intense thunderstorm that soon rushes off the barren mountain slopes. In order to trap all available moisture, the saguaro has an extensive root network and is able to store sufficient water within its stem to last for a year. After rain has fallen, the cactus rapidly fills with water and increases its girth. It blooms at night, and each white flower, rich in nectar, survives for about 24 hours. Saguaros

Above, right: Burrowing owls hunt both day and night for the insects, rodents, and reptiles on which they prey.

Opposite: The 2,500 species of plants occurring in the Sonoran Desert include cacti species such as *(clockwise from bottom right)* organ pipes cactus, the gigantic saguaro, prickly pear, fishhook cactus, and beavertail cactus.

Location: Southern Arizona, adjoining the city of Tucson.

Climate: There are two rainy seasons a year (July–September and January–March). Between the rainy seasons, several months may pass without a drop of rain. In summer, temperatures can rise to 115°F (46°C) in the lower-lying Saguaro West, but evenings are cool and the peaks of the Rincon Mountains in Saguaro East are cooler.

When to go: Winter and spring are best.

Access: Interstate 10 passes through the city of Tucson. Exit 279 provides a direct access to the eastern section of the park along Old Spanish Trail; the western section can be reached on Gates Pass Road at Exit 257.

Facilities: Red Hills Visitor Center in Saguaro West is located near the well-known Arizona–Senora Desert Museum. In this section of the park are five picnic areas and three interpretive trails. Saguaro East Visitor Center is situated on Old Spanish Trail Road. Two picnic areas are along the Cactus Forest Drive and the Desert Ecology Trail. A network of 128 miles (205 km) of hiking trails explores the mountain wilderness that is inaccessible to vehicles.

Outstanding features: This park protects groves of the largest cactus found in North America, the saguaro, which grows to a height of 50 feet (15 m) and weighs as much as 10 tons. The eastern section preserves forests of oak and fir and part of the Rincon Mountains.

Visitor activities: Scenic drives, hiking, short walks, overnight backpacking, cycling, horseback riding, and bird-watching.

produce seeds only when they are 40 years old. In the inhospitable desert, only one seed in 12 million reaches adulthood. Each cactus plant can produce as many as 40 million seeds in its lifetime.

Cactus Viewing

The access road to the west unit passes through the Tucson Mountain County Park. Just before the national park entrance, the 12-acre (5-ha) Arizona–Sonora Desert Museum is known throughout the world for its naturalistic animal enclosures—this zoological park exhibits only species native to the southwestern United States. The west unit's Red Hills Visitor Center provides a panoramic view of the surrounding desert and offers a short trail exploring a cactus garden. From the center, a 9-mile (14-km) loop road passes Signal Hill Picnic Area, where Hohokam Native American petroglyphs can be seen on the rocks. Several hiking trails crisscross the terrain east of the loop road.

In the larger eastern unit, Cactus Forest Drive, near the visitor center, is a circular 8-mile (13-km) route that passes through a mature saguaro cactus grove and includes stops at Mica View Picnic Area and a short interpretive trail. The remainder of the eastern unit is a wilderness area that is accessible only to hikers or to visitors on horseback. A network of trails leads hikers through several vegetation zones and ascends Mica Mountain—8,666 feet (2,641 m)—and the 8,482-foot (2,585-m) Rincon Peak.

Above: Although the teddy-bear cholla *(foreground)* is covered in sharp spines, cactus wrens nest in the branches to protect their chicks.

Right: Saguaro cacti dotted around the Sonoran Desert are evocative of the American West, their distinctive silhouette having been featured in many Western movies.

CARLSBAD CAVERNS NATIONAL PARK

Deep in the Guadalupe Mountains, subterranean passages and enormous underground caverns decorated in dazzling stalactites, stalagmites, and helictites are among the delights of this national park. The origins of the limestone from which the caverns in the park are formed can be traced back to a horseshoe-shaped reef of some 400 miles (650 km) in length that was deposited in a shallow ancient sea about 250 million years ago. Over time, the reef was built up as lime precipitated from seawater or was deposited by lime-secreting algae and other marine organisms. Eventually, the ocean retreated, and the reef was covered by sediments. About 10 million years ago, uplift produced the Guadalupe Mountains and exposed part of the reef to erosion. As rainwater seeped through the ground, it dissolved certain elements and became slightly acidic. This water percolated through the overlying rocks and gradually ate out caverns in the limestone reef. The beautiful stalactite and stalagmite formations in the Carlsbad caves were created about 500,000 years ago by limestone dissolved in water.

In 1923, a national monument was proclaimed to protect Carlsbad and another 75 caves located nearby. The monument was redesignated as a national park, covering 73 square miles (188 sq km), in 1930 and declared a World Heritage Site in 1995. Guadalupe Mountains National Park, in Texas, is located 4 miles (7 km) to the southwest; the two parks are separated by the Lincoln National Forest. Carlsbad is quite isolated and is situated in the southeastern corner of New Mexico near the city of the same name.

Cave Tours

Over 30 miles (50 km) of passages have been surveyed in Carlsbad. At Lechuguilla Cave in the wilderness area, a total of 85 miles (140 km) of passages have been discovered, but this cave will not be developed for general public access.

There are two self-guided tours of the Carlsbad caverns; cave temperature averages 55°F (13°C) throughout the year. The Blue Tour enters the cave at the natural entrance and zigzags down a winding path into Bat Cave. The trail then continues to descend for 550 feet (170 m) into the heart of the cave. The Red Tour explores the caverns from the elevator, rest area, and lunchroom located 755 feet (230 m) below the surface. This one-hour tour passes many famous features in the Big Room including the Rock of Ages, Giant Dome, and Bottomless Pit (which is actually 138 feet, or 42 m, deep). The Big Room, the second largest cavern ever discovered anywhere in the world, is 1,800 feet (550 m) long and 1,100 feet (335 m) across at its widest point.

On the Green Tour, rangers guide visitors on a 90-minute walk into four chambers, including King's Palace and Queen's Chamber. The tour descends to the deepest part of the cave open to the public.

Above, right: During summer, Mexican free-tailed bats roost in Bat Cave and exit the cave at sunset in search of insect prey. This mass exodus, estimated at 5,000 bats per minute, is one of the park's major attractions.

Location: Southeastern New Mexico, near the city of Carlsbad.

Climate: Summers are warm, and the average high in July is 92°F (33°C). Rain falls mainly in the form of thunderstorms in summer, which occur on an average of 30 days. Winters are mild and daytime temperatures in January average 60°F (15°C), with an overnight low of 24°F (−4°C).

When to go: The park is open throughout the year and the temperature in the caves remains constant at 55°F (13°C). The bats are active from spring to autumn and migrate to Mexico for the winter.

Access: When approaching from the north or south, take U.S. Highway 285 to Carlsbad, then head southwest on U.S. Highway 62/180 to El Paso, Texas. This road passes the main entrance to the park near White's City.

Facilities: The visitor center at the cave entrance, 7 miles (11 km) from White's City, has a restaurant and picnic area. An elevator descends to a lunchroom in the cave 755 feet (232 m) below the surface. A picnic area is also located along Walnut Canyon Desert Drive. The remainder of the park is a wilderness area that can be explored only on 50 miles (80 km) of hiking trails.

Outstanding features: The park protects an extensive limestone cave system that shelters a large population of Mexican free-tailed bats as well as a portion of the surrounding Chihuahuan Desert.

Visitor activities: Scenic drives, cave tours, bat viewing at dusk, hiking, short walks, overnight backpacking, cycling, and bird-watching.

Right: The delicate Temple of the Sun can be visited on the self-guided Red Tour.

Opposite, top: The Big Room covers 14 acres (56,000 sq m) and is the largest cavern open to the public.

Opposite, center: Immense caverns were exposed when groundwater dissolved the same limestone reef that formed the nearby Guadalupe Mountains.

Opposite, bottom: Hiking trails explore the surrounding Chihuahuan Desert.

Other Activities

A booklet available at the visitor center describes the circular, 9-mile (15-km) Walnut Canyon Desert Drive that winds through the desert mountains near the visitor center. This one-way gravel road can be traveled in an ordinary car but is not suitable for trailers and mobile homes. The Desert Nature Trail, to the right of the natural cave entrance, is a fascinating walk that illustrates traditional Native American uses of the desert plants. There are three picnic areas in the park and over 50 miles (80 km) of backcountry trails.

From the amphitheater at the natural entrance, a multitude of Mexican free-tailed bats can be seen leaving the cave each evening from April to October. In 1903, the exodus of the bats alerted an entrepreneur to the nitrate-rich bat guano that was a guaranteed supply of fertilizer. Over the next 20 years, thousands of tons of guano were removed from the cave. An estimated nine million bats lived in the cave. However, their population has declined over the years to less than one million, possibly due to the widespread use of insecticides. During the day, bats sleep in Bat Cave, 200 feet (60 m) below the ground surface, and at night they leave the cave at a rate of 5,000 per minute in search of their insect prey.

Ranger-led tours of Slaughter Canyon Cave allow visitors to see the 89-foot-high (27-m) Monarch, one of the tallest columns in the world. This two-hour tour allows visitors to discover a part of the cave that is free of paved paths, lighting, or any convenience, with flashlights providing the only source of light.

THE PACIFIC COAST

This is the most diverse natural region in America and contains a wide range of habitats that include the driest deserts in the country, jagged snow-crowned peaks, and forests of oak and fir. The Sierra Nevada, running the length of California's eastern boundary, support ever-changing bands of forest with increasing altitude, among them relic groves of giant sequoia, the largest living thing on earth. In the north, moisture-laden winds from the Pacific Ocean sustain luxuriant forests of cedar, hemlock, and fir. The world's tallest trees, the redwood, grow along a coastline of sheltered coves. Here, too, the many snow-capped volcanic peaks of the Cascades Range protrude above the surrounding forests.

In the nineteenth century, settlers were drawn to this region by the allure of gold and fertile land. Nowadays, mild weather and a vibrant economy still attract settlers from other parts of the country. This region supports 15 percent of the total American population on 8.6 percent of the land. California alone is home to one in eight Americans. However, despite population pressures, the state has the second largest area of proclaimed wilderness of any state—21,808 square miles (56,264 sq km) in total, a figure surpassed only by Alaska. A continuous band of forest reserves runs the entire length of the Sierra Nevada. Even Los Angeles is hemmed to the north by forest reserves. California has eight national parks—including Death Valley National Park, the largest in the lower 48 states—and an estimated 5,000 mountain lions still inhabit its rugged realms. In the northern states of Oregon and Washington, designated wilderness covers 7,200 square miles (18,600 sq km) of land, and road construction and logging will soon be outlawed in many areas.

The Pacific Ocean teems with life. Nutrient-rich currents cultivate kelp forests that sustain an abundance of fish, crabs, lobsters, seabirds, and seals. Gray and humpback whales migrate along the coast to the Arctic. An expanding population of the once critically endangered sea otter is at home in the surf near Monterey. To safeguard the ocean's bounty, five large marine reserves have been established, while three national parks help protect natural habitats and marine life along one of America's most beautiful coastlines.

Left: Olympic Coast National Marine Sanctuary protects the bountiful resources of the Pacific Ocean and adjoins the coastline of Olympic National Park.

NORTH CASCADES NATIONAL PARK

Situated in the center of one of the least developed regions of the 48 states is the Cascade Range, a chain of snow-capped volcanic mountains that form a jagged spine running through Washington and Oregon. In 1968, a national park was established at the northern edge of the range in Washington, one of three parks that border Canada. The park owes its existence to the commitment and determination of Senator Henry Jackson and protects some of the most spectacular mountain scenery in the country. To many it is known as the American Alps. Rugged peaks and raw teeth of black rock tower to heights of over 9,200 feet (2,800 m), while deep snowfields and 318 known glaciers cling to sheer crags. With a raw wilderness of extreme weather conditions and subzero temperatures, much of the park is accessible only to experienced mountaineers.

The Cascade Range is renowned for its countless waterfalls. Spring melts produce copious runoff that tumbles down steep cliffs in glistening curtains. Along Highway 20, the only road route through the northern Cascade Mountains, miniature falls plunge down steep banks lining the road.

The ruggedness of the Cascade Range discouraged development in the past. Setting aside 93 percent of the park as a wilderness area was therefore possible. In addition, five wilderness areas were established on national forest lands surrounding the park, two of which are the largest in Washington State, and together they quadruple the size of the protected area.

North Cascades is divided into two sections by the narrow Ross Lake National Recreation Area, which surrounds three dams built along the Skagit River before the park was established. Adjoining the South Unit at its southernmost point is the scenic Lake Chelan National Recreation Area. It encompasses the largest lake in Washington, Lake Chelan, a glacial lake 1,528 feet (466 m) deep.

Cedars, Hemlocks, and Firs

Moisture from the Pacific rises up the western slopes of the mountains and produces 110 inches (2,750 mm) of precipitation per year. However, on the eastern slopes, at Stehekin, precipitation decreases to just 34 inches (850 mm). On the mountains' lower western slopes, luxuriant forests of western hemlock (*Tsuga heterophylla*), red cedar (*Thuja plicata*) and Douglas fir (*Pseudotsuga menziesii*), occur. This forest's dense understory attracts many birds and mammals. With an increase in altitude, these tree species are replaced by the Pacific silver fir (*Abies amabilis*), mountain hemlock (*Tsuga mertensiana*), and subalpine fir (*Abies lasiocarpa*).

At higher altitudes, only alpine tundra can survive the extremes of temperature and the lack of available

Above, right: The lynx lives in the colder regions of North Cascades National Park, ranging widely in the mountains.
Opposite: In spring, the mountain slopes are transformed by thousands of silvery cascades.

Location: Northern Washington. Darrington is the nearest small town, and Burlington and Mount Vernon are large towns on the interstate to the west.

Climate: In July, the average high temperature ranges from 64° to 72°F (18° to 22°C) and the high peaks are covered in permanent snowfields.

When to go: Best visited from April to September.

Access: From Interstate 5, take Exit 230 and head east on Highway 20. Heavy snow closes this road east of the park from mid-November to April.

Facilities: North Cascades Visitor Center is located near the village of Newhalem. There are two campgrounds on the banks of the Skagit River and facilities for launching boats. Several interpretive trails are accessible along Highway 20. Diablo Lake has a campground, picnic area, and boat-launching facilities. Ross Lake Resort accommodates visitors in floating units during summer. A campground is at the top end of the lake on the Canadian border. In the South Unit are seven campgrounds and five picnic areas reached by shuttle bus from Stehekin in the adjacent Lake Chelan National Recreation Area.

Outstanding features: An untamed wilderness of jagged mountains, permanent snowfields, over 300 glaciers, alpine meadows, and forests of red cedar, western hemlock, and Douglas fir.

Visitor activities: Scenic drives, hiking, short walks to historic buildings, overnight backpacking, mountain climbing, cycling, horseback riding, boat tours, river rafting, kayaking, fishing, wildlife viewing, and birdwatching. Cross-country skiing and snowshoeing are winter activities.

Above: Although flowering from May to August, the mountain phlox grows on rocky slopes and alpine meadows.

Above, right: Abundant rainfall on the Cascades' western slopes encourages the growth of red cedar forests.

Below: The mountain goat's thick coat and excellent camouflage enable it to survive on snow-clad mountains.

water. Alpine plants grow close to the ground to avoid cold winds. During the brief summer, many produce colorful flowers to attract pollinators such as flies and spiders, as bees are absent at high altitudes.

Wildlife in the Cascades

North Cascades is a remote park and sustains a wide variety of wildlife, including many species that are rare in other national parks. Common mammals include black bear, black-tailed deer (subspecies of mule deer), red fox, lynx, porcupine, Townsend's chipmunk, and Douglas squirrel. At extremes of altitude, wildlife is restricted to pika, hoary marmot, grey-crowned rosy finch, and birds of prey. Although the mountains are blanketed in snow during winter, hundreds of bald eagles concentrate on the Skagit River along the western border of the park to feed on spawning kokanee and chinook salmon.

The mountain goat, mountain lion, grizzly bear, and gray wolf are some of the park's more unusual mammals. The mountain goat, with its square hooves and dense coat of white hair, is superbly adapted to the sheer mountain slopes and cold conditions and is well camouflaged against predators. Mountain lions, although they are not often seen, are at home in the park's rugged terrain, preying mainly on deer and smaller mammals. Grizzly bears are occasionally sighted, although they prefer the drier environment of the Pasayten Wilderness located east of the park. Both black and

grizzly bears feed on salmon during the annual spawn. After a long absence, gray wolves have returned to the park from Canada, and their calls can sometimes be heard at night.

Ross Lake and Lake Chelan

Highway 20 closely follows the Skagit River through Ross Lake National Recreation Area. There are no roads in the North Unit and only one gravel road in the South Unit. Few hiking trails ascend the mountain's icy peaks. From the town of Concrete, the road follows the Skagit River into the mountains. Near the village of Newhalem are two campgrounds on the banks of the river. Cherry trees line the streets of the village; in spring their blossoms add bright splashes of color to the valley. From Newhalem, the road follows the shoreline of Gorge and Diablo Lakes and offers splendid views of the surrounding mountains. Parking areas are along the road and trailheads for some of the 386 miles (618 km) of trails that cross the forested valleys. Accommodations are available at Ross Lake, which is the largest of the three reservoirs, and boating and trout fishing are permitted. However, fishing for salmon is not allowed in the park.

Left: Picturesque Diablo Lake is surrounded by snow-crowned summits that rise to over 8,100 feet (2,500 m).

Below, left: Cherry trees line the streets of the village of Newhalem in North Cascades.

Below: Snow dominates the landscape near the tree line on the high Cascade Mountains.

From Highway 20, a rough gravel road leads to Johannesburg Mountain in the South Unit. At the end of the road, a hiking trail climbs Cascade Pass and leads to Cottonwood Campground where a Park Service bus completes the 23-mile (37-km) journey back to Stehekin on the isolated northern shore of Lake Chelan, passing nine other campgrounds along the route. The only other way to get to Stehekin is by boat, and the 50-mile (80-km) journey across the lake takes four hours. Information on backcountry hiking can be obtained from the Golden West Visitor Center, and North Cascades Lodge is a well-known meeting place. Fishing, hiking, boating, and cycling are popular pastimes. Visitors can also visit many of Stehekin's historic buildings.

OLYMPIC NATIONAL PARK

The sixth largest national park in the lower 48 states, Olympic preserves high mountains, glaciers, moss-festooned rain forests, dozens of streams and rivers, and a scenic coastline renowned for its isolated beaches and hidden coves. The major portion of the park consists of the forested slopes surrounding 7,965-foot-high (2,428-m) Mount Olympus, and eight glaciers cling to rugged valleys at the mountain's summit. The summit is the focal point of the park. It receives 200 inches (5,000 mm) of precipitation per year, mostly in the form of snow. On the lower sea-facing slopes, moisture-laden winds from the Pacific sustain a temperate rain forest where towering specimens of western hemlock, Sitka spruce (*Picea sitchensis*), and bigleaf maple (*Acer macrophylum*) are draped in a hairy coat of moss, lichen, and ferns.

Covering 1,440 square miles (3,717 sq km) of mountain and unspoiled coastline, Olympic was proclaimed a national park in 1938 and declared a World Heritage Site in 1981. Of the park's surface area, 96 percent is designated wilderness, and five small wilderness areas extend protection to national forests along the east and south boundaries. A separate narrow strip of land protects 62 miles (100 km) of the coastline from Kalaloch northward almost to the tip of the peninsula. The Olympic Coast National Marine Sanctuary extends 30 to 45 miles (48 to 72 km) out to sea from Pacific Beach, south of the park, to Cape Flattery on the northwestern tip of the Olympic Peninsula.

Highway 101 circles the park, briefly passing through the northwestern corner and the southern section of the coastal strip. Nine side roads deviate from Highway 101, ending at campgrounds tucked into the mountain's lower valleys. However, apart from these minor tracks, the only way to explore the mountain's higher slopes is along the hiking trails that continue from the roads.

Rain Forest and Endemic Fauna

During the Ice Age the peninsula was isolated from the mainland, and 16 species of plants and animals, such as the pocket gopher, marmot, and a species of minnow, occur only on Mount Olympus. There are four types of forest in the park, of which the temperate rain forest is the most interesting. Large quantities of rain fall onto the mountain's western slopes. On average, total precipitation varies from 140 to 167 inches (3,500 to 4,175 mm) at the base of the mountain. An abundance of moisture and moderate temperatures give rise to a temperate rain forest. The dominant trees in this dense forest are Sitka spruce and western hemlock. Other species present include Douglas fir, black cottonwood

Above, right: Flying squirrels are strictly nocturnal and rely on skin flaps to glide between trees in the forest.
Opposite: Club moss adorns bigleaf maples in the Hoh Rain Forest on the wet western slopes of Mount Olympus.

Location: Northwestern Washington, near Port Angeles.

Climate: Heavy rains sustain the lush rain forests on the mountain's western slopes and the snowfields on its summit. At lower altitude, in July, the average high is 76°F (19°C), while in January the average low is 28°F (−2°C).

When to go: Throughout the year. July to September are the driest months.

Access: U.S. Highway 101 encircles the park. From Interstate 5, take Exit 108 at Olympia to connect to this highway, or take Highway 16 north from Tacoma.

Facilities: There are several visitor centers in the park as well as two information stations and another in the town of Forks. Three lodges adjoin Lake Crescent. A hot springs resort is in the Sol Duc Valley. Apart from the lodges, there are no restaurants in the park. There is another lodge and service station at Kalaloch Rocks and a nearby campground. The two campgrounds in the northern coastal section of the park have boat-launching facilities, and there are 12 campgrounds on the lower slopes of the mountain. Interpretive trails and picnic areas are located at most of the roads that provide access to the mountain.

Outstanding features: Ice-capped mountains, glaciers, waterfalls, three large lakes, impenetrable rain forests, and one of the most beautiful coastlines in the United States.

Visitor activities: Scenic drives, hiking, beach walks, walks to waterfalls, overnight backpacking, mountain climbing, cycling, boating, river rafting, kayaking, windsurfing, swimming, fishing, horseback riding, wildlife viewing, and bird-watching. Cross-country skiing and snowshoeing are winter activities.

(*Populus trichocarpa*), and several trees restricted to the Pacific Coast, such as western red cedar, bigleaf maple, and vine maple (*Acer circinatum*).

Although they are difficult to detect in the dense foliage, the forest is home to many mammals, including black-tailed deer, raccoon, Douglas squirrel, northern flying squirrel, snowshoe hare, and mountain beaver. An estimated 5,000 Roosevelt elk, the largest population in America, inhabit the forest. At high altitudes above the tree line, the hardy mountain goat commonly occurs. These animals were introduced in the 1920s from Alaska and successfully increased to the point where surplus animals now need to be regularly removed. Because the park contains a variety of suitable habitats, it is being evaluated under the Wolf Recovery Program as a possible home for the gray wolf.

Below: The park incorporates a beautiful coastline with countless sea stacks and undeveloped beaches.

Visiting Olympic

Heading northwest from Seattle through Tacoma and Bremerton, Highway 101 leads to the Olympic National Park Visitor Center, located in the seaside town of Port Angeles on the Strait of Juan De Fuca. A 18-mile (29-km) side road climbs from the town up Klahhane Ridge to a picnic area on Hurricane Ridge. At an altitude of 5,500 feet (1,670 m), strong winds often blow across the ridge. Refreshments can be obtained at the Hurricane Ridge Visitor Center. A network of hiking trails explores the valleys on the eastern side of the mountain. An 8-mile (11-km) trail winds down the valley below to Lake Mills, and a 44-mile (71-km) trail follows a broad curve up the Elwha and North Fork Quinault Valleys to the North Fork Campground near the park's southern boundary.

West of Port Angeles, another side road leads to Lake Mills and the Altaire Campground. Boating and fishing are permitted, and no fishing license is required. After another 9 miles (14 km), Highway 101 enters the park and closely follows the southern shore of Lake Crescent. This is the second largest lake in the park. Lodges, restaurants, picnic areas, and boat-launching sites are situated along its wooded shoreline. To the north and south, high hills enclose this picturesque lake. Just beyond the lake, a side road leads to the Eagle

Campground and Sol Duc Hot Springs Resort where accommodations are available. A short walk leads to the Sol Duc Falls where, flanked by towering trees and with its banks draped in dense vegetation, the Sol Duc River plunges through a narrow gap and down one of the most beautiful waterfalls in the country.

After traveling 43 miles (69 km) farther through national forest and timber plantations, a side road leads for 19 miles (30 km) to the Hoh Rain Forest Visitor Center. Short trails explore the luxuriant forest where enormous red cedar, western hemlock, Sitka spruce, and bigleaf maple trees grow. From the end of the road, the impressive Blue Glacier on the north slope of Mount Olympus can be reached after a hike of 17 miles (27 km) up the Hoh River Valley.

When returning to Highway 101, the road bends toward the ocean and closely follows the coastline from Ruby Beach to the southern boundary at South Beach. Six streams flow through dense forests to meet the ocean, and the beaches are piled with pebbles and driftwood. At Ruby Beach, several prominent sea stacks provide a home for roosting birds. These sea stacks once formed part of the mainland, but erosion has resulted in the prominent rocky isles found today.

Near Beach 6, a turnoff leads to an enormous cedar tree. There is a campground, lodge, and information station at Kalaloch Rocks, and the wide sandy beach is ideal for walks. Highway 101 then turns inland again, and a side gravel road follows the Queets River and ends at a campground. From the road, a short trail leads to the park's largest specimen of Douglas fir.

Opposite, right: A dense carpet of ferns and vine maple is sustained by moisture-laden winds from the Pacific Ocean.

Top: The Sol Duc River arises on the northern slopes of Mount Olympus and flows past the Sol Duc Hot Springs Resort in its upper valleys.

Left: Pebbles and driftwood on Ruby Beach.

Left: Glacial action formed freshwater Lake Crescent on the park's northern boundary. A range of hills separates the lake from the ocean 4 miles (7 km) to the north.

MOUNT RAINIER NATIONAL PARK

Mount Rainier is the highest and most prominent volcanic peak in the Cascade Range, and at 14,410 feet (4,392 m) it is also the highest peak in Washington State. The national park was established in 1899 to protect Mount Rainier, its 25 glaciers and glacial features, and the surrounding slopes, which give rise to over 20 rivers, and is therefore one of America's oldest parks.

Although the park is situated just 40 miles (65 km) from Seattle, the city's close proximity does not detract from its appeal. Mount Rainier is the centerpiece of the 368-square-mile (949-sq-km) park, and its snow-crowned summit dominates the landscape. The mountain's slopes rise steeply to the summit, increasing 12,500 feet (3,800 m) in elevation over 12 miles (19 km), and producing significant changes in vegetation. Dense forests of red cedar, hemlock, and Douglas fir clothe the lower slopes and black bear, elk, and black-tailed deer feed on the undergrowth. With increasing altitude, forests are replaced by grassy meadows and snow-covered ridges. In hidden valleys, hundreds of streams of pure, frigid water, fed by melting snow, rush over beds of polished volcanic rock.

National forests act as a buffer against development around the park. Three small wilderness areas have been designated on forest lands surrounding the park. Much of the eastern boundary adjoins the large William O. Douglas Wilderness.

Paradise and Longmire

The mountain traps moisture-laden winds from the Pacific Ocean, and snowstorms are a frequent occurrence on the higher slopes. At Paradise on the southern slope, annual precipitation totals an incredible 126 inches (3,150 mm), making many of the park's roads accessible only between June and October. Of the five entrances to the park, only the 18-mile (29-km) stretch from the Nisqually Entrance to Paradise Inn, the 2-mile (3-km) road from the southern boundary to Ohanapecosh, and a gravel road in the northwest corner remain open during winter.

After passing through forest for 7 miles (11 km), the road reaches Longmire, where a mineral spring resort was established in 1883. The park's headquarters were originally located here in 1899; the building now houses a museum. The cozy 25-room National Park Inn here is open throughout the year. From Longmire, the road climbs steeply through many sharp bends and gains 2,700 feet (820 m) in altitude over 11 miles (19 km) before reaching the settlement of Paradise. This area is

Above, right: Black-tailed deer, a subspecies of mule deer, occur only in the forests of the Pacific Northwest.

Opposite: In spring, the pure waters of the Ohanapecosh River surge over boulders still capped in snow.

Location: Central Washington, southeast of the city of Tacoma.

Climate: The mountain slopes receive heavy snows in winter. Altitude reduces temperatures in summer, and an average high of about 70°F (21°C) can be expected.

When to go: Throughout the year, but the majority of roads are open only in summer.

Access: When approaching from the south on Interstate 5, take Exit 68 and head east on U.S. Highway 12. At the junction in Morton, Highways 7 and 706 head north to the Nisqually Entrance, and U.S. Highway 12 continues east to the Stevens Canyon Entrance, which is open only from June to October. From Seattle, head south on Interstate 5 and take Highway 7 in Tacoma to the Nisqually Entrance.

Facilities: The Henry M. Jackson Memorial Visitor Center at Paradise is open on weekends year-round and daily from May to mid-October. Longmire Wilderness Information and both Sunrise and Ohanapecosh Visitor Centers are open from May or June until late September, depending on weather conditions. Two lodges on the southern slopes of the mountain can be accessed from the Nisqually Entrance. Paradise Inn is open only from May to October. Six campgrounds are located on the mountain's north and south slopes, and there are ten picnic areas and a number of interpretive trails. Gasoline is not available in the park.

Outstanding features: A massive ice-capped volcano surrounded by glaciers and snowfields.

Visitor activities: Scenic drives, hiking, short walks, overnight backpacking, mountain climbing, cycling, fishing, horseback riding, wildlife viewing, and bird-watching. Cross-country skiing and snowshoeing are popular winter activities.

Map labels

N

Ipsut Creek

Mount Rainier NP

Olympia

Mowich Lake

Sunrise Visitor Center

White River

WONDERLAND TRAIL

Mount Rainier

Columbia Crest
14,410 ft
(4,392 m)

WONDERLAND TRAIL

Henry M. Jackson Memorial Visitor Center

Paradise

Cougar Rock

Nisqually Entrance

Longmire Museum

Stevens Canyon Entrance

Ohanapecosh Visitor Center

Sunshine Point

William O. Douglas Wilderness

renowned for its splendid views of the mountain and summer displays of wildflowers. The Henry M. Jackson Memorial Visitor Center is open throughout the year, but the historic Paradise Inn is open only in summer. Many short hiking trails explore the mountain slope above Paradise. The 93-mile (149-km) Wonderland Trail, which circles the entire mountain, passes just south of the road. Paradise is also the starting point for those wishing to scale the peak of Mount Rainier, although this is recommended only for experienced climbers. A local operator provides three-day courses, including a supervised climb, for the less experienced. Cross-country skiing and snowshoeing are popular winter activities.

Ohanapecosh River

When approaching on Highway 12 from the south, Cayuse Pass, on Highway 410 that heads north to Seattle, is open only from May to November. However, even when the road is closed, the Ohanapecosh River, with its surrounding old-growth forests of red cedar, western hemlock, and Douglas fir, is well worth the journey. Icy waters tumble over cascades, and many tributaries rush through dense forests to join the river. Hiking trails are along both banks of the river. The largest of eight campgrounds in the park is located near the entrance. The campsite and adjacent Ohanapecosh Visitor Center are open during summer. The nearby Grove of the Patriarchs Trail is a short walk that explores an island of towering ancient trees, formed where the river divides into two channels.

Opposite: The year-round ice-crowned summit of Mount Rainier overshadows Mineral Lake.

Below: Old-growth forests of cedar, hemlock, and fir on the mountain's southern slopes.

CRATER LAKE NATIONAL PARK

About 500,000 years ago, Mount Mazama was an impressive volcano rising to a height of 12,000 feet (3,660 m). Then, 7,700 years ago, an eruption occurred that was 42 times more powerful than that which occurred in 1980 on Mount St. Helens in Washington State. The top 4,000 feet (1,200 m) of the mountain were blown off. On the northern slopes, now included in the park, ash from this eruption was deposited to depths of 50 feet (15 m). Scientists have found ash from this eruption in eight states and as far north as Canada. The volcanic activity depleted the mountain's chambers of magma, and the core collapsed to form a caldera. The focal point of this national park is Crater Lake, which formed when snow and rainwater flooded the caldera.

The Klamath tribe probably witnessed these tumultuous events; pumice from Mount Mazama has been found elsewhere in Oregon, in caves used by Native Americans. Yet they offered no hint of the lake to white settlers, and many were forbidden by their spiritual leaders to visit it. Only in 1853 did gold prospectors stumble upon the lake. A decade after Yellowstone was established, William Steel began lobbying to have the crater declared a national park. Steel finally appealed to President Theodore Roosevelt. In 1902, a national park of 286 square miles (738 sq km) was proclaimed. The Steel Information Center, on the south rim of the crater, commemorates his 17-year campaign.

Crater Lake, covering 21 square miles (54 sq km), is the deepest lake in America and the seventh deepest in the world. Inflow of water to the lake is balanced by evaporation, and the annual variation in lake level is less than 3 feet (1 m). The crater rim rises high above its waters. In the northeastern corner, the water is 1,932 feet (589 m) deep, more than three times the depth of Lake Mead on the Colorado River. The lake's water appears a deep cobalt blue. The water is very pure and contains very few minerals. As sunlight penetrates the water, the water molecules absorb all the colors of the spectrum. Blue, with the shortest wavelength, is reflected back.

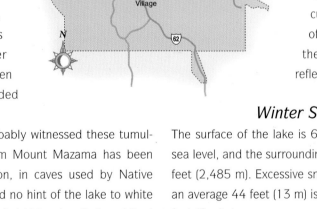

Winter Snowdrifts

The surface of the lake is 6,180 feet (1,880 m) above sea level, and the surrounding crater walls rise to 8,150 feet (2,485 m). Excessive snowfalls occur in winter, and an average 44 feet (13 m) is recorded. Snowdrifts of 20 feet (6 m) deep are common, and the four-story Crater

Above, right: The bobcat feeds mainly on hares and rodents but may catch animals as large as deer.

Opposite: Although deformed by wind and cold, a whitebark pine stands like a sentry above the cobalt blue lake.

Location: Southern Oregon. Medford is the closest large town.

Climate: In winter, this is one of the coldest places in Oregon and an average low of 6°F (−14°C) can be expected. Summers are short and in July, a high of 80°F (26°C) is average.

When to go: Summer is the best time of year.

Access: When approaching from the south on Interstate 5, take Highway 62 north from Medford to the west entrance to the park. If winter snows have not closed the north access road, take Exit 124 on the Interstate and head east on Highway 138.

Facilities: Rim Village Visitor Center is open daily June to September. A cafeteria is located nearby and Crater Lake Lodge, open from late May to mid-October, has a restaurant. Most facilities in Mazama Village, including a lodge, general store, service station, and campground, are open from early June to mid-October. A second campground, at Lost Creek, is open from mid-July to the end of September. Seven picnic areas are located on the Rim Drive, and three interpretive trails are between Rim Village and Mazama. The Steel Information Center, south of Rim Village, supplies hiking maps. The post office is open throughout the year.

Outstanding features: A cobalt blue lake, the deepest in America, floods the caldera formed by a volcanic eruption on Mount Mazama 7,700 years ago.

Visitor activities: Scenic drives, hiking, overnight backpacking, mountain climbing, cycling, horseback riding, wildlife viewing, and bird-watching. Cross-country skiing and snowshoeing are additional winter activities.

Lake Lodge is often half-buried by snow. However, despite the cold and the excessive snowfalls, the lake rarely freezes over. In summer, the water stores energy from the sun, maintaining a temperature of around 55˚F (13˚C). In winter, this stored energy is sufficient to prevent ice from covering the lake, an event last recorded in 1949, when temperatures reached an all-time low.

Forest Wildlife

Much of the park is clothed in a dense forest of western hemlock and Douglas fir. A forest of ponderosa pines can be seen in the south. At higher altitudes mountain hemlock, subalpine fir, and Shasta red fir (*Abies magnifica*) grow near the crater rim. On exposed slopes at the edge of the crater, the twisted trunks of whitebark pines are evidence of the harsh conditions.

Some of the birds often seen in the park's coniferous forests include Steller's jay, Clark's nutcracker, black-headed grosbeak, barred owl, blue grouse, western tanager, and mountain chickadee. The park also falls within the range of the rare northern spotted owl, and an estimated 4,000 pairs are restricted to the forests of the Northwest. Mammals include black bear, black-tailed deer, red fox, bobcat, Townsend's chipmunk, Douglas squirrel, northern flying squirrel, yellow-bellied marmot, and pika.

Visiting the Crater

During winter, only the southern and western access roads are open and the Rim Drive is closed to traffic. Both of the park's lodges are closed, and no fuel is sold during winter. The circular 33-mile (53-km) Rim Drive

Below: The caldera formed by a violent volcanic eruption is now flooded by the deepest lake in America, Crater Lake.

offers the best views of the crater and is usually accessible from June to October. Seven picnic areas are situated along the Rim Drive. From June to mid-September, guided boat trips depart from a landing on the northern shore, accessible only along Cleetwood Cove Trail. Wizard Island is a miniature volcano complete with a summit crater, rising 764 feet (234 m) above the water near the western shore of the lake. The 100-minute boat tours of the lake stop at Wizard Island, where a hiking trail from the shore climbs to the crest of the cone. Several species of fish were introduced to the lake toward the end of the ninteenth century, and rainbow trout and kokanee salmon are still present. The waters of the lake are so pure that seeing fish in the depths below is possible. Fishing is permitted, and no license is required.

The Pacific Crest National Scenic Trail runs down the middle of the park, following the western edge of the crater for 5 miles (8 km). Additional hiking trails are in the northwest and southern sections of the park, and several shorter trails climb significant peaks. Between Crater Lake Lodge and Mazama Village, which offers lodge and campground accommodations, are three short trails. The Castle Crest Wildflower Trail is a 0.5-mile (800-m) stroll through a forest of mountain hemlock and red fir that gives way to a meadow clothed in wildflowers during summer. Close to Mazama Village, the Godfrey Glen Trail passes the Duwee Falls and explores a forested canyon. Annie Creek Canyon Trail is a circular 2-mile (3-km) trail that follows a creek through the delightful canyon below Mazama Village Campground.

LASSEN VOLCANIC NATIONAL PARK

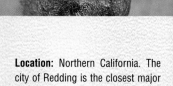

This park was established in 1916 and protects 165 square miles (427 sq km) of the mountains in northern California. Lassen Peak, a dormant volcano 10,457 feet (3,187 m) high, is the highest point in the park. The volcano has erupted several times over the past 300 years, but the most recent period of volcanic activity took place in 1921. A seven-year period of volcanic explosions began in May 1914. Over 150 eruptions occurred during that year, causing a large vent to appear in the mountain. Lava flowed down the slopes, melting snow and sending a flood of mud and boulders down the valleys. Then, on May 22, 1915, a massive eruption took place. It sent a mushroom cloud of smoke 7 miles (11 km) into the air. Three days later a superheated blast of steam and gas knocked over trees and left a 3-mile-long (5-km) corridor of devastation.

Lassen Peak is visible from 50 miles (80 km) away. During the gold rush of the mid-nineteenth century, wagon trains heading for Sacramento used the mountain as a landmark. Sections of the Nobles Emigrant Trail, which brought settlers to California from the East, can still be seen in the park. A 17-mile (27-km) section of the Pacific Crest National Scenic Trail, which follows national forests and mountains from the Canadian border to southern California, passes through the center of the park.

Natural Diversity

Lassen Peak lies in a transition zone between the Sierra Nevada to the south and the Cascade Range of mountains to the north. As a result, 779 plant species have been recorded, while nearby mountains have less than 500 species. Mammals in the park include mule deer, black bear, coyote, bobcat, Douglas squirrel, northern flying squirrel, and pika.

Bumpass Hell

Highway 89 follows a meandering route through the western half of the park, passing many geothermal features and six mountain lakes. At the road's highest point, a hiking trail climbs to the summit of Lassen Peak. Nearby Bumpass Hell, a thermal basin of boiling mud and steam vents, was named after a hunter who explored the area in 1865. Wooden walkways lead to the mudholes and fumaroles.

Above, right: Mule deer are common throughout the parks in the western half of the United States.

Opposite, top: Barren lava beds are evidence of the major eruption that took place during 1915.

Opposite, bottom left: Upper Meadows near the summit of the 10,457-foot-high (3,187-m) Lassen Peak.

Opposite, center right: The Painted Dunes, created by volcanic activity, are located in the northeast portion of the park.

Opposite, bottom right: Wooden boardwalks lead to the hot springs and fumaroles of Bumpass Hell.

Location: Northern California. The city of Redding is the closest major center.

Climate: High elevation reduces temperatures. In summer, a high of 80°F (27°C) can be expected. In winter, the average low drops to around 8°F (−13°C) and heavy snowfalls are common. Annual precipitation is high. An average of 70 inches (1,750 mm) falls, mostly as snow.

When to go: In winter, heavy snowfalls close the road through the park. The best time to visit is from May to September.

Access: From Interstate 5, take Highway 44 east from Redding.

Facilities: Five campgrounds along the road that meanders through the park and another two campgrounds in the eastern part of the park. Interpretive trails explore the volcanic features along the roadside. Food outlets are at the south entrance and at Manzanita Lake Campground at the north entrance. Drakesbad Guest Ranch, open in summer only, is situated in a valley in the south of the park and can be reached only along a separate access road.

Outstanding features: The park preserves the volcanic Lassen Peak and the intriguing evidence of 1914–1915 eruptions. Steam rises from vents at Bumpass Hell, and many mountain lakes and high peaks to the east can only be reached on foot.

Visitor activities: Scenic drives, hiking, short walks to geothermal features, overnight backpacking, mountain climbing, cycling, swimming, canoeing, fishing, wildlife viewing, and bird-watching. Cross-country skiing and snowshoeing in winter.

REDWOOD NATIONAL PARK

Location: Northern California, adjoining the coastal center of Crescent City.

Climate: Winter is wet and windy. In January, an average low of 36°F (2°C) can be expected. Summer is the driest time of year, when temperatures in the forest range from 70° to 85°F (21° to 29°C). However, the coast is cooler, and fog is common.

When to go: Throughout the year. Spring and autumn are the best seasons for viewing the forests.

Access: From San Francisco, take U.S. Highway 101 north to the northern Californian coast and the southern entrance to the park. From Interstate 5, several roads head west through national forests to the coast, although there is no direct route.

Facilities: Prairie Creek Visitor Center is situated in the southern section of the park. There is an information center on the beach near Orick, one at the northern entrance, one on Crescent Beach, and another at park headquarters in Crescent City. There are four campgrounds in the park and 14 picnic areas. Several interpretive trails explore the redwood groves from the scenic drives. Although there are no lodges, restaurants, or service stations in the park, adjacent Crescent City has a full range of services.

Outstanding features: Silent, sheltering groves of towering redwoods, a scenic stretch of sandy beaches and rocky coastline, and the mouth of the Klamath River.

Visitor activities: Scenic drives, hiking, short forest and beach walks, overnight backpacking, cycling, swimming, fishing, canoeing, horseback riding, wildlife viewing, and bird-watching.

Gigantic redwood trees, deep dappled shade, and 34 miles (54 km) of unspoiled beaches and sheltered coves are among the attractions of this picturesque national park in northern California. Groves of ancient redwoods grow so tall that they block out the sun. The old-growth forests are interspersed with secondary-growth forests and meadows. Highway 101 meanders through the park, but side roads and walking trails allow visitors to experience the true beauty and solitude of this treed zone. Several streams rush through the forest, and the Klamath River enters the ocean near the middle of the park. During the height of the coho and chinook salmon season in September, many congregate on the lagoon in the hopes of catching the prized fish.

The park stretches from the delightful seaside town of Crescent City south to Stone Lagoon. Three state parks are incorporated within the national park, totaling an area of 169 square miles (437 sq km). The entire area is managed as a single unit. In 1980, the park was declared a World Heritage Site.

Ancient Giants of the Park

About 40 species of sequoia were abundant in North American forests many millions of years ago, but now only two species survive: the giant sequoia (*Sequoiadendron giganteum*) and the redwood (*Sequoia sempervirens*). These trees display a remarkable resistance to fire, disease, and insects, which partly accounts for their great age. Redwoods are evergreen trees that grow to exceptional heights. They can grow as much as 2 feet (60 cm) per year, and reach maturity at about 400 years of age. The annual rings on one tree indicate that the trees can live for over 2,000 years. Redwood seeds are exceptionally small and light—1,350 seeds can fit into a teaspoon—and each one is capable of producing a towering giant.

Climatic changes since the Ice Age have restricted the tree to a narrow coastal strip, from 5 to 35 miles (8 to 50 km) wide, that stretches from Monterey in California to southern Oregon. As redwoods require large quantities of water for growth, the moisture-laden winds produced by the Pacific Ocean are needed by the trees. They produce excellent timber, resistant to insects and rot. From the 1850s onward, loggers began cutting down the redwoods. Less than one-tenth of the original forests now remain. In 1908, President Theodore Roosevelt proclaimed the Muir Woods National Monument near San Francisco to save a tract of the redwoods, the first attempt to protect the trees. However, coastal lands where these trees grew in California were sold by the government for a pittance to private owners, and felling of redwoods continued. Only in 1968 was a national park established to protect a few of the remaining old-growth groves.

Along Redwood Creek in the south of the park, logging had scarred the hillsides and silted the streams. In 1978, the federal government bought 75 square miles (194 sq km) of land and added it to the park. Workers

Above, right: Forests of tall redwoods are the major appeal of this northern Californian park.

Opposite: At False Klamath Cove, the road through the park runs parallel to the breaking waves.

Above: South of the mouth of the Klamath River, this World War II radar station was disguised as an ordinary house.

Below: At Big Tree Wayside a short trail leads to a 304-foot-tall (93-m) Redwood that is estimated to be 1,500 years old.

then planted 700,000 redwood saplings throughout the area in an experiment to reestablish the forest. Along the same creek, the world's tallest known tree was discovered in 1963. Soaring to the height of a city skyscraper, the National Geographic Society Tree has been accurately measured as standing 365.5 feet (111.4 m) tall, with a massive girth of 44 feet (13 m).

Wildlife of the Forest and Ocean

Although the park is renowned for its plant life, herds of Roosevelt elk are often seen, especially in the meadows at Elk Prairie in the south. Although they are not always easy to detect in the dense forest, other mammals present include mountain lion, bobcat, red fox, northern flying squirrel, Townsend's chipmunk, black-tailed deer, and black bear. The redwoods fall within the range of the endangered northern spotted owl. The rare marbled murrelet builds its nest on the tops of tall trees, carrying fish from the ocean to feed its young.

Most of the 300 bird species recorded in the park are marine species. The California current flows south along the coast, drawing nutrients to the surface from the ocean's depths. Birds such as the common murre, pigeon guillemot, rhinoceros auklet, Brandt's cormorant, and south polar skua can be seen searching for food or skimming across the waves. On the beaches and on lagoons flocks of willet, snowy plover, lesser yellow-legs, sanderling, western gull, and double-crested cormorant congregate, and the rare brown pelican visits in summer. Many marine mammals are found in the ocean, including California sea lion, harbor seal, gray whale, humpback whale, killer whale, and common dolphin.

Scenic Drives and Walking Trails

The park headquarters and an information center are located just east of Crescent City. In summer, kayaking on the Smith River is a popular sport. The river rushes over several rapids and is home to chinook and coho salmon and to cutthroat and steelhead trout.

Driving south on Highway 101, the road passes Crescent Beach. A coastal trail begins at the beach, runs through forest, and follows the coastline to False Klamath Cove and the mouth of the Klamath River.

South of the Klamath Lagoon, an 8-mile (11-km) scenic drive hugs the high cliffs above the ocean, providing a splendid view across grassy hillsides and of the wave-trimmed rocky shore. Near the end of the coastal

drive, a hiking trail leaves the road, ending near Orick on the southern border of the park.

One of the finest groves of redwoods can be seen along the 9-mile (14-km) Newton B. Drury Scenic Parkway, which follows a shorter route than Highway 101. There are places to park along the narrow road flanked by towering trees, and many hiking trails explore the surrounding forest. The Prairie Creek Visitor Center and a campground are located near the end of the road before it rejoins Highway 101. Davidson Road, 2 miles (3 km) south of this junction, passes through the forest and follows the coast to Fern Canyon, passing Gold Bluffs Beach Campground along the route. This road coincides with a section of the coastal trail, where the canyon's 30-foot-high (10-m) walls are covered in ferns.

A number of trails are along Redwood Creek and through the southern section of the park, which was acquired in 1978. The world's first, second, third, and sixth tallest trees are found within a short distance of each other in the Tall Trees Grove. Access to the grove is restricted—a limited number of permits are issued free of charge. The Lady Bird Johnson Grove, 2 miles (3 km) east of Highway 101, can be accessed along a short trail that reveals one of the most impressive sections of the forest. For visitors approaching the park from the south on Highway 101, the Redwood Information Center overlooks a wide sandy beach dotted in driftwood near the southern entrance. Permits for the Tall Trees Grove can be obtained only from the rangers here, and a number of displays are in the building.

Above: Redwood National Park encompasses the Jedediah Smith (north), Del Norte Coast (central), and Prairie Creek (south) State Parks.

Below, left: Young herring gulls on the beach at False Klamath Cove.

YOSEMITE NATIONAL PARK

Known throughout the world for its sheer granite cliffs that were sliced vertically by an ancient glacier, Yosemite is one of the oldest and most popular national parks in America. The park was established in 1890, but President Abraham Lincoln had already granted the area to the people of California in 1864. Yosemite Valley, dominated by the 3,600-foot-high (1,100-m) El Capitan and 8,842-foot-high (2,695-m) Half Dome, is the park's focal point. It attracts the vast majority of the four million visitors, who are drawn by its natural beauty.

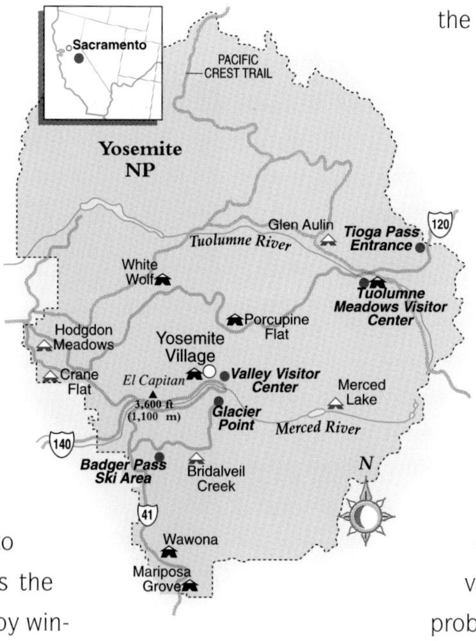

Three roads enter the park. The most popular ends in the Yosemite Valley, Highway 41 follows the western boundary to Wawona, and a high road crosses the Tuolumne Meadows and is closed by winter snows. Apart from these access routes, 94 percent of Yosemite is rugged wilderness crossed only by some 800 miles (1,100 km) of hiking trails. The park covers an area of 1,169 square miles (3,017 sq km) and is bordered by three wilderness areas of forest land. In 1984, Yosemite was declared a World Heritage Site.

Domes and Waterfalls

Yosemite's fascinating landmarks began to form about three million years ago when the Merced River cut a deep canyon through the mountains. During the Ice Age, an enormous glacier filled the Yosemite Valley. The immense mass of ice gouged and scoured the sides of the valley, producing its characteristic U shape. When the ice melted some 10,000 years ago, the meltwater formed a lake in the valley, which was filled by sediment washed down from the surrounding mountains.

The abrasive force of the ice produced the sheer cliffs and monoliths of granite that rise more than 3,000 feet (1,000 m) above the valley floor. Tributaries of the Merced now tumble down the sides of the U-shaped valley that has been left behind by the glacier. From Valley View on the Merced River at the entrance to the valley, El Capitan dominates the horizon on the left and Bridalveil Fall drops into the valley below Cathedral Rocks. Farther up the valley, prominent Half Dome was probably formed when a glacier undermined the base of an enormous granite outcrop and a section fell away along a weakness in the rock.

On the north side of the valley, Ribbon Falls plunges 1,612 feet (491 m) down the cliffs. Farther up, the Yosemite Falls drop a total distance of 2,425 feet (739 m) in two spectacular waterfalls. The 620-foot-high (189-m) Bridalveil Fall on the south side of the valley, unlike the Yosemite and Ribbon, never dries up, although its flow can be reduced to a misty plume. On

Above, right: Lichen on a giant sequoia in Mariposa Grove.
Opposite: Nevada Falls on the Merced River plunges down rocks polished by Ice Age glaciers.

Location: Central California. The city of Fresno is the nearest major center.

Climate: In Yosemite Valley the average high in July is 90°F (32°C). In January, the average low reaches 26°F (–3°C), but higher elevations are much colder.

When to go: Autumn is a good time to avoid the crowds.

Access: When approaching from the north on Highway 99, take Highway 140 east from Merced; from the south take Highway 41 north from Fresno.

Facilities: Valley Visitor Center is open throughout the year; Tuolumne Meadows Visitor Center is open in summer only. Yosemite Valley has a range of services, including a general store, several restaurants, lodges, and campgrounds. There are two lodges at Wawona and another at Tuolumne. At White Wolf, on the Tioga Road, is a lodge and campground. Lodges at higher elevations are open only during summer, but those in Yosemite Valley and Wawona are open throughout the year. Apart from Yosemite Valley, there are eight campgrounds in the park. Five service stations and 14 picnic areas are located at convenient intervals along the park's roads.

Outstanding features: Yosemite Valley is the park's most visited attraction. North of the valley lies a wilderness of granite domes and high meadows; to the south lie forests of oak and fir and a grove of sequoias.

Visitor activities: Scenic drives, narrated tram tours, hiking, short walks to sequoia groves and Indian Village, overnight backpacking, mountain climbing, rock climbing, cycling, golf, swimming, fishing, horseback riding, wildlife viewing, and birdwatching. Cross-country skiing and snowshoeing during winter.

Map labels: Sacramento · PACIFIC CREST TRAIL · Yosemite NP · Tuolumne River · Glen Aulin · Tioga Pass Entrance · 120 · White Wolf · Tuolumne Meadows Visitor Center · Porcupine Flat · Hodgdon Meadows · Yosemite Village · Crane Flat · El Capitan · Valley Visitor Center · Merced Lake · 3,600 ft (1,100 m) · Glacier Point · Merced River · 140 · Badger Pass Ski Area · Bridalveil Creek · N · 41 · Wawona · Mariposa Grove

Right: The Merced River meanders through the valley framed by El Capitan *(left)* and the Dewey Point *(right)*.

Below, right: Vernal Falls on the Merced River in the upper Yosemite Valley.

Below: The yellow-bellied marmot makes its home under loose rocks.

the Merced River are two impressive waterfalls at the east end of the valley that can be reached only on hiking trails. The first, Vernal Falls, plunges 317 feet (96 m). Upstream, the Nevada Falls drops 594 feet (181 m) over a wall of polished granite. The valley waterfalls are best viewed in late May when the river swells with runoff produced by melting snow.

Wildlife in Yosemite

In the Sierra Nevada, the variety of trees present and the abundance of plants in the understory, in particular berry-producing plants such as the blackberry and bitter cherry, enable the forests to support many species of mammals. Mule deer, black bear, Townsend's chipmunk, western gray squirrel, Douglas squirrel, northern flying squirrel, and golden-mantled ground squirrel inhabit the forests. The yellow-bellied marmot and pika occur at high altitudes. In 1986, bighorn sheep were reintroduced, and a small population today inhabits the high mountains.

Predators include the mountain lion, coyote, gray fox, river otter, short-tailed weasel, pine marten, fisher, badger, ringtail cat, spotted skunk, raccoon, and wolverine. The wolverine is a fierce predator that has a very limited distribution in the country.

An estimated 250 to 500 black bears live in the park. They have become experts at locating food in campgrounds. Special steel containers are now

provided, but bears still caused damage to property estimated at $190,469 in the first nine months of 1999. Many vehicles were broken into in parking lots, and incidents involving bears and visitors totaled 569 for that year. The Park Service continues to seek ways to minimize and control contact between bears and visitors.

The occurrence of four distinct vegetation zones in the park provides habitats for many bird species. Some of the common birds to be observed include pine grosbeak, robin, dark-eyed junco, mountain chickadee, pine siskin, olive-sided flycatcher, and Steller's jay.

Yosemite Valley

Many facilities are provided for visitors in Yosemite Village, including a garage, village store, and medical and dental clinic. Behind the store, a walkway leads past a restaurant, the post office, the wilderness center, and the Ansel Adams Photographic Gallery to the visitor center. An adjacent building houses the Yosemite Museum, and the Ahwahnee Indian Village is located behind the museum. This reconstructed village contains traditional houses and storage areas from the valley as they would have appeared in 1872.

Accommodations in the valley are provided at Curry Village, The Ahwahnee, and Yosemite Lodge. Three campgrounds are located on the banks of the Merced River near Curry Village, and there is a large stable for horses. North of the river, Sunnyside Campground is located at the base of the Three Brothers Rock Formation, near Yosemite Lodge. A free shuttle bus service follows a figure-eight route between Yosemite Lodge and the east end of the valley, stopping at 19 points along the route. A number of picnic areas are in the forests bordering the river, and 12 miles (19 km) of bicy-

Left: The reconstructed Ahwahnee Indian Village depicts the culture of the Yosemite Valley's former inhabitants.

Below: Ranger-led tours highlight the most important features of the valley.

Right: Yosemite's granite domes and valleys are traversed by 800 miles (1,300 km) of hiking trails.

Below: The 8,842-foot-high (2,695-m) summit of Half Dome is the highest of the impressive peaks flanking the Yosemite Valley.

Tuolumne Meadows

Highway 120 crosses the center of Yosemite and provides access to the largest subalpine meadow in the Sierra Nevada. The 39-mile (62-km) route passes a number of small glacial lakes with side roads leading to four campgrounds. The road then skirts the northern shore of the large Tenaya Lake where impressive granite domes, often capped in snow, tower above the water and the surrounding coniferous forests. Because the Tuolumne Meadows are situated at an altitude of 8,400 feet (2,560 m), the air can be icy, and the growing season is limited. However, during early summer the grassy steppe is clothed in bright displays of wildflowers. The visitor center overlooks the meadows, and hiking trails lead to lakes tucked into the mountains.

This is the best starting point for backcountry hiking in the High Sierras, and camping permits are available from the visitor center. Farther east are a picnic area, campground, lodge, restaurant, and facilities for horseback riding. At the park's eastern boundary, the road crosses Tioga Pass, which, at 9,945 feet (3,031 m), is the highest pass open to vehicles in California. This is one of five passes across the Sierra Nevada from Yosemite northward to Interstate 80 between Sacramento and Reno. Like many of these, the road is closed from November to May, when heavy snows make it impassable. However, in summer, this is a scenic drive through the adjoining national forest.

cle paths have been laid out. Bicycles can be hired at Curry Village and Yosemite Lodge. Visitors can walk along bike paths. However, an additional 13 popular trails are in the valley ranging from a 30-minute ramble to a 17-mile (27-km) round-trip hike to the summit of the impressive Half Dome.

Climbers from around the world are drawn to El Capitan's 3,600 feet (1,100 m) of sheer granite. Five to eight days are needed to reach the summit, and this impressive landmark was scaled for the first time only in 1958. During summer, the Yosemite Mountaineering School holds climbing classes in the valley and at Tuolumne.

Glacier Point and Sequoia Groves

From the Yosemite Valley, Highway 41 climbs steeply and heads south. Just before the tunnel, a view site offers an incredible panorama over the valley.

At Chinquapin, 14 miles (22 km) from Yosemite Valley, a side road leads to Glacier Point, with an unmatched view over the valley. From an altitude of 7,200 feet (2,200 m), the granite cliffs plunge 3,200 feet (980 m) to the valley floor. Four waterfalls can be seen cascading down the valley sides.

A 4-mile (7-km) hiking trail zigzags from the view site to the foot of Sentinel Rock. During winter, this trail is closed and the road is kept open only as far as the Badger Pass Ski Area.

Returning to Highway 41, the road passes Wawona after 27 miles (43 km), where there is a store and a hotel overlooking a golf course. The Mariposa Grove, one of the three groves of giant sequoia in the park, is a short distance from Wawona near the southern entrance to the park. A short walking trail winds through the 200 trees in the grove, where you can see the 2,700-year-old Grizzly Giant. A cabin built by an early pioneer now houses a museum.

Left: The vertical face of El Capitan attracts rock climbers from around the world.

Below: The base of a giant sequoia in the Mariposa Grove near the park's southern boundary.

Overleaf: Glacier Point offers an exceptional view of the Yosemite Valley and the Upper and Lower Yosemite Falls, the two highest waterfalls in North America.

SEQUOIA & KINGS CANYON NATIONAL PARKS

These two contiguous national parks protect the high Sierra Nevada in central California. Sequoia was established in 1890 as America's second national park. Support for the park came from people who wanted the forests protected against logging and others who wished to preserve the catchments of important rivers. Sequoia is named after a famous Native American leader who developed the Cherokee alphabet. In the same year, a national park was established to protect the sequoia trees in Grant Grove. When Kings Canyon was inaugurated in 1940, Grant Grove became a separate unit of this new park. The combined area of the parks preserves 1,348 square miles (3,479 sq km) of oak woodlands, coniferous forests, spectacular rivers and canyons, and the high mountain peaks of the Sierra Nevada.

Some of America's most beautiful and least developed country exists in these parks. Highway 198 twists through sharp bends that climb from oak woodlands to coniferous forests in Sequoia. Only one road enters the untamed wilderness of Kings Canyon where the erosive power of water has carved the deepest canyon in the country. Apart from these roads, the parks consist of vast wilderness areas crossed only by hiking trails. No road passes are across this section of the Sierra Nevada, where roads that end in deep valleys are hemmed by towering peaks. Mount Whitney, the highest peak in the lower 48 states, rises to 14,495 feet (4,418 m) on the eastern border of

Sequoia. A dozen peaks along the Palisade Crest in Kings Canyon and around Mount Whitney exceed 14,000 feet (4,200 m) in height, and hikers can take at least a week to hike to the high summits. Even the shortest route along the Pacific Crest National Scenic Trail from Kings Canyon to Mount Whitney requires a round-trip expedition of 75 miles (120 km).

Since 1943, both national parks have been managed as a single unit. Four wilderness areas have since been designated in the mountains to the south and north. An unbroken corridor of wilderness links the parks with Yosemite National Park 40 miles (65 km) to the north.

Forests of the Sierra Nevada

The coniferous forests in the Sierra Nevada are the most diverse in the world. In low-lying valleys, summer temperatures are high and rainfall is low, and an oak woodland characterized by trees such as the California black oak (*Quercus kelloggii*) and blue oak (*Quercus douglasii*) is the dominant vegetation type. Chaparral scrub occurs in regions too dry for woodland. Above the oak woodlands, the ponderosa pines grow on dry mountain slopes. With an increase in alti-

Above, right: The Californian ground squirrel, important prey for many predators, nests and hibernates among boulders and depends on its coloration for camouflage.
Opposite: Kings Canyon in the high Sierra Nevada is a rough, untamed wilderness of awesome mountains and rugged canyons.

Location: Central California, east of Fresno.

Climate: In January, the average low temperature is 16°F (–9°C). In summer, highs of 80°F (27°C) can be expected, but temperatures decrease markedly at higher elevations.

When to go: April to October provide the best opportunities for outdoor recreation.

Access: From Highway 99 take Highway 180 east from Fresno, or take Highway 198 east from Visalia.

Facilities: Foothills Visitor Center at Sequoia's southern entrance and Lodgepole Visitor Center close to Wuksachi Village. In Kings Canyon, Grant Grove Visitor Center is situated near a grove of sequoias, and Cedar Grove Visitor Center borders the South Fork Kings River along its upper course. Only Foothills and Grant Grove are open year-round. There are three lodges in Sequoia and two in Kings Canyon, generally open from May to September. Food is available at Wuksachi and Grant Grove throughout the year and at Cedar Grove and Lodgepole in summer. There are six campgrounds in Sequoia and seven in Kings Canyon and endless opportunities for backcountry camping and hiking. Interpretive trails explore the giant sequoia groves, and six picnic areas are located along the main roads.

Outstanding features: The deepest canyon and some of the highest peaks in the United States, extensive forests of oak and fir, and scattered groves of gigantic sequoias.

Visitor activities: Scenic drives, hiking, short walks to sequoia groves, overnight backpacking, mountain climbing, cycling, swimming, fishing, horseback riding, wildlife viewing, and bird-watching. Cross-country skiing and snowshoeing are additional winter activities.

tude, the winds that are forced up the mountains drop their moisture. The white fir (*Abies concolor*), incense cedar (*Libocedrus decurrens*), and sugar pine (*Pinus lambertiana*)—the tallest American pine—become the dominant trees. These trees, and the giant sequoia, require cooler areas where soil moisture is adequate throughout the dry summer months.

Sequoias are found on nonglaciated ridges at altitudes ranging from 4,500 to 8,400 feet (1,500 to 2,550 m). About 2.5 million years ago, a significant change in global climate caused nearly 40 members of the family to become extinct. Only 75 groves of sequoias remain in the world. They are all confined to the western slopes of the Sierra Nevada, mostly within a 60-mile-long (95-km)

belt south of the South Fork Kings River. The total area covered by all the sequoia groves amounts to just 57 square miles (147 sq km) of the mountain's vastness.

Sequoias are the largest living trees on earth. The General Sherman Tree, at 274.9 feet (83.8 m) high, is the largest in the park. Even the slightly smaller General Grant Tree has a diameter of 40 feet (12 m), and towers to a height of 267 feet (81.5 m) above its base. The sequoia's bark may be as thick as 2 feet (60 cm) at the base of the tree, and protects it from forest fires, diseases, and insects. These gigantic trees can weigh as much as 1,200 tons and can live for more than 3,000 years. However, their shallow roots mean that they are easily toppled by strong winds and storms. Cones remain on the tree for up to 20 years, and fire is essential for seed germination.

In the coniferous forests where sequoias are found, the Jeffrey pine (*Pinus jeffreyi*) grows above 6,500 feet (2,000 m), where low temperatures, frequent snow, and deep shade make it impossible for the ponderosa pine to survive. Above altitudes of 8,000 feet (2,400 m), moisture levels begin to decline sharply. The California red fir (*Abies magnifica*) is found in the upper montane

zone above the mixed coniferous forests. At higher altitudes, the lodgepole pine (*Pinus contorta*) and mountain hemlock struggle to survive before extreme cold and a lack of available moisture make tree growth impossible. At this high altitude, nearly all precipitation falls as snow.

Opposite: A tourist is dwarfed by the General Sherman Sequoia. As earth's largest living organism, these trees are equivalent in weight to a herd of 1,800 adult bison.

Below: Variations in thickness of the concentric rings on a fallen giant can pinpoint climate changes as far back as the days of the Roman Empire.

Right: A roadside picnic area in Kings Canyon adjoins the delightful Grizzly Falls.

Below right: The Fallen Monarch, in General Grant Grove, has been lying in this position for over a century and was used in the past as a home, hotel, and stable for 32 horses.

Winding Passes and Awesome Canyons

From Fresno, Highway 180 enters the national parks just south of Grant Grove Visitor Center. A short circular walking trail explores this famous grove of sequoias, and a booklet describes points of interest along the trail. There are 33 named trees along the length of the walk. Apart from those named after generals Grant and Lee, most of the trees are named after individual American states from Arizona to Wyoming.

Continuing north, the road loses 2,000 feet (600 m) in altitude, descending through chaparral vegetation, then follows the south fork of the Kings River to Cedar Grove Village. The road descends in a series of tight bends, passing through a narrow canyon flanked by rugged, lofty peaks. The views of the folded mountains and the deep canyon are truly magnificent. In some places, the surrounding mountains rise 8,000 feet (2,400 m) above the rushing river.

After running parallel to the river for some distance, the road reaches a pleasant picnic area at Grizzly Falls in Sequoia National Forest, which borders the park. At Cedar Grove, 2 miles (3 km) after the park boundary, are four campgrounds, horseback-riding facilities, and a lodge and restaurant that overlook the rapidly flowing river. Hiking trails follow the riverbanks before heading north into the wilderness.

The only way out of Kings Canyon is to retrace the journey along Highway 180 to Grant Grove. From Grant Village, Highway 198 winds through the forest and passes the Redwood Mountain Grove, which covers 4.5 square miles (12 sq km). The grove contains 15,800 gigantic sequoias with a diameter of more than 10 feet (3 m) at their bases.

From Wuksachi Village, the road reaches General Sherman Tree, which is the largest living thing on earth. The tree weighs 1,256 tons, the diameter at its base measures 36.5 feet (11 m) and its crest soars high above the many visitors who come to see it each year. It is estimated to be between 2,300 and 2,700 years old. Although the General Sherman Tree is very old, and can therefore be expected to be so large, sequoias are, in fact, among the fastest growing trees in the world. They

Below: The South Fork Kings River flows gently past Cedar Grove Lodge before entering Kings Canyon, the deepest canyon in the United States.

can reach an astounding height of 100 feet (30 m) in less than a century.

From the General Sherman Tree, the circular 2-mile (3-km) Congress Trail leads first to another tree named after General Lee, then to the House Group and the Senate Group, and then passes the President Tree, with a diversion to a tree named after Chief Sequoyah. The President Tree is the fourth largest sequoia, while the General Lee Tree stands 250 feet (76 m) tall. Since 1940, the practice of naming trees after famous people has been discontinued.

From the grove, the road skirts prominent Moro Rock and descends rapidly, losing 4,700 feet (1,435 m) in altitude over 15 miles (23 km). After leaving the coniferous forests, the road passes through oak woodlands that clothe the hill slopes and valleys, then exits the park at Ash Mountain.

Below: The untrammeled inner wilderness of the high Sierra Nevada can be visited only by hikers and mountaineers.

DEATH VALLEY NATIONAL PARK

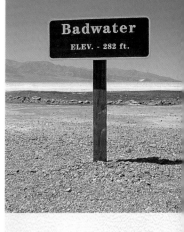

A sun-baked wilderness of parched flats, salt pans, sand dunes, and desert mountains, this is the largest national park in the lower 48 states and the least hospitable. Death Valley is an immense park extending over 5,214 square miles (13,450 sq km). It is the hottest, driest, lowest-lying region in America. The highest temperature in the United States—134°F (57°C)—was recorded in the valley in 1913. Rainfall is meager and an average of 1.5 inches (40 mm) falls in winter. Near Badwater, the dusty floor of the 120-mile-long (190-km) valley descends to 282 feet (86 m) below sea level, the lowest point on the continent of North America. However, just 15 miles (20 km) west across the salty flats, the terrain rapidly rises to 11,049 feet (3,368 m) at Telescope Peak—a dramatic increase in altitude of around 11,300 feet (3,500 m) over a short distance. Further west, across an expanse of desert, Mount Whitney, the highest peak in the country outside Alaska, reaches its summit at 14,495 feet (4,418 m) above sea level. The close proximity of the highest and lowest points in the country is due to fault lines that have allowed a block of land to sink below the surrounding strata.

Death Valley was named in 1849 by pioneers in search of a shortcut from Salt Lake City to the California gold fields. After crossing the Amargosa Mountains, they were forced to venture onto this inhospitable wasteland. The expedition was unable to cross the jagged salt crystal bed of the Devil's Golf Course and did not find the refreshing oasis at Furnace Creek. In 1933,

a national monument was proclaimed to protect the valley and surrounding desert. Additional land was added along the eastern and western borders in 1994, and the monument was redesignated a national park.

Desert wildlife, while not always apparent, includes mountain lion, kit fox, bobcat, desert bighorn, ground squirrel, desert cottontail, kangaroo rat, and many species of reptiles. Among the most fascinating desert animals are the pupfish, relics from an ancient lake that can live in water that is heated to 108°F (42°C) by the intense sun. Pupfish survive by staying near the edge of the pool where the water is fractionally cooler. The Nevada pupfish is found in fewer than 20 pools, while the Devil pupfish is restricted to only one side of the Devil's Hole sinkhole.

Bullfrog, Borax, and Scotty's Castle

Attempts by humans to settle the valley over the past 150 years are some of the most interesting facets of Death Valley. In 1880, borax was discovered by Aaron and Rosie Winters, two poor desert settlers. Borax was mined for use in pottery making. For six years, teams of

Above, right: The lowest point in the Western Hemisphere is situated near Badwater in Death Valley.

Opposite: From Dante's View, the lower-than-sea-level floor of Death Valley is a conspicuous landmark.

Location: Southeastern California, bordering Nevada. Barstow is the nearest major town.

Climate: Summers are exceptionally hot, and the American record high temperature of 134°F (57°C) was recorded in the valley. In some parts of Death Valley, annual rainfall averages a paltry 2 to 4 inches (50 to 100 mm).

When to go: It is best to avoid the park in summer; October to April are the best months to visit.

Access: From Interstate 15, take Highway 127 north from Baker to Shoshone, and then head west on Highway 178.

Facilities: Furnace Creek Visitor Center is the park's focal point. There are two lodges (both with restaurants), a service station, a post office, and three campgrounds in the vicinity. There are nine campgrounds in the park and a picnic area at the sand dunes. In the north of the park is a restaurant and service station at Scotty's Castle. Stovepipe Wells Village, near the sand dunes, has a lodge, campground, service station, and airport. Farther south along Highway 190 there is a lodge, campground, and service station at Panamint Springs. Radiator water is available at eight points along the main roads through the park.

Outstanding features: Desert features include salt pans, sand dunes, and barren mountains. In some places the valley floor sinks to 282 feet (86 m) below sea level, the lowest point in North America.

Visitor activities: Scenic drives, four-wheel-drive excursions, hiking, short walks to historical buildings and geologic features, overnight backpacking, cycling, horseback riding, and bird-watching.

20 mules hauled wagons loaded with 12 tons of the mineral. A water wagon was towed as well, and the journey to the railway station at Mojave took ten days to complete. The crumbling ruins of the Harmony Borax Works can be explored on an interpretive trail.

In the mountains surrounding Death Valley, gold, silver, copper, and lead claims attracted fortune seekers, giving rise to mining towns such as Ballarat, Skidoo, Leadfield, and Bullfrog. Panamint City was founded in 1893 after silver was found but was destroyed by a flash flood three years later. When the ores were exhausted, the towns died as quickly as they had sprung up.

In the north of the park, Scotty's Castle is a legend in itself. In 1905, Walter Scott emerged from Death Valley carrying sacks of gold and scattered money on the streets of Los Angeles. Scott carefully cultivated the legend of a secret gold mine in Death Valley. A miner and a one-time rider in Buffalo Bill's Wild West Show, Scott was the friend of a Chicago millionaire, Albert Johnson. When Johnson later built a lavish Spanish-style mansion in Death Valley at the cost of $2 million, Scott claimed that the villa was financed by the mine. The tale drew many fortune seekers to the area. Scotty's Castle still retains its original furniture, and the mansion was added to the park in 1970. Rangers conduct tours on the hour through the fascinating mansion. A restaurant is also on the premises.

Above, left: In this inhospitable, sun-seared valley, the Harmony Borax Works defied the elements for six years.

Above: Near Stovepipe Wells Village, sand dunes have been formed by winds blowing across the desert.

Traveling in Death Valley

Because Death Valley is an immense arid area, visitors are warned of the dangers of heat exhaustion. At sites along the four roads crossing the park, barrels store emergency water for car radiators. As summer temperatures of 125°F (52°C) are common, the park is best visited from November to February. The easiest route to Death Valley is along Highway 127 from Interstate 15. In this parched, lightly populated region distances are great. Shoshone is 56 miles (90 km) from the Interstate and Badwater 57 miles (91 km) farther north.

Many of the park's most interesting aspects are located along the 45-mile (72-km) stretch of Highway 190 between Badwater and Stovepipe Wells Village. They include the salt crystals of the Devil's Golf Course, the palm-fringed oasis at Furnace Creek—which yields 600 gallons (2,400 L) of water per minute—Harmony Borax Works, the Salt Creek pools, and the red sand dunes. The road passes the Furnace Creek Visitor Center, four campgrounds, and several interpretive trails. Accommodations are provided by two lodges at Furnace Creek and at Stovepipe Wells Village. Of the nine campgrounds in the park, only Furnace Creek, Wildrose near Telescope Peak, and Mesquite Spring, in the north near Scotty's Castle, remain open throughout the year.

JOSHUA TREE NATIONAL PARK

In southern California, the Mojave and Colorado Deserts meet west of the Little San Bernardino Mountains near Palm Springs.

Joshua Tree, a former national monument and comprising 1,239 square miles (3,196 sq km), is one of three parks that preserve the deserts of California. Located just north of Interstate 10 near Palm Springs, it is the national park closest to Los Angeles and its rapidly expanding neighboring cities in southern California. Joshua Tree was established in 1994 and is named after a species of branched yucca (*Yucca brevifolia*).

At higher altitudes on the mountains, where the air is cooler and annual rainfall can be as high as 7 inches (175 mm), plants typical of the Mojave Desert occur, in particular the Joshua tree. Open woodlands of these Joshua trees grow among eroded outcrops of granite, while on higher slopes pinyon pines become the dominant species. Below 3,000 feet (1,000 m) on the sunbaked Pinto Basin in the east of the park, rainfall decreases to about 3 inches (75 mm). The arid plains are dotted with creosote bushes and many species of cactus typical of the Colorado Desert.

The Joshua Tree

The many-branched Joshua tree is restricted to the hillsides and desert plains of southern California, Nevada, and Arizona and may grow to 30 feet (9 m) in height. It provides important nesting sites for the cactus wren, Scott's oriole, and Gila woodpecker. The larvae of the yucca moth feed only on the developing seeds of the plant. The female moth gathers pollen from the anther of one plant, rolls it into a ball, and takes it to the stigma of another plant, thereby pollinating the plant. One or two eggs are laid, and the larvae feed on the seeds. The tree also provides food and cover for the wood rat and night lizard, which, in turn, attract predatory snakes such as the spotted night snake.

Desert Oases

Although temperatures in the desert soar to 110°F (43°C) in summer, five oases are in the park and water flows to the surface in two of these. A 1.5-mile (2.5-km) hiking trail from the town of Twentynine Palms leads to the Fortynine Palms Oasis situated south of Highway 62. Bighorn sheep and many species of birds depend on this precarious water supply.

In the south of the park, near Cottonwood Visitor Center and Campground, the Cottonwood Springs are surrounded by fan palms, the only indigenous palm that occurs in this desert. This oasis attracts many species of birds, such as white-winged dove, verdin, black-tailed gnatcatcher, summer tanager, Scott's oriole, and Lawrence's goldfinch.

Visiting Joshua Tree

From Highway 62, Park Boulevard runs between the western and northern entrance gates and includes several points of interest. This road passes three campgrounds, three picnic areas, and several short interpre-

Above, right: The Joshua tree thrives in the scorching Mojave Desert in southern California.

Location: Southern California, near the city of Palm Springs

Climate: In midsummer temperatures of 120°F (49°C) have been recorded, and the average high in July is around 112°F (44°C). Temperatures in the mountainous western section of the park are lower than in the eastern Colorado Desert. In winter, the days are mild at around 60°F (15°C) and drop below freezing at night.

When to go: Best visited in the cooler months from September to May.

Access: Interstate 10 passes the park's southern entrance. To enter the park at the western or northern entrance, take Highway 62 north from Palm Springs.

Facilities: Oasis Visitor Center, in the town of Twentynine Palms and the Cottonwood Visitor Center in the south of the park are open throughout the year. There are eight campgrounds in the park, seven picnic areas, and a number of interpretive trails. Although no lodges, restaurants, or service stations are in the park, the neighboring towns of Palm Springs, Indio, Yucca Valley, and Twentynine Palms have a range of services.

Outstanding features: Granite monoliths and rugged mountains provide the geologic backdrop to a park located at the junction of two major deserts. Apart from inconspicuous and often nocturnal desert animals, the park protects unique desert plants such as the Joshua tree and other cactus species.

Visitor activities: Scenic drives, four-wheel-drive excursions, hiking, rock climbing, short walks through the cactus garden, overnight backpacking, cycling, horseback riding, and bird-watching.

Above: As one of the highest points in the park, Keys View provides panoramic views across the Little San Bernardino Mountains and the Coachella Valley. The San Andreas Fault runs through the center of the valley.

Center, right: The park was established to protect groves of Joshua trees and the surrounding desert.

Bottom right: The presence of water at the Cottonwood Springs, near the southern entrance, attracts many species of birds.

Opposite: Granite boulders in the Hidden Valley once served as the perfect hideout for cattle rustlers.

tive trails leading to points of interest. A 5-mile (8-km) side road ends at 5,185-foot-high (1,580-m) Keys View, which offers a splendid panorama over the surrounding countryside, the Salton Sea, and as far south as Mexico. The Salton Sea in the valley below is one of two regions in California that is below sea level. The lake attracts large numbers of wild fowl, and its southern portion is protected by a national wildlife refuge. In the past, this area of the Imperial Valley was part of the Gulf of California. However, sediment deposited at the mouth of the Colorado River acted as a dam, and the seawater evaporated, leaving a dusty depression. In 1905, an irrigation canal carrying water from the Colorado broke and flooded the depression, creating a body of water that has endured the sun's relentless rays.

Many granite formations are in the park. Hidden Valley, once used as a cattle rustler's hideout, and Jumbo Rocks attract many rock climbers.

From the southern entrance off Interstate 10, the Pinto Basin Road passes Cottonwood Visitor Center and the nearby oasis and the arid Pinto Basin before joining Park Boulevard near the northern entrance. Away from these two main roads, a number of tracks, suitable only for four-wheel-drive vehicles, traverse remote corners of the park. Many of these tracks were built during the gold rush. Eighty percent of the park has been set aside as a wilderness area where hiking and backcountry camping are permitted. Hikers should avoid camping in desert washes where flash floods can occur and need to carry all their own drinking water.

CHANNEL ISLANDS NATIONAL PARK

Located off the coast of southern California, this national park encompasses five scenic islands, provides a home to 85 endemic plants, and is renowned for an abundance of birds and marine mammals. The park was proclaimed in 1980. Its boundary extends 1 nautical mile (1.8 km) offshore, embracing 388 square miles (1,001 sq km) of land and sea. The Channel Islands National Marine Sanctuary extends a further 5 nautical miles (9 km) out to sea and offers protection to 1,658 square miles (4,277 sq km) of the surrounding ocean.

Anacapa, the closest of the five islands, is 11 miles (18 km) west of the mainland, while the island of Santa Barbara is located 40 miles (65 km) southwest of Los Angeles. Santa Cruz, the largest of the islands, covers 96 square miles (247 sq km), the major portion of which is maintained as a strict sanctuary where public access is limited.

Six species of seals congregate on the islands, including an estimated 150,000 California sea lions, and 10,000 northern elephant seals raise their young on San Miguel Island. The rich diversity of marine life that surrounds the islands is due to cold water from the north being forced by the landmass to rise to the surface. Rich in nutrients, these currents encourage a proliferation of kelp and marine organisms. The underwater kelp forests nourish and shelter many forms of marine life ranging from the luminous orange garibaldi to blue rockfish, kelp bass, California sheephead, senorita wrass, giant kelpfish, surfperch, and giant squid as well as starfish, anemones, sea urchins, lobsters, and crabs. Over 20 species of sharks inhabit the surrounding ocean, and

sightings of dolphins and gray whales draw whale-watchers from nearby coastal cities. About 200 species of birds have been recorded on the islands, and Anacapa and Santa Barbara are important nesting sites for the endangered brown pelican. Among the unusual birds present, bird-watchers will observe black oystercatcher, ashy storm-petrel, pelagic cormorant, elegant tern, tufted puffin, Xantus' murrelet, and Cassin's auklet.

Visiting the Islands

There is a visitor center at the park headquarters, situated at Ventura Harbor on the mainland, and museums on Anacapa and Santa Barbara Islands. Boat trips depart from the adjacent harbor daily depending on weather conditions. There are campgrounds on all the islands, but visitors must carry their own food and water. Although sections are reserved as special breeding reserves for rare birds and marine mammals, there are hiking trails on all the islands, and the tidal pools teem with marine life. Sanctuary areas along the coastlines of most of the islands are closed to fishing, and certain of the tidal pools are specially protected.

Map labels: Sacramento; N; Ventura Visitor Center; San Miguel; Santa Cruz; Anacapa Island Lighthouse; Anacapa; Santa Rosa; **Channel Islands NP**; Lighthouse; Santa Barbara

Above, right: Colonies of around 150,000 California sea lions are based on the five scenic islands.

Opposite: The Channel Islands National Park safeguards giant kelp forests, hundreds of fish species, 85 endemic plants, and breeding colonies of seabirds and seals.

Location: Off the coast of southern California, south of Santa Barbara.

Climate: Winds off the ocean reduce the temperature, and rain falls mainly in winter. In January, the average low is around 44°F (7°C). In July, a high of 80°F (27°C) can be expected.

When to go: The park is open year-round.

Access: Only by boat from Ventura Harbor.

Facilities: The visitor center is situated at the entrance to Ventura Harbor on the mainland and is open throughout the year. Visitors in private boats must obtain permits from park rangers for visiting Santa Rosa and San Miguel Islands. The islands are undeveloped and facilities for visitors are limited. There are basic campgrounds and restrooms on all the islands, but visitors must carry their own food and drinking water. Interpretive trails and museums are located on Anacapa and Santa Barbara Islands, and there are lighthouses on both.

Outstanding features: Five unspoiled islands off the Californian Coast that safeguuard important populations of marine mammals and seabirds. Marine life abounds in the surrounding ocean, and sightings of whales peak during summer and winter.

Visitor activities: Boat tours, sailing, hiking, short beach walks, overnight backpacking, fishing, swimming, scuba diving, snorkeling, whale-watching, wildlife viewing, and bird-watching.

HAWAII

Among the most isolated islands in the world, the Hawaiian Islands are strung for 1,640 miles (2,625 km) across the central Pacific. This archipelago of eight large islands and 124 smaller isles and atolls sustains 8,800 plant and animal species that occur nowhere else on earth.

Born from volcanoes erupting on the ocean bed, these far-flung islands were colonized over millions of years by plants and animals. No reptiles ever reached the islands, and only two mammals—a monk seal and hoary bat—made the long journey. Plants and insects blew in on the winds from Asia, while most birds arrived from North America. With no predators, and nurtured by moisture-laden winds, species adapted over time to their new environment. A total of 2,500 plants emerged from 275 immigrants. Fifty different species of honey-creeper, a finch-sized bird, filled many vacant niches on the islands and developed bills specialized at cracking nuts, feeding on nectar, or boring into bark.

In the fourth century, Polynesians from the Marquesas Islands colonized the Hawaiian Islands, bringing with them pigs, dogs, coconuts, bananas, and sugar cane. An estimated 35 species of endemic birds became extinct at this time. During the 1820s, European settlers introduced goats, pigs, and many plants. Cats and mongooses were introduced to control the rats that had escaped from ships. Instead, though, they devastated the islands' bird populations.

The danger of extinction in Hawaii is partly due to its small size. As the fourth smallest state, its combined land surface covers 6,423 square miles (16,674 sq km). With its incredible diversity of plants and animals, many species are restricted to a single mountain. On Oahu, each of five separate valleys contains a different species of achatinella snail. Of the United States' threatened and endangered species, Hawaii heads the list with 31 of the 88 birds and 199 of the 526 plants listed. Of the original 50 honeycreeper species, only 21 remain; 14 are endangered. Despite the ever-present threat of extinction, over one-quarter of the islands still remain in their natural state. Two significant national parks and 40 preserves protect a rich diversity of life. Park rangers and researchers continuously combat alien species and breed endangered species in captivity.

Left: The Hawaiian Islands were formed by volcanic activity on the bed of the Pacific Ocean, which still continues to build new islands and alter existing landforms.

HAWAII VOLCANOES NATIONAL PARK

Located on the eastern side of Hawaii Island, the largest and youngest in the Hawaii archipelago, this park includes the high summits of two of the most active volcanoes in the world, Kilauea and Mauna Loa. Established in 1916, just 16 years after the Hawaiian Islands became American territory, the park covers 358 square miles (924 sq km). Altitude varies from sea level to the lofty summit of 13,680-foot-high (4,169-m) Mauna Loa, the most rapid increase in elevation in any American national park. Apart from the impressive volcanoes, other attractions include endemic birds and plants, dense rain forests, and a stretch of coastline where sea turtles come ashore to nest.

Four wilderness areas have been designated in the park, while six forest reserves and two nature reserves protect the adjoining forests and mountains, acting as important buffer zones. The luxuriant 'Ola'a Forest is protected as a separate block of land north of Kilauea Visitor Center. The park was declared a World Heritage Site in 1987.

Island-Building Volcanoes

Hawaii, also known as the Big Island to avoid confusion with the entire archipelago, covers 4,038 square miles (10,458 sq km) and was formed by four volcanoes. A fifth volcano, Kilauea, has formed on the southeastern slopes of Mauna Loa. Some 12 miles (19 km) north of the park, another volcanic mountain, Mauna Kea, is the highest peak of.all the islands, rising to a massive 13,796 feet (4,205 m) above the surrounding ocean.

The origins of the Big Island, which emerged from the ocean during the past 400,000 years, lie in pools of magma located 50 miles (80 km) underground. Far below the earth's surface, currents of heat cause pools of magma to move upward. The surrounding rocks are kept in a plastic state by heat and pressure. The lighter magma pools rise and find routes to the surface through cracks and fissures in the overlying crust. Over time, this constant outpouring of molten rock accumulates and builds a new island. Measuring from the ocean bottom to the crest of the mountains, these volcanoes represent an accumulation of billions of tons of magma. Mauna Loa, one of the largest mountains on earth, rises 32,000 feet (9,800 m) from the ocean floor, surpassing even Mount Everest in height. The mountain has slowly been built up over thousands of years, with each century adding about 300 acres (1.3 sq km) of new land. About 20 miles (30 km) offshore, another volcano and future island, Loihi, is slowly taking shape on the ocean floor some 3,300 feet (1,000 m) below the surface.

Above, right: Honeycreepers are endemic to the Hawaiian Islands, but of the original 50 species, only 21 remain and many are listed as endangered.

Opposite: Molten lava from one of Hawaii's active volcanoes enters the sea.

Location: Southeast coast of the island of Hawaii, south of Hilo.

Climate: The coastal area is usually warm and dry, and there is little fluctuation in daily temperatures throughout the year. Kilauea is often cool and wet as winds blowing across the ocean are forced up the mountain. At higher elevations, temperatures drop below freezing and snow may occasionally fall on Mauna Loa.

When to go: The park is open throughout the year. Weather conditions vary considerably depending on altitude and aspect, with the least amount of rain falling during autumn.

Access: From Hilo, head south on Highway 11 to the park entrance. Lava flows have closed off the coastal access road.

Facilities: Kilauea Visitor Center adjoins the caldera, and Volcano House Hotel is situated across the road. There are two campgrounds in the park and six picnic areas. Several interpretive trails have been laid out on the edge of the caldera. Jaggar Museum is situated on the western rim of the caldera. For hikers, there are two cabins along the hiking trail leading to the summit of Mauna Loa.

Outstanding features: The park's irrefutable focal point is the two active volcanoes. However, other significant attractions include a long stretch of beautiful coastline, lava desert, and lush rain forests.

Visitor activities: Scenic drives, hiking, short walks into the crater, overnight backpacking, cycling, fishing, horseback riding, and bird-watching.

Unlike classic volcanoes, where sudden violent eruptions produce steep, cone-shaped mountains, the regular flow of magma to the surface creates rounded mountains in Hawaii. Largely fluid in nature and less likely to produce gaseous explosions, the eruptions on Mauna Loa and Kilauea give rise to intriguing fiery fountains and rivers of molten lava. These rivers of lava are extremely hot, usually about 2,000°F (1,100°C) at the eruption, and flow about 20 miles (30 km) before they cool and harden.

The summits of the two volcanoes in the park have collapsed, and broad calderas have replaced the conical peaks common on many mountains. On Kilauea, the caldera is 2.5 miles (4 km) long and 2 miles (3 km) wide, with the cliffs ringing it rising 400 feet (120 m) above a floor of bubbling lava. On Mauna Loa, lava flows from eruptions that took place from 1942 to 1984 are visible. On Kilauea, an extensive lava field formed between

1969 and 1974 is up to 3 miles (5 km) wide in some places. The current eruption of Kilauea began in 1983, and a broad river of lava flows down from the mountain's southeastern slopes to the ocean.

Endemic Species

Winds blowing from the northeast across the Pacific are forced to rise up the mountains and drop their moisture on the northern and eastern slopes of Kilauea where rainfall can exceed 150 inches (3,700 mm). A lush rain forest of ferns and tall trees grows on these wet slopes. Some of the forest's many plants include the bright red blossoms of 'Ōhi'a lehua (*Metrosideros polymorpha*), the fan palm (*Pritichardia schattaueri*), leafy hāhā (*Cyanea recta*), and several species of geraniums. On the southwest slopes of the mountain, rainfall decreases to about 30 inches (700 mm) and on these hot, dry slopes, some areas of lava, known as the Ka'u Desert, are almost devoid of vegetation.

On the Big Island, a total of 14 bird and 51 plant species are listed as endangered or threatened in terms of the Endangered Species Act of 1973. Many species are threatened by animals and plants that were either deliberately introduced to the island as food sources or were accidentally introduced. Mosquitoes, an example of an accidental introduction, arrived in the 1820s in water casks on whaling ships. They carry avian malaria, which threatens the endemic honeycreeper birds. To combat the destructive effect of exotic species, such as feral pigs, ginger from Asia, and South American banana poka and strawberry guava, park rangers regularly hunt pigs and cut down these exotic plants. An estimated 4,000 pigs still inhabit the park. Once they have been eliminated from a certain area, fences are erected to protect the forests. Rangers have erected 70 miles (110 km) of fences that now protect one-third of the park's rain forests.

On the Volcano's Edge

From the town of Hilo, the access road climbs 4,000 feet (1,200 m) in 30 miles (50 km) to Kilauea. The Kilauea Visitor Center and Volcano House Hotel overlook the northern rim of the caldera. A network of hiking trails crosses the caldera floor, while the circular 12-mile (19-km) Crater Rim Trail closely follows the edge of the caldera. Visitors can complete the same route by road, and the 11-mile (18-km) Crater Rim Drive includes stops at seven view sites. Along this drive there is a turnoff to the Chain of Craters Road (19 miles; 32 km), which ends

abruptly at the coast where a recent lava flow blocks its path. Trailheads for four trails are located along this road, and there are many view sites. An extensive trail system explores the wilderness area extending 17 miles (27 km) west of the road.

North of Kilauea, a winding road ends at the Mauna Loa Lookout after 14 miles (22 km). From this point, the Mauna Loa Trail climbs to the summit of the mountain where two cabins are provided for hikers. The return hike of 43 miles (69 km) takes several days to complete.

Opposite, top left: Like toffee in a gigantic confectionery factory, twisted strands of pahoehoe lava add new contours to the mountain slopes.

Left: Steam and volcanic gases billow above the lava flow as it enters the ocean.

Below and opposite, bottom: Measuring 2 miles (3 km) across, Kilauea Caldera is bordered by sheer cliffs rising up 300 feet (100 m) above its floor.

HALEAKALA NATIONAL PARK

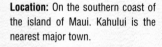

Two volcanoes dominate the island of Maui, and erosion has cut deep canyons into the mountains. Haleakala is the largest and highest of the volcanoes, and its crown rises to 10,025 feet (3,055 m) above the Pacific Ocean. Below its summit, the Ko'olau Gap, a huge bowl that is 2,720 feet (830 m) deep and 2.5 miles (4 km) wide, drops away to the east and is dotted with cinder cones. The park touches the coast at its eastern end and, from the waterfalls near the Kïpahulu Visitor Center and Campground, the terrain rises steeply to the crest of the mountain, gaining 10,000 feet (3,050 m) over 13 miles (21 km).

Air temperatures vary from an average 75°F (24°C) at the coast to 40°F (4°C) on the high summits. Four distinct vegetation zones are contained within the park, ranging from luxuriant rain forest to dry forest on leeward slopes. Subalpine shrub occurs at high altitudes. On the summit, few plants can become established in the harsh conditions. Yet within a short distance, waterfalls plunge down valleys clothed in dense vegetation.

Established in 1916, this park covers 45 square miles (115 sq km), forming a 3-mile-wide (5-km) corridor that extends from Kukui Bay up the Kipahulu Valley to the awesome Ko'olau Gap and the volcano's lofty summit.

Lush Rain Forest and Alpine Shrub

On Maui, 12 birds and 64 plants are listed as threatened and endangered. While nonnative plants such as bamboo and guava have taken over the lower coastal valleys where trails lead to two impressive waterfalls, at elevations above 1,000 feet (300 m), indigenous plants continue to hold their own. Parts of the Kïpahulu Valley receive an average rainfall of 250 inches (6,250 mm) and a dense carpet of ferns, mosses, lichens, and the enormous umbrella-shaped leaves of the 'Ape'ape grow under forest trees. As this valley contains pristine rain forest, it has been set aside as a strict reserve and is closed to the public. Apart from damage to plants, visitors inadvertently transport plant seeds on their boots and clothing. Fences have been erected to prevent feral goats and pigs from destroying endemic plants, and helicopters ferry rangers to the upper valleys to combat alien plants.

At higher altitudes near the crest of the mountain, the feathery leaves and tall flower spike of the 'ahinahina, or silversword (*Argyroxiphium sandwicense*), cling to rocky slopes. The silvery appearance of the leaves is due to a covering of tiny hairs that help to conserve moisture and protect the plant from high-altitude solar radiation. Several species of lobelia, closely related to members of the family found in high mountains in other parts of the world, are visited by the 'i'iwi, a brilliant red honeycreeper that uses its narrow, curved bill to suck nectar from the plant.

Above, right: The Hawaiian goose, or nēnē, was saved from extinction by a captive breeding center in western England.
Opposite: The silversword grows on the barren volcanic slopes near the summit of Haleakala.

Location: On the southern coast of the island of Maui. Kahului is the nearest major town.

Climate: The average high in July in coastal areas is 83°F (28°C), and in January 78°F (26°C), though on the high mountains, the temperature may drop below freezing.

When to go: Throughout the year. The lower-lying portions of the park receive considerable amounts of rain, mainly during winter.

Access: From Kahului, take Highway 37 south to the junction of Highway 377. Follow this road, then head east on Highway 378 to the summit of the mountain. To access the coastal section of the park, head east from Kahului on Highways 36 and 360. From Hana, Highway 31 winds along the coast to enter the park at Kipahulu.

Facilities: Three visitor centers are located in the park, one on the coast and two at the summit of the volcano. There is a picnic area and campground at Hosmer Grove on the mountain and another on the coast near Kukui Bay. There are no food services, lodges, or service stations in the park. In the wilderness area are three cabins for hikers.

Outstanding features: Altitude in the park varies from sea level to 10,025 feet (3,055 m), reflected in a diversity of habitats from rocky coastline and high waterfalls to dense rain forests and an arid alpine zone at the summit of the volcano. Several rare birds inhabit the island.

Visitor activities: Scenic drives, hiking, short walks to waterfalls and along the coast, overnight backpacking, swimming, horseback riding, and bird-watching.

(835 m) in 9 miles (14 km) to Haleakala Visitor Center near the summit.

In the wilderness area that has been designated in Ko'olau Gap are 27 miles (43 km) of hiking trails. Trailheads for two trails depart from the campground and summit area. Three cabins are provided for hikers. From Kaupō Gap, on the eastern edge of the wilderness, a trail exits the park and crosses private land before ending at the coast.

To explore the coastal section of the park and the Makahiku and 400-foot-high (122-m) Waimoku Waterfalls requires a journey from Kahului on Highway 360 along the northern coast of Maui. After entering the park, the 4-mile (7-km) round-trip trail leaves the road and follows the Pīpīwai and 'Ohe'o Streams to the waterfalls. On the other side of the road, two short trails follow the coast to Kīpahulu Campground, passing a thatched Hawaiian cultural village en route. Just before it enters the ocean, the 'Ohe'o Stream flows through a delightful series of pools framed by dense vegetation. Swimming in the pools is popular among visitors, particularly those who need to cool off after hiking to the waterfalls.

Above: Hardy pioneer plants colonize an apparently barren wasteland of cinder near the mountain's lofty summit.

Right: Cinder cones punctuate the Ko'olau Gap on the upper reaches of Haleakala.

The nēnē, or hawaiian goose, is another endemic bird found in the park. By 1950 the wild population in Hawaii had decreased to 30 birds and was in grave danger of extinction. A few birds were flown to the Wildfowl Trust in Slimbridge, England, and successful captive breeding made it possible to reintroduce birds to Hawaii. The total population now exceeds 800.

In the past, many 'ahinahina, or silverswords, were destroyed by goats. After the goats were removed, rangers discovered that ants from Argentina were preying on native yellow-faced bees, important pollinators of silverswords. Preserving Hawaii's endemic plants and birds is proving to be a difficult and expensive undertaking.

Visiting Crater and Coast

There are two approach roads to the park and two campgrounds but no connector roads within the park or short hiking trails between these two entrances. From Kahului, Highway 37 heads south to the north entrance, and Highway 378 climbs steeply, ending at view sites overlooking the awesome Ko'olau Gap. There is a campground near the entrance and two visitor centers. From the park headquarters, near the entrance, the road zigzags steeply up hairpin bends, climbing 2,740 feet

Above: Moisture-laden winds from the Pacific Ocean sustain lush tropical jungles on the mountain's lower slopes.

Left: With a life span of up to 20 years, the silversword, or 'ahinahina, flowers only once and then dies.

ALASKA

A merica's last wild frontier, Alaska is a harsh, icebound land where winter temperatures in the Arctic average −11°F (−24°C) and where record lows have dropped to −80°F (−62°C). Over many centuries, native Aleuts and Inuits perfected a culture dependent on Alaska's bounteous fish and wildlife, but it was only in 1784 that the first European fur traders established an outpost here. The United States government bought Alaska from Russia in 1867 for the sum of $7.2 million, a paltry amount considering the state's tremendous natural resources.

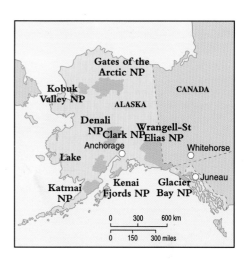

Alaska accounts for 16 percent of America's surface area but is home to only 0.2 percent of the country's people. Wild animals are abundant, both on land and in the ocean. An estimated 400,000 caribou migrate across the tundra, walruses and sea lions crowd remote islands, while sea otters and humpback whales surface in sheltered coves. With the passing of the Alaska National Interest Lands Conservation Act in 1980, the area set aside for national parks in America doubled in size. Eight Alaskan national parks were proclaimed, covering 64,840 square miles (167,300 sq km), an area equal in size to the state of Washington. Five of these parks are larger than the largest national park in the lower 48 states. Wrangell–St. Elias could accommodate six Yellowstones within its 20,600 square miles (53,160 sq km) of soaring mountains and glaciers. The national park system also includes seven national monuments and preserves in the Alaskan wilderness.

Apart from the park system, 17 national wildlife refuges cover 14 percent of Alaska and preserve wildlife ranging from Kodiak and polar bears to snow geese. The Yukon Delta National Wildlife Refuge, the largest refuge in America, covers an area the size of Maine and is known for its herds of musk oxen. In southeastern Alaska, the Tongass National Forest, where rainfall averages 200 inches (5,000 mm) a year, protects dozens of islands and nearly 11,000 miles (17,500 km) of shoreline.

As home to the grizzly bear, gray wolf, snowy owl, and king salmon, Alaska appeals to the intrepid traveler and the lover of unbounded wilderness.

Left: The immense Harding Icefield feeds the rivers of ice that terminate in Aialik Bay, Kenai Fjords National Park. This ice field, a relic from the Ice Age, covers more than half of the park and conceals a mountain range under ice that is up to 1 mile (1.6 km) thick.

227

ALASKAN NATIONAL PARKS

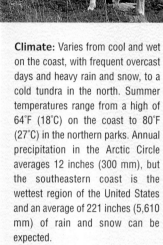

Denali National Park

Two mountain ranges shape the southern and northern regions of Alaska. In the north, the Brooks Range is a high gateway to the remote northern Arctic. Southward, the Alaska Range forms a long spine that extends from Attu Island, at the far western tip of the Aleutian Islands, for 1,470 miles (2,350 km) along the chain to the mainland. Over 75 volcanoes, part of the Ring of Fire that encircles the Pacific Ocean, have fashioned the high peaks of the islands and Alaska Peninsula. Where the land broadens into the mainland, the mountains continue eastward in an arc 700 miles (1,100 km) long, that includes three-quarters of the 16 highest peaks in North America.

Located in the center of this range is Mount McKinley, one of the tallest summits in the world. Towering to 20,320 feet (6,194 m), this ice-crowned mountain overshadows Kilimanjaro in Africa and all the high mountains in Europe and Australasia. It is surpassed only by peaks in the Andes and Himalayas. Where Mount Everest is surrounded by many lofty peaks, much of McKinley's splendor is due to its sudden and dramatic rise of 18,200 feet (5,550 m) above the surrounding country, one of the greatest variations in altitude in the world. The mountain's summit was scaled for the first time in 1913. In midsummer, the temperature at the base can reach 78°F (25°C), but on the summit, daytime temperatures rarely exceed 10°F (−12°C). In this land of perpetual winter, deep snow forms a permanent white cap that feeds the mountain's 20 glaciers. Approximately 1,000 people a year attempt to climb the mountain during the brief climbing season from April to early July. However, only about half of them survive the harsh conditions to finally make it to the summit.

In 1917, a national park was established primarily to protect the wildlife of the northern tundra, which was being hunted to supply mining towns. The park was tripled in size in 1980 to 9,419 square miles (24,300 sq km) and renamed Denali, an Athapaskan Native American word meaning "the High One."

Denali is the fourth largest national park in America and the most accessible of Alaska's large parks. The entrance, and the park's only road, is located on Highway 3 some 210 miles (340 km) north of Anchorage. Only the first 15 miles (24 km) of the road, which follows the northern face of the mountain, is open to tourists in private vehicles. For the remaining 74 miles (118 km), a shuttle bus service travels a gravel road that ends at an airstrip. Apart from a lodge at the entrance and six campgrounds, only two accessible by private vehicle, there are no facilities in the park and no marked trails.

Above, right: The only all-white wild sheep, dall sheep, are perfectly camouflaged in Alaska's snow-capped mountains.
Above, middle: Where migrating fish swim upstream to spawn, bald eagles find a ready supply of protein in Alaska's remote wilderness.
Opposite: The highest summit in North America and one of the highest in the world, Mount McKinley can be scaled only by experienced mountaineers for three months in summer.

Climate: Varies from cool and wet on the coast, with frequent overcast days and heavy rain and snow, to a cold tundra in the north. Summer temperatures range from a high of 64°F (18°C) on the coast to 80°F (27°C) in the northern parks. Annual precipitation in the Arctic Circle averages 12 inches (300 mm), but the southeastern coast is the wettest region of the United States and an average of 221 inches (5,610 mm) of rain and snow can be expected.

When to go: Late May to mid-September; from May to August the sun remains above the horizon for 16 to 18 hours a day. In the northern parks, the sun does not set at all during June.

Access: Denali, Kenai Fjords, Wrangell–St. Elias, and Gates of the Arctic can be reached by road from Anchorage. In Denali, there is a station on the railway from Anchorage to Fairbanks. Lake Clark and Katmai can be reached only by boat or seaplane. Cruise ships from Vancouver to Alaska regularly visit Glacier Bay. To reach remote Kobuk Valley, it is necessary to fly to the Inuit village of Ambler. From Ambler, the only approach is downriver by boat.

Facilities: All parks have visitor centers or information offices, with the exception of Gates of the Arctic and Kobuk Valley. Lodge accommodations are available during summer in Denali, Kenai Fjords, Lake Clark, Katmai, and Glacier Bay. Campgrounds are provided in Denali, Kenai Fjords, Katmai, Glacier Bay, and Wrangell–St. Elias. There are no facilities in the far-north Gates of the Arctic and Kobuk Valley parks.

Visitor activities: Narrated bus tours, hiking, overnight backpacking, mountain climbing, horseback riding, aerial sightseeing, boat tours, fishing, kayaking, whale-watching, river rafting, wildlife viewing, and bird-watching. Winter activities include cross-country skiing, snowshoeing, snowmobiling, and dog sledding.

Denali is renowned for its abundance of wildlife and has been nicknamed "the Subarctic Serengeti." All the mammals that occurred historically are present today and predator/prey relationships have been little affected by human activity. A total of 37 mammal species are known to occur, including Dall sheep, grizzly bear, gray wolf, wolverine, arctic fox, ground squirrel, and hoary marmot. During May, about 2,700 caribou migrate up the mountain slopes to give birth to their calves. Grizzly bears are estimated to number about 200, and areas where bears are often sighted are closed to hikers, because bears have been known to attack. Dall sheep, the only pure white wild sheep, are closely related to bighorn sheep, and are restricted to Alaska and north-western Canada. An estimated 2,500 of these sheep inhabit Denali's high mountains and ridges.

A total of 159 species of birds have been recorded. The park protects the largest breeding concentration of golden eagles in Alaska and 120 nests have been identified. Other notable birds include the short-eared owl, northern harrier, gyrfalcon, merlin, sandhill crane, trumpeter swan, and snow bunting.

Kenai Fjords National Park

Located on the southeastern coastline of the Kenai Peninsula, this picturesque park of 950 square miles (2,450 sq km) adjoins several national wildlife refuges and state parks. It incorporates an immense ice field, active glaciers, and five major fjords that were scoured by ice. The Harding Icefield, a relic from the last Ice Age, dominates higher elevations in this park and hides a mountain range under a cold shroud of ice. As snow and ice accumulated, 32 glaciers were born on the high slopes, seven of which enter the ocean. In the past, glaciers carved the deep valleys, which were then flooded by

Above: Katmai National Park protects the largest population of Alaskan brown bear, a subspecies of the grizzly, in the United States.

Right: Exit Glacier, in Kenai Fjords, plunges 2,500 feet (750 m) in less than 3 miles (5 km) before reaching its terminus.

the rising sea to form the five major fjords that are included within Kenai Fjords National Park.

In the narrow band of coniferous forest between the ocean and ice-capped peaks, wildlife includes black bear, moose, and wolverine, while mountain goats are superbly suited to the sheer mountain peaks. The cold waters of the Pacific sustain plankton and fish such as cod, rockfish, pollock, and pink salmon, which in turn support marine mammals like the harbor seal, northern sea lion, sea otter, and gray whale. Flocks of sea birds nest on rocky cliffs, and the abundance of marine life sustains many species, including the horned puffin, northern fulmar, red-faced cormorant, common murre, Aleutian tern, rock sandpiper, and black turnstone.

Highways 1 and 9 from Anchorage end at the coastal town of Seward. The only road into the park is a gravel route that ends at a parking area near Exit Glacier. Regular boat trips from Seward offer the best opportunities for viewing sea birds and marine mammals. During summer three cabins are available in the fjords, and the cabin at Exit Glacier can be used in winter.

Lake Clark National Park

The 32-mile-wide (51-km) Cook Inlet separates the Kenai Peninsula from the mainland. Flying west from Seward across 100 miles (160 km) of rock, ice, and ocean, Lake Clark and Katmai National Parks preserve a

wilderness of mountains, lakes, coastline, and volcanic activity. Lake Clark, named after the largest of its glacial lakes, is dominated by two active volcanoes that overshadow the Cook Inlet. Redoubt Volcano, the higher of the two, last erupted in 1990 and rises 10,197 feet (3,108 m) above the bay of the same name, just 14 miles (22 km) east of the mountain.

Above: Steller's sea lions feed mainly on pollock and congregate on the rocky shores of southern Alaska.

Below, left: Once persecuted for their pelts, an estimated 140,000 northern sea otters now live along the southeastern coast of Alaska all the way to the Aleutian Islands and Russia's Kamchatka Peninsula.

Above: Small herds of woodland caribou occur in the forests of southern Alaska. However, in the Arctic Circle, mass migrations of thousands of these animals are a seasonal phenomenon.

Below, right: Katmai's Valley of Ten Thousand Smokes was named after the thousands of fumaroles that appeared in the valley floor after the violent volcanic eruption of 1912.

Opposite, top: In summer, wildflowers enhance the unspoiled beauty of Glacier Bay.

West of the mountains, many rivers flow across valleys clothed in tundra and spruce forests before emptying into glacial lakes. Three free-flowing rivers have been designated wild rivers. The park is a vital spawning ground for sockeye salmon, and four other salmon species occur in its rivers and lakes. Because habitats range from high mountains to low-lying valleys, many wild animals are present, including Dall sheep, caribou, moose, black and grizzly bear, lynx, and gray wolf.

The park and the adjoining Lake Clark National Preserve cover 6,320 square miles (16,306 sq km), of which 60 percent is designated wilderness. Winter in the interior of the park is severe, and there are no facilities or marked trails. Because there is no access by road, most visitors to this wilderness arrive by seaplane, drawn by activities that include hiking in the foothills, camping, river running, and fishing along rushing rivers and glacial lakes.

Katmai National Park

On June 6, 1912, one of the most violent volcanic eruptions ever recorded took place after several days of earthquakes had shaken Mount Katmai. When the eruption finally ended, volcanic ash and rock covered nearly 40 square miles (110 sq km) at depths of up to 300 feet (90 m). When a group of scientists ventured into the area four years later, they found a valley filled with thousands of fumaroles. Steam rose 1,000 feet (300 m) into the air from numerous fissures, and the valley was named after

the "tens of thousands of smokes." Since then, the fumaroles have died, and erosion has carved canyons through the deposits. This created a lunar landscape where, in the past, astronauts were trained. Although it is not the highest peak in Katmai Park, Mount Katmai is one of the most interesting, and a lake has since filled the crater on its summit.

In 1918, a national monument was proclaimed to protect the valley. In 1980 it was redesignated a national park and expanded to 6,390 square miles (16,488 sq km). Apart from the active volcanoes that form a range bounded by the coast, Katmai is known for its large numbers of Alaskan brown bears, a subspecies of the grizzly. The 1,500 bears represent the largest protected population in America. During July and August, as many as 20 brown bears can be seen fishing for sockeye salmon in the McNeil River on the northern boundary of the park.

By plane, the park headquarters at King Salmon are 290 miles (460 km) southwest of Anchorage. During summer, seaplanes fly to Brooks Camp, which is located 33 miles (53 km) inside the park. The lodge and campground are situated on a narrow spit surrounded by the largest of the park's 18 major lakes. Five small lodges occupy prime locations on lakes to the north, reached only by seaplane. At Brooks Camp, brown bears can be seen fishing for salmon at the nearby rapids. A gravel road heads south for 23 miles (37 km) to the Valley of Ten Thousand Smokes.

Glacier Bay National Park

In 1794, when British explorer George Vancouver sailed along the southeastern coast of Alaska, he encountered a wall of ice that towered above the ocean. Glaciers such as this have since then retreated by 65 miles (105 km), and forests have colonized land that was once under ice. The 12 glaciers that end in the bay are the remnants of a minor ice age that began 4,000 years ago. Some of these glaciers advance as much as 7 feet (2 m) per day, and massive cliffs of ice sheer away from the glacier's snout, plunging into the water. Between Glacier Bay and the Pacific Ocean, the Fairweather Mountain Range includes peaks that rise to heights of 15,320 feet (4,670 m) within 15 miles (24 km) of the ocean. Moisture-laden winds from the ocean are forced to rise up these mountains, and produce large quantities of snow that supply the glaciers.

In the 11-branched bay that has been revealed since 1845, the seven glaciers in John Hopkins Inlet are the most active. One of the largest populations of harbor seals in the Pacific Ocean occurs in the park, and in summer the seals give birth in this inlet. Several small islands in the bay that have been exposed by the retreating ice now host nesting seabirds and sea lions. In summer humpback whales gather to feed on an abundance of krill and shrimp, and killer whales hunt seals in the bay. In autumn, the world's greatest concentration of bald eagles, estimated at 2,500, gathers in Alaska Chilkat Bald Eagle Preserve north of the park.

Below: Icy Strait, which links Glacier Bay to the Gulf of Alaska, offers superb opportunities for watching humpback whales.

Above: In 1750, Glacier Bay lay hidden beneath an immense glacier that has since retreated inland by 65 miles (105 km), with most of the retreat having occurred by 1890.

The bay's spectacular icebergs, active glaciers, and marine animals attract many cruise ships and charter boats. Glacier Bay Lodge and Campground, situated near the mouth of the bay, are accessible only by airplane or boat and are the only facilities provided inside the park—the major portion remains an icebound wilderness. In recognition of its unique attributes and importance for marine conservation, this park of 5,125 square miles (13,223 sq km) was declared a World Heritage Site in 1992.

Wrangell–St. Elias National Park

Dominated by three snow-capped mountain ranges, the largest park in America is known for its enormous glaci-ers and broad, fast-flowing rivers. In the Wrangell and St. Elias Mountains, seven peaks rise above 14,800 feet (4,500 m), and 9 of the 16 highest summits in America soar above the valleys. In the southeastern corner near Icy Bay, the loftiest peak, Mount St. Elias (18,008 feet; 5,489 m), straddles the boundary between Alaska and Canada.

Covering an area twice the size of New Hampshire, Wrangell–St. Elias consists of national park land bordered by national preserves. The national park mostly covers the high peaks. The preserves incorporate valleys to the north and west and an area along the Chitina River in the center where two tiny settlements are served by a 61-mile (98-km) gravel road. Two campgrounds and a

Gates of the Arctic National Park and Kobuk Valley National Park

Within the Arctic Circle, two national parks and adjacent preserves and wildlife refuges safeguard an immense expanse of tundra and mountain that is equal in size to the state of Pennsylvania. Stretching 250 miles (400 km) west of the Alaskan oil pipeline is Gates of the Arctic. It protects important summer feeding grounds for some of the 200,000 caribou that comprise the western arctic herd. The park, named after the narrow passage carved through the Brooks Range by the North Fork Koyukuk River—Gates of the Arctic—is a true wilderness area: 13,281 square miles (34,266 sq km) of spruce forest, ice-shrouded mountain and tundra, and one of the most unspoiled corners of the earth.

In the far west near Kotzebue Sound, Kobuk Valley is one of the most inaccessible corners of Alaska. At a latitude of 67.5°N, it is somewhat surprising to encounter forests of spruce that give way suddenly to a sea of high sand dunes extending over 25 square miles (65 sq km). Kobuk Valley receives the lowest number of visitors and can be accessed only by boat or airplane from nearby Inuit villages.

Below: Barren ground caribou migrate twice a year over vast distances across the tundra in the Arctic Circle. Both sexes grow antlers, the only deer species where this occurs.

Overleaf: At the height of summer, extended hours of daylight finally yield to darkness in Glacier Bay, an isolated wilderness refuge that safeguards whales and marine life.

lodge are in the center of this wilderness park, but all other visitor facilities are extremely limited. Wild animals include an estimated 16,000 Dall sheep, confined with the mountain goat to mountainous terrain, while moose, caribou, black bear, and gray wolf roam across the valley forests.

To safeguard its heartland, 73 percent of the park has been designated a wilderness area. Wrangell–St. Elias adjoins the Kluane National Park and the Tatshenshini–Alsek Wilderness Park in Canada, which form a direct link to Glacier Bay. Conserving a combined vast wilderness of 37,500 square miles (96,750 sq km), these contiguous parks have recently been declared a World Heritage Site.

PLANNING A VISIT

The United States is an enormous country and distances between major cities can be considerable. With a few exceptions, the speed limit on highways is 65 miles (104 km) per hour. Roads are well marked and rest areas are located along major routes at regular intervals. Motels, restaurants, and fast-food outlets can be found at virtually every off-ramp, and even in small towns in lightly populated regions. Gasoline, car rental, fast food, groceries, and accommodations are usually reasonably priced, and driving is the best way to discover America's national parks. A detailed atlas is an essential companion.

Air Travel

Several airlines offer ticketless air travel with all bookings and payments conducted via the Internet. This allows the visitor to take advantage of the lowest fares; there are additional discounts for reservations placed more than one month in advance. All the major car rental companies have desks at airports, either at the terminals or in close proximity, and shuttle buses transport passengers to the car rental lots.

Credit Cards

Every credit card transaction first requires authorization from the visitor's home bank. Although the latest technology and telecommunication systems are in operation, disruptions in computer systems do occur and credit cards are often rejected. It is therefore essential that some other form of payment—either travelers' checks or cash—be carried at all times.

When to Go

Many of the national parks can be crowded during summer months and over weekends. The best time of year to plan a visit is during April or May and September or October, subject to local weather patterns. Winter snowfalls close many roads and facilities in national parks in the higher elevation and northern regions, but offer greater opportunities for solitude and wilderness activities.

National Park Accommodations

Where lodge accommodations are available in a national park, restaurants, general stores, and other amenities are generally included.

Campgrounds typically have a 7- or 14-day limit but this may vary. Most operate on a first-come, first-served basis. Facilities in some campgrounds are rather basic: cold water, toilets, and picnic tables. Some have pay showers but these are not generally open during winter. In many parks, there is no water available at campgrounds during winter. Certain sites may close seasonally depending on the climate. Camping fees vary, and some parks have reduced rates during winter.

Entrance Fees

Entrance fees are charged at 33 of the parks described in this book, and are collected even where a marked highway passes through a park. Fees are normally charged per vehicle but a per-person fee is charged where a visitor enters on foot, bicycle, motorcycle, or as part of an organized group or commercial tour.

Other user fees such as camping, boating, cave tours, special interpretive activities, and guided tours apply in certain parks.

The National Parks Pass costs $50 and admits the holder and any accompanying passengers in a private vehicle where a park has a per-vehicle entrance fee. Where a per-person entrance fee is charged, the pass admits the holder, spouse, children, and parents. It can be purchased at any park where entrance fees are payable, and allows entry to any national park for one year from the month of purchase. The pass is nontransferable and does not cover charges for camping, parking, tours, and concessionaire-operated facilities.

Precautions

Visitors should not underestimate the dangers of severe winter weather. Any visitor who attempts to hike in mountainous areas, even in midsummer, must be well equipped with thermal clothing and the correct hiking gear. Thorough planning and preparation are necessary, and park rangers must be informed of your route.

Grizzly bears occur in parks in Alaska, and in Glacier and Yellowstone, and black bears are widely distributed. Under no circumstances should they be fed because this increases the chances of an attack and causes bears to lose their fear of humans. Backcountry hikers should take proper precautions to avoid contact with bears, including avoiding certain strong-smelling foods and toiletries that attract bears, and taking care to hang food on a pole at least 10 feet (3 m) above the ground. Where bears are present, park rangers issue detailed guidelines that, if followed, will guarantee safety. Similarly, mountain lion numbers are increasing throughout much of the country and fatal attacks have been reported. It is unwise to hike alone in areas where mountain lions are present, and children must not be allowed to run ahead of the hiking party.

In mountainous areas, water is usually plentiful. However, wild animals can spread the parasite giardia; symptoms of an infection include diarrhea, swelling, and cramps. To avoid contamination it is best to boil water.

Additional Information and Addresses

The National Park Service maintains a comprehensive website at http://www.nps.gov that includes maps and up-to-date information and advice. This site also lists the addresses and telephone numbers of all the regional National Park Service offices, as well as information about all the parks, preserves, and national monuments that fall under their management. Free detailed maps and brochures are available at the entrances to every national park or can be ordered from the head office in Washington, DC, either by telephone or by e-mail, although not more than 10 maps can be mailed at any one time.

National Park Service Head Office:
National Park Service
1849 C Street NW
Washington, DC 20240
Telephone: (202) 208-6843

INDEX